7
b
tele

26.

Playleadership

PLAYLEADERSHIP

Bernard S. McGovern, F.N.A.R.L., M.Inst.P.L.
Games Organizer, London Borough of Lewisham

with a Foreword by Joan Pearse, M.B.E., S.R.C.N.
formerly Organizer of Playgroups for
the Save the Children Fund

FABER AND FABER LIMITED
3 Queen Square London

First published in 1973
by Faber and Faber Limited
3 Queen Square London WC1
Printed in Great Britiain by
Western Printing Services Ltd Bristol
All rights reserved

ISBN 0 571 10184 4

Leisure is both the occasion and the capacity of the whole personality to open up in itself

JOSEPH PEIPER

To my wife, Hilda,
and our daughters, Patsy, Dinky and Liz

Foreword

When I first met Bernard McGovern I quickly realized that he was a person who was deeply interested in his work. He showed a determination to provide effective help for the energetic youngsters of today so that their leisure would be creative, absorbing and wholly satisfying.

A vast amount of knowledge and much useful and detailed information is available in this readable and instructive book. Through it all there runs a thread of understanding sympathy for the many daily problems which the playleadership staff have to cope with. Part-time leaders will be especially glad of the tribute paid to them.

This book will be of infinite value to those just starting their career in Playleadership. Experienced workers will also find much to help them, as will local authorities who would like to implement a playleadership scheme. The book makes fascinating reading. Someone like myself who has little understanding of music will, nevertheless, learn much from the two chapters devoted to this subject. Everyone will be sadder and wiser after reading the chapter 'Drugs and Rebellion'.

Playleadership is a complex subject and, alas, still not fully appreciated in this country. One would like to feel that all sections of the community who are concerned with the daily problems of our young people will have the opportunity to study this book.

If Playleadership is undertaken with the thoroughness that is emphasized throughout these pages, surely more of our youngsters will be kept off the streets and away from trouble. One would hope, too, that this would lead them towards a clearer understanding of fellowship and a sense of belonging.

February 1973   JOAN PEARSE

Contents

Illustrations

Acknowledgements

For their wholehearted support during the pioneering years of playleadership in Lewisham I am indebted to members of Lewisham Borough Council, and to my Chief Officers, Mr. J. Carr, B.Sc.(Eng.), M.I.C.E., M.I.M.E., Borough Engineer of the old Metropolitan Borough, and Mr. John Turner, F.R.I.C.S., F.I.C.E., M.I.M.E., Borough Engineer of the new London Borough of Lewisham.

I should like to thank the International Recreation Association for permission to publish extracts from the Declaration of the Rights of the Child and the Charter for Leisure, and the International Playground Association for permission to publish extracts from their Newsletter, particularly Heinrich Rupprecht's enquiry in Ulm, Germany (Vol. 3 No. 4, September 1968) and, also from their Newsletter, Linda Cottam's report in the Phoenix Gazette of Madam Tanon's talk 'Junk playgrounds are in'.

I should also like to thank the following for permission to quote from their work.

Councillor Simon Randell of Bromley Borough Council who wrote *Drugs in your Town*.

Mr. John James of Bolingbroke School, Battersea, who has researched into the leisure-time activities of local children.

The Oxford University Press for permission to quote from *Children's Games in Street and Playground* by Iona and Peter Opie.

The Pre-School Playgroups Association in whose publications Beverley J. Morris, M.A., Dip.Ed., writes about the Hutt Valley Play Centres, Wellington, New Zealand.

Mr. W. D. Abernethy, Secretary to the Children's Playground and Playleadership Committee of the National Playing Fields Association, for his valuable writings on the setting up of Adventure Playgrounds.

Mr. S. J. Fraser, M.I.M.S.O., Safety Officer, Lewisham Borough Council, who has contributed 'Safety in Adventureland'.

15

Mr. Pat Hanna, some of whose games' inventions I publish.

Mr. Leslie Carling, who has made suggestions about buildings for indoor play.

I quote also from 'Allow a little humour to creep in', from *The Times Educational Supplement* (21 May 1971) by courtesy of *The Times* and the author Gerald Haigh.

For advice on the technical aspects of equipment construction I am indebted to Mr. A. Gierth, an active playleader with the Lewisham scheme for fifteen years.

Mr. Colin Mayne, Dip.P.E.(Oxon), Tutor, Playleadership Course, Thurrock Technical College, has given valuable advice on the manuscript content in relation to its value to students of playleadership, and I thank Mr. J. E. Birkhead, D.I.C., B.Sc., for his guidance during the last fifteen years in the administrative aspects of a Local Government Play Scheme.

I should also like to thank the Central Council of Physical Recreation for help with details of various sporting organizations.

My thanks are extended to Sportsmark Ltd. for permission to publish details from their list of dimensions of courts and pitches; to Mrs. Win Malyan who read the manuscript and gave helpful suggestions; to officers of various sections of the Borough of Lewisham Surveyors' Department for their helpful advice on the section dealing with contacts and to the young people of the Lewisham Playleadership Scheme who took part in discussions to clarify their own points of view. To Miss P. Jean Cunningham, B.A., S.R.N., S.C.M., H.V.Cert. and Mrs. Pat Barefoot, B.A., who undertook the editing of the manuscript and who both gave me much assistance.

Finally, my grateful thanks are due to the many playleaders of the Lewisham Playleadership Scheme who were instrumental in collating information for this book, but particularly I am indebted to Mrs. Elsie Thomas, F.N.A.R.L., my able assistant who is responsible for all matters appertaining to the feminine point of view in the book, and who unselfishly gave up so much of her own time in sifting through the mass of literary material which had to be accomplished to produce this book.

Introduction

The potential in any child defies measurement. A child's character will be moulded by various influences, and it follows that the adults he is in contact with in his early years will be largely responsible for the way in which he develops. First and foremost until he is of school-age, he will depend entirely on his parents, or perhaps too on other adults in his immediate family or household. Then, when he is older, his teachers at school may exert a great influence. Home and school will account for much of his time but will not cover every activity. There is also play.

Play has many aspects and all must be given scope. There is purely imaginative play. A solitary child may play by weaving fantasies in his mind. At other times a child needs to play with companions of his own age, and it is important that there should be outdoor play.

Play is not time wasted. It is a way of stretching a child. He learns to enjoy doing and performing. He gains satisfaction from actual achievement. He is learning to appreciate values that will last him throughout life.

Although some form of recreational leadership has always existed simply because from time immemorial every group of children who came together at play have chosen their own leader, the designation 'playleader' did not creep into our vocabulary until the middle of the present century.

Many attempts to establish playleadership in one form or another took place in various parts of the country during the early years of the twentieth century but very little information is recorded about these projects to benefit the student in his search for enlightenment.

Possibly the nearest approach to organized playleadership enjoying any degree of public acceptance was that devised by Baden Powell which is now accepted throughout the world and known as the 'Boy Scout' movement. Bound by a special code of rules, its uniformed members had to pay subscriptions and were attached to various Christian churches in small units.

Discipline, although not too severe, was enforced and the threat of expulsion always hung over the heads of any would-be non-conformists. The penalty seldom had to be enforced as most of its members came from homes with good family backgrounds. Baden Powell's organization provided its members with plenty of adventure, personal challenge and comradeship and most certainly paved the way towards good citizenship.

Playleadership as we know it today has much in common with the aims of the Scout movement when it first began but has also other qualities. During the past ten years or so rapid progress has been made but it was not until the mid 1940's that local authorities began to anticipate the values of playleadership as a full-time public amenity. The alarming increase in vandalism and juvenile delinquency demanded a quick solution.

During these early post-war years a large number of boys and young men who had been raised during the absence of their fathers away on national service made their presence felt in no uncertain manner to the annoyance of the general public.

Two local authorities, both of them in the London Area, decided to combat this problem by introducing free facilities for young people to take part in recreational activities in their local parks. These schemes were publicized as 'organized games in the parks'. Although both projects had much in common they were nevertheless somewhat different. Beckenham, in Kent, decided to redesignate a number of its younger men who were employed as park keepers and name them 'Games Wardens'. Their extra duties would include organizing games for local children. These wardens would come under the jurisdiction of the parks superintendent and would be directed in their duties by a newly appointed chief games warden.

The Metropolitan Borough of Wandsworth in Surrey, whose problem with vandalism had become widely publicized, appointed an ex-army warrant officer from the Army Physical Training Corps. He tackled the problem by going out into certain districts in a van which carried a quantity of sports and miscellaneous recreation equipment. His objective was to persuade groups of young people who were playing in the streets to come to their local parks and use the equipment.

After a slow start this system began to prove successful with the result that it became rather difficult for the games organizer to cope with the demand which had steadily increased. The council provided additional part-time assistance for him by employing a small number of games assistants. It soon became apparent that even more help was required so a number of senior boys and girls who had shown signs and qualities of leadership were appointed by the games organizer as voluntary playleaders.

Therefore it can be accepted that in England playleadership was officially launched on a full-time basis as a direct result of conditions which prevailed after the second world war and that our first playleaders were senior boys and girls.

The Metropolitan borough of Wandsworth published the following reasons for introducing its scheme in 1947:

... 'To encourage young people to play in parks instead of in the streets in order to reduce the risk of accidents, curb the growth of juvenile delinquency and also the amount of damage to public and private property. ...'

In recent years playleadership has been bandied backwards and forwards as being the possible solution to a number of social and educational problems. Because of this, responsibility for its implementation has not fallen into a national pattern and throughout the country local government responsibility for this service is borne by any one of the many departments. Some local authorities have two schemes organized by different departments. Usually administered from the department which controls parks, many are known to come under the control of departments of education, housing, welfare, surveyors, health and town clerks.

Playleadership has been criticized as duplicating the work of other professions; it has been the subject for discussion at conferences and seminars all over the world, yet its full worth has not been recognized in this country. Even its title, which has been accepted internationally, is somewhat controversial in England but no matter what one's concept is, the fact remains that its values have been apparent in many different ways.

An increasing demand for this service will provide opportunities for more people to take up its challenging work. As always there will be those who for reasons best known to themselves will decry my methods and objectives; my reply is that where my projects have not been successful I try to keep visitors and students fully informed on such failures in the hope that they will benefit by my lessons and in their turn put them to good account – my methods are not foolproof and I try to make sure that a false impression is not given.

I maintain that a playleader's foremost contribution to society is to lead the way in showing children and young people how to use their leisure time. The most important aspect of leisure is its freedom – freedom for a person, especially a youngster, to be himself, to round out his life with that which he cannot find in his school or his work. Leisure covers a vast number of activities; it encompasses everything done outside work or school.

No other reason than this need be sought as a basis for implementing a playleadership scheme. It is not sufficient that the educational requirements of our young are provided and enforced by us, because they only meet the needs halfway. Out of school leisure needs are also of great importance if we are to develop the 'whole person'. But, as Town Planner F. J. C. Amos tells us, we have no such 'Whole Service' to encourage this.

Most playleadership schemes in this country, unlike the Continent and the U.S.A., are implemented for the express purpose of combating juvenile delinquency and vandalism, and comparatively few owe their beginnings to the foresight of people in authority who have seen the need from a purely recreational amenity standpoint.

During recent years the role of a playleader employed in the adventure playground has been shown more or less as that of a social worker, because so many of them have involved themselves in all kinds of social work which is not really their responsibility. Unfortunately this misconstrues the whole concept of the designation of playleaders who work in places other than adventure playgrounds or community play centres.

As a playleader I do not consider myself to be a social worker, or my job as being social work, although a degree of parallelism does exist. The social worker must surely be an expert in his field; he should be highly trained and not involved in matters outside the orbit of his work.

I am of the opinion that playleadership should be classified as 'occupational recreation' and that its main function be directed towards providing for the leisure-time needs of normal children and young people. I emphasize, normal children and young people.

The provision of play and occupational facilities for groups of physically handicapped children should be supervised by a fully qualified social worker who has also had some training in play provision and not by a playleader who knows little about physically handicapped children. I feel that this is a highly specialized subject and should be left in the capable hands of experts. Handicapped children who come to a play area frequented by normal children should be encouraged to take part in those activities of which they are capable.

Some authorities expect the introduction of a playleadership scheme to solve its immediate problems of vandalism and delinquency overnight. But it won't. Its benefit will not become apparent in this respect for two or three years or even longer, and maybe not at all. Any benefit which society may derive by way of the retarding of delinquency is purely incidental, but to set up schemes solely to combat vandalism or the like is insufficient reason.

To my way of thinking, a playleadership scheme should not come within the orbit of an educational body but rather it should be controlled from that section which deals with parks and open spaces. A scheme will benefit all the more if the parks section is controlled by the District Surveyor and Engineer. This department usually contains adequate facilities within itself to meet all the many needs of a playleadership scheme.

As the Charter for Leisure (announced in Geneva in 1970 by the International Recreation Association) states:

> 'Leisure time should be unorganized in the sense that official authorities, urban planners, architects and private groups of individuals do not decide how others are to use their leisure time. The above mentioned should create or assist in the planning of the leisure opportunities, aesthetic environments and recreation facilities required to enable man to exercise individual choice in the use of his leisure, according to his personal tastes and under his own responsibility.'

Playleadership is a demanding profession; demanding of its full-time workers and of its part-time workers alike. No place exists within its ranks for those who are not sympathetic to the needs of a young society. Nor does a place exist for the character who sees himself as heaven's gift to the community. But one does exist for the ordinary down-to-earth family man or woman who likes youngsters and who has some knowledge of bringing them up. This type of experienced playleader would be aware that he must constantly be one step ahead of the children. During an actual playleading session where such a leader is personally participating in the activities, he will always be drawing on the resources of his experience to decide what the next activity will be, and to be able to do this successfully he will need to have a good repertoire of activities on which he can call. Of course knowing what these activities are is of little use if he is unable to take the initiative and actually take the lead himself.

He must know how to 'pace' himself, and arrange his programme so as not to 'play out' his charges too quickly. Coupled with this he must maintain interest and create atmosphere.

Certain activities are known to appeal to youngsters at specific times, and occasions arise when it becomes necessary to promote a series of short-lived activities one after the other. The art of knowing or of deciding what a particular sequence of activities will be only comes through having the experience of working in a particular area over a long period of time.

In this respect no formula for success – which will apply anywhere – exists. Every playleader will find it necessary to tailor his own capabilities to the needs of his young people.

Concepts differ enormously, as do the needs of our young. There are those of us who would advocate providing complete freedom of expression, or alternatively just single activities like art or drama, sport, adventurous activities or just organized games, to mention a few. Because of some of these short-sighted concepts of ours, our young are being unintentionally denied some of the things they really need most.

They should be given a wide choice, because if the choice is limited good results are likely to be still more limited. I speak of choice of real values such as that of association with mature adults, choice of being able to help their associates and of witnessing good sportsmanship and seeing good examples set as against the doctrine of win at all costs and damn the losers.

To those unfamiliar with legitimate playleadership it might be as well if I explained that play activities of any description – except of course games matches – seldom command the total interest of a group of children for much longer than twenty minutes.

It might be as well too to take a look at a cross-section of a typical group of young people one would find at a play unit. Some desire to borrow small items of play equipment such as skipping ropes, play balls or stilts with the object of playing individually; others wish to amuse themselves with quiet activities such as painting, etc., or are content to lounge around chatting or listening to music; there are the older group on the lookout for contact with the opposite sex; some are bent on having a giggle or maybe are potential vandals; a few are on the lookout to thieve whatever is obtainable; some are spectators, come to see specific games played; some come with their parents, particularly the 'under fives'. Last but in all probability the most important is the 'loose' crowd or hard core of the play area. Here in this loose crowd are the youngsters who are most in need of a playleader's attentions.

The purpose of this book is to offer the benefit of my experience which is extensive but by no means all-embracing, in the hope that it will benefit its readers and cause them to think and discuss and try out new ideas for themselves and for the advancement of children's recreation and playleadership.

1 · Scope and Structure

The initiative for starting a playleadership scheme and responsibility for its organization rests generally with the local authority.

Their interest may have been aroused in a number of ways. The National Playing Fields Association and the National Association of Recreation Leaders are two of several bodies who send literature, films and speakers. Other local authorities too may stimulate interest by holding training courses for their playleader staff and inviting neighbouring authorities to send observers. Some small schemes, especially adventure playgrounds, are organized and maintained by voluntary bodies.

Legislation allowing for expenditure is very permissive. No fewer than twenty-one Acts of Parliament, passed since 1875, make provision for this (see page 263, Appendix 2).

Generally, within the local authority, control and management is delegated to the Parks Committee. The chief officer responsible to the committee is the Parks Officer, and the playleadership organizer or games organizer is responsible to him for its direction and organization.

Place of operation

Playleadership schemes can operate almost anywhere and if planners intend to provide an all-embracing scheme then experience so far has proved that the most suitable place is a public park preferably one containing purpose-built accommodation (this will enable the scheme to operate throughout the year and not only during the summer months as do many schemes in England) a grass area for full dress sports, a hard surface area for multipurpose recreational activities and an area set aside for adventurous activities.

It is envisaged that in the not too distant future parks will become centres for family recreation where facilities for all members of the family will be available.

In several European countries these facilities are already in existence and a number of progressive local authorities in this country have made a start with the same objective in view. One way is to commence with a playleadership scheme for children then periodically extend facilities to cater for a higher age group.

Types of schemes

All types of schemes operating in this country have proved beneficial to the needs of the community in more ways than one but no type of scheme yet devised can guarantee success in its entirety.

Playleadership is still very much in the experimental stage and therefore certain failures can be expected but a great deal of knowledge has already been gained by those authorities who took the initiative a few years ago and who exchange their experiences with each other.

Several different concepts of play provision exist in England which include:

1. Playleadership schemes
2. Organized games schemes
3. Adventure playgrounds
4. Under-fives play clubs

BRIEF DEFINITIONS

Playleadership schemes

To play is to perform acts not part of the immediate business of life.

Nearly all activities provided in centres are of an outdoor nature. Playleaders always actively participate in the activities.

Some of the many activities provided in play areas are:

Children's sports	Stilt walking
Miming	Painting and drawing
Table games	Flower arranging
Teni-quoits	Play producing
Word games	Cooking
Choreography	Treasure hunts
Films	Dancing
Embroidery	Concert parties

'Collecting' competitions	Dressmaking
Table tennis	Slide shows

Percussion bands

Organized Games

Organized games are the pivot on which a comprehensive play-leadership scheme revolves. Such schemes embrace organized leagues and competitions for children of a wide age-range, catering for those who are competition-minded. Undoubtedly these schemes attract seventy per cent of those youngsters who take advantage of play amenities. Participation in such games is purely voluntary, with no attempt being made to compel youngsters to play.

Chambers' English Dictionary gives a definition of the word 'play' as being 'to engage in a game and to contend against in a game'.

The important value of this type of provision lies in the opportunity afforded to youngsters to arrange their own affairs.

Activities mainly include full dress games, but other free-play interests are also provided for and may include:

Shinty
Five-a-side soccer (during the summer months)
Association football (during the football season)
Netball
Vaulting and gymnastics
Basketball
Rounders, baseball
Rugby fives
Cricket
Sports meetings
Football team management
Dancing and movement groups
Small team games
Batinton (not to be confused with badminton)

Games centres

These operate during winter evenings as an extension of park schemes offering a wide choice of activities and catering for older children.

Adventure playgrounds

These controversial play areas are provided successfully in many parts of Britain. The town of Emdrup in Denmark produced the first adventure playground during the German occupation in 1943. Professor C. T. Sorensen had the inspiration and John Bertelsen was appointed as the first leader.

Without going into detail here about the value of such playgrounds I shall simply say they are play areas where little if any prohibition exists. Surplus industrial waste materials are provided for young people and with these things they are able to take part in activities not normally allowed in other places.

By involving themselves with each other in their playwork they have the opportunity to counteract their inhibiting environment.

In all types of play schemes it is vital that as many activities as possible be provided but obviously some activities may only take place under certain conditions. Adventure playgrounds prove invaluable by providing some of the leisure-time needs of young children for very little cost.

Typical activities which take place in adventure playgrounds are:

a. Tree climbing
b. Den building
c. Fire lighting
d. Digging
e. Gardening
f. Cooking
g. Water play

Under-fives play clubs

These are open almost every afternoon throughout the year for under-fives accompanied by parents.

It is of course generally accepted that if a scheme is to serve the whole community it should be very comprehensive so far as activities are concerned and should embrace certain characteristics of all those types of schemes so far mentioned.

Times of opening

Parks are usually open from early morning till nearly dusk but playleadership buildings which are situated in them usually open from about 10.00 or 10.30 a.m. until 8.00 or even 10.00 p.m.

If play areas have floodlighting obviously the youth community will derive great benefit. During darkness older members of the community may utilize indoor facilities.

Activities

About the most successful and popular male activity is soccer. Boys of various age groups (from about six years) are encouraged to form their own teams, appoint a manager and organize games within their own age group.

One authority registers nearly six hundred teams during the summer months. Cup competitions are arranged for each group and league winners are presented with medals or certificates.

Provision is made for a wide range of interests, covering individual sports and group work. Cultural, creative and adventurous activities are usually given a degree of priority. Competition is permitted in only a limited number of these because of the possible dangers of over-exuberance, particularly in physical activities, but nevertheless it is realized that healthy competition can benefit a scheme provided such competition is not organized on too high a plane.

2 · Playleaders

RECRUITING AND TRAINING

Staffing a playleadership scheme varies according to local conditions and demand; it involves the recruitment of both professional
and part-time staff. Selection of playleaders is undoubtedly the
most important factor of all and the success or failure of a play
scheme will reflect the qualities and personalities of those employed.

It is recognized that leaders, whether they lead in industry,
politics or any other sphere, have much in common and playleaders
are no exception. The word 'playleader' makes sense only when one
is aware of what is expected of one by the children. Common sense
and a 'down-to-earth' approach are basically what is required.
Experience has shown that the most important and natural factor
of all is that successful playleaders have a healthy enthusiasm for
their vocation, a 'positive attitude' and confidence in themselves.

Each unit is usually staffed with a senior playleader, he or she
being a person possessing the right personality and experience to
work with children and young people; an assistant playleader who
should be a very versatile and adaptable person; also a number of
reliable trainees – boys and girls who possess qualities of good
leadership. A number of voluntary leaders usually make up the
team because this is really what is required – 'a team of people
interested in the development of recreational facilities for the
young' – people who are far-sighted enough to foresee the problems
that could arise in the future in the age of more leisure and less work.

Some schemes have a monitor or prefect system whereby young
boys and girls are selected by the senior playleader, their duties
being to issue and recover items of play equipment, to maintain
and check it and to see it is safe for future use, to compile league
tables for the press, produce their own magazine and a host of other
duties that only reliable youngsters can do.

Recruiting staff

Recruiting staff to work in playleadership is no simple matter as many who appear really promising at interview are most disappointing at the work.

Many are employed for term-time evening sessions. A record of part-timers employed by one Local Authority showed that they followed the following occupations:

School teachers	Shop assistants
Swimming pool attendants	Waiters
Printers	Professional footballers
Skating rink attendants	and scouts
Hospital workers	Musicians
Cinema workers	Sports coaches
Housewives	Students
Firemen	Insurance agents

Policemen

Their lengths of service in playleadership varied from between two hours and fourteen years and their motives and attitudes to work proved to be:

To earn pin money for their holidays
To gain experience in the work
To kill time and seek companionship
To create a new interest for themselves
To keep themselves fit
Their interest in sport
To buy a car
Their own children use the scheme
To do a 'child survey'
As a service to the community

The National Playing Fields Association have issued a pamphlet giving the following list of questions which they suggest could be asked of potential full-time Organizers:

Questions suggested for use by those interviewing playleader applicants

1. Why are you interested in working with children and young people?

2. What age-range of boys and girls do you prefer to work with and why?
3. Why do you think that supervision is necessary at all?
4. How would you deal with the problem of aggressive teen-agers?
5. Explain your views of the function of play in a child's development.
6. Should boys and girls be segregated in play?
7. What is the most important aspect of playleadership?
8. What do you consider your duties would be as a Recreation Organizer.
9. Have you any experience in dealing with parents?
10. With what other child, social and recreational services would you consider it necessary to be in close contact?
11. What is your present staff position?

I think that the National Playing Fields Association list of questions is quite searching up to a point but I feel that such questions might only satisfy a committee who are concerned with a voluntary playground scheme, and that a Local Authority might need to ask in addition:

How many different kinds of playleadership schemes are you familiar with, and can you give brief definitions of them?
How do you see playleadership fitting in as part of the social life of the community in the future?
How would you implement the scheme in this area?
How much equipment and major games furniture would you require to begin?
What is your concept of playleadership?
Would you be capable of organizing a training course for Junior Leaders?
Would you require any staff in the first instance?
Would you organize any special events?

The kind of questions which might be asked of a potential playleader seeking work with a Local Authority could well include the following examples:

What kind of relationship would you strive to create with the parks staff?
What kind of public relations would you advocate?

What action would you take if you found yourself in a difficult situation?

Would you provide any facilities for very young children?

Would you seek the co-operation of outside bodies?

How would you cater for the play needs of girls?

How many hours per play session would you advocate when a scheme first starts?

The above examples are by no means standard questions from any one authority.

'Do school teachers make good playleaders?'

The frequency with which the question occurs may be due, in part, to the scarcity of 'natural' playleaders. The school teacher is, of course, one of the few people who might be available to work during school holidays. A discussion into the suitability of school teachers as playleaders leads one directly into the question of 'what is a playleader?'

Playleaders are classified into three groups:

a. Full-time professional
b. Part-time semi-professional
c. Voluntary

The designations of full-time professional playleaders differ throughout the country, although all do the same job. Here are a few examples:

Beckenham — Chief Games Warden
Dagenham — Chief Games Organizer
Lewisham — Games Organizer
Sunderland — Recreation Leader
Wandsworth — Games Organizer
Coventry — Playleadership Organizer

At the present time few people are qualified in playleadership except by experience, although people employed as professionals are carefully selected by a committee fully competent in selecting officers who have the right personality and mental capacity to fulfil any duty which they may be called to perform in the public interest.

When selecting people for this kind of work it should be borne in mind that one should be looking for those who possess the right

33

personality for it. It is abundantly clear by now that in this con-
nection personality means that the playleader should understand
the need for sympathy, sympathy in the sense that one must like
young people and understand their points of view. The playleader
should be mentally and practically adaptable. Adolescence shows
itself in strong likes and dislikes, and the leader must be in sympathy
with these feelings. There is the type of sympathy possessed by the
experienced leader who can sense and feel the reponse of children
and young people to various situations. Playleaders are up against
the full force of canned entertainment, television, cinemas, juke
boxes, etc., and should be able to offer something that these pastimes lack, they must create a happy atmosphere and a friendly
community. The most painstaking and sincere work is useless
unless the children and young people have accepted the leader,
and only his personality will effect this. The difficulty is that it is
practically impossible to judge correctly whether a candidate has
these qualities or not until he has done a period of work. In spite
of this a 'type' pattern has been established which is by no means
foolproof and not nearly complete. It shows us that a fair proportion
of successful professional playleaders have come from the Armed
Forces; this is understandable when one takes into account that
they are used to mixing and are well disciplined. They are also
pretty well used to judging character and can usually 'size up'
a situation quickly and accurately.

Married women often make good playleaders, but again it is
difficult to get the right type of person who can afford to give the
time, when they have a family to look after. Usually the husband
objects to his wife giving up so much of her time, especially when
the hours of work are so irregular, but undoubtedly the best source
of recruitment is married women: of the different types of recruit
that are known to me they are the most loyal, hardworking and
sincere.

Housewives are, as a rule, devoted to the children they are
working with, and experience has shown that they appreciate and
understand young children much better than do men playleaders.
They seem to gain the respect of older boys far more quickly than
men. I have known of two women playleaders who recruited 120
five-a-side football teams; looked after the fixtures and leagues;
sent results of literally hundreds of games to the press; I have even
seen one conduct a league meeting and referee the games. This

did not stop them from looking after their girls' netball games, dancing troupes, etc. Age does not seem to matter very much. I have known a woman playleader in her sixties – and she was excellent.

If the full-time playleader is the inspiration of a scheme, the part-time leader is most surely the backbone. Very little recognition or credit is given to part-time leaders and yet if it were not for them many schemes would be unable to continue successfully. Some appointments have been made whereby people are responsible for implementing new schemes without ever having worked as playleaders. Of course this is not very good for playleadership at all. In order to ensure constant progress I feel that those people responsible for making appointments should endeavour to implement a system whereby only applicants who have worked as part-time leaders for at least three years – including winters – can even be considered for full-time posts. In time this would ensure that all organizers would be aware of the difficulties in the work, and particularly the difficulties facing part-time leaders.

The 'type pattern' also indicates that students have been employed successfully but much depends on the subject they are studying, because this undoubtedly affects their approach to the job.

Those students who are specializing in physical education are without doubt the most successful and surprising though it may seem, the sociologist does not do so well. The sociologist seems to become too engrossed in other aspects of community life, so consequently his playleading efforts suffer. Art students are more at home in the adventure playground, but take a long time to settle down, they have proved to be fairly unreliable in attendance and several have not set good examples to the children.

Owing to the special intermittent nature of their usual classes at various schools, supply teachers adapt themselves far more quickly than do full-time teachers. In the past they have been a great asset, the reason being that they treat this job as semi-professional, as their living partly depends on it.

As can be expected professional coaches usually find time to offer a few sessions each week. Swimming, cricket, soccer and tennis coaches have been employed but not as specific sport coaches, only as ordinary playleaders. Always they tend to lean towards their own particular interest, which is to be expected, and care

35

must be taken to ensure that they do become involved with other activities and do not create a group of children in the play area who are one-track-minded as far as activities are concerned.

Certain day-time occupations give scope for lots of freedom, and as long as the work is completed within the working week, it does not matter a great deal when it is carried out. One such occupation is insurance agency work. Several insurance agents have worked as playleaders but not with any great degree of success. All of them stayed for only short periods of time, which really was a pity, as they all had good personalities and won acceptance by the children.

Another occupation which gives scope for freedom is music. Several professional musicians were accepted as playleaders but again they stayed for only a week or so.

To get back to the all-important question about whether school teachers make good playleaders; well – the answer is that some do and some do not. Unfortunately for playleadership the vast majority do not, but providing a teacher has the correct outlook, he will make playleading become 'child's play' to use an appropriate phrase. In addition to all the natural requirements of a playleader the following points will need to be carefully considered where teachers are concerned.

His 'staying power' bearing in mind that he already works for most of his time with children and should really be recovering from the great pressures of school work. Playleading is a very strenuous occupation and will take a great deal more out of the teacher than does teaching. It should also be considered whether his normal occupation of teaching will suffer when he returns to school after a bout of playleading.

His ability to 'shelve' the fact that he is a school teacher and to be able to get along without the use of forced discipline or a classroom attitude.

Where he is to be employed as a playleader in relation to the school at which he teaches.

His sense of humour and his attitude to leniency.

His ability to give loyalty to his own play charges instead of expecting loyalty from them as his due right.

His ability to come down to the children's level if needs be.

His ability to adopt a pseudo-parental attitude in place of his normal one of being in authority.

His ability to talk to the children instead of at them and to know that they have much to offer him and to accept that he and they can learn together.

Considerable time could be spent writing on the personal qualities that a good playleader should possess be he teacher, tailor, tinker or sailor, but I feel this to be the correct procedure for the selection of a playleader from any walk of life.

Observe him at work with children under a variety of conditions particularly with a group of children of the opposite sex.

Give the new playleader a chance to express his ideas without any undue interference – within reason of course – from other members of the staff.

Note how he responds to pressures from the older age group.

Try him out with extra chores which must be done in his own time.

Attempt to involve him with awkward parents and see how he copes.

Delegate responsibility to him whereby he becomes involved with a fairly large mixed age group in the organization of a major local event.

Plant ideas in him and observe the results.

Leave him 'holding the baby' at some important event and observe his actions.

Listen to the children discussing him.

Observe his ability to improvize with materials and activities.

Listen carefully to his discussions with the children.

Note how he 'paces' himself in physical activities.

If he should be reasonably good in all the above suggestions I feel that he is a good playleader potentially and that after a local course on playleadership should make the grade. My own experience indicates that only one out of two hundred employees turns out to be a good playleader.

ABOUT PARENTS

The best type of voluntary helpers are parents, who can contribute lots of valuable help to a play scheme, but they can also prove to be somewhat of a drawback. Much depends on how they are initiated when they first come on the scene. The playleader should train himself to assess new parent acquaintances accurately. This takes time of course.

It is not unknown for parents to offer their help for selfish reasons, basically to favour their own offspring, so care must be taken when Mr. J. Smith volunteers to referee a game which involves J. Smith, junior. Invariably this leads to trouble even if the game is controlled with complete impartiality. The trouble is usually started, not by the youngsters competing, but by other parent spectators. Every playleader knows that there are always more 'qualified by experience' referees on the touch line than on the playing fields, and nearly every Dad seems to be an ex-professional soccer player. Many of them start complaining even before the game begins after appraising the opposition potential.

'He is a big lad for Division Four, have you checked his age?'

'Look how he hits that ball, more like fourteen than eleven.'

'This competition seems poorly organized to me.'

'Oh no I'm not complaining, but I think you should keep them in their proper sizes.'

Afterwards, if and when his boy's team is victorious the mood is apt to change.

'Yes! very good game, you've got some good lads here.'

'Must be a bit of a job to get it all sorted out.'

'Oh, I didn't realize the winners receive medals.'

Too many parents do not take sufficient interest in their children's out-of-home interests as it is, so the playleader should also guard against damaging any relationship which may exist between parents who do come to the play area and their children.

Most normal children seem to have a certain amount of natural aggression. This is particularly evident in an under-five playgroup where children often fight for the possession of a toy. Whether this aggression can be harnessed successfully is a matter of opinion but certainly serious consideration should be given to the views of the national coach of an American team which took part in the Mexico Olympics in which he says, 'I am not interested in coaching any youngster who is not a "BAD LOSER".' If aggression therefore is an ingredient in the make-up of world class athletes it should be regarded as a natural asset which can be of value in other walks of life. During the early years parents should play an important part in the slow process of teaching their children to control their aggressive tendencies.

Quite unintentionally some parents are apt to spoil their young-sters by being over-protective and not letting them fight their own battles. In later years this shows itself when they tend to have little if any confidence in themselves. Such parents are sometimes seen with their children in the play area, because seldom if ever are these youngsters allowed out on their own, Mum or Dad are always around to see that 'fair play' is exercised so far as their young are concerned. They choose his activities, watch his every move and even interfere with other children in the play area if they think things are getting rough.

If one over-protects a child from the rigours of childhood it will run the risk of becoming socially isolated and may grow into a shy ineffective adult. No one teaches a child more effectively than the children he associates with in his everyday life so it is unwise to prevent him from mixing. If for example he cheats, brags, cries and argues every time he is the loser, his associates are usually capable of reforming him with their own methods. Childhood is essentially a rough and tumble period of one's life, where one learns to give and take, so that too much sheltering could prove to be harmful in other ways. They will be denied some of the everyday attentions that all children need, with the result that they grow up into bullies and will try to take from society whatever they need irre-spective of where it comes from or who is hurt in the process.

Other parents have a different attitude entirely in that they goad their children and young into fostering their aggressiveness. They encourage their offspring to fight at any given opportunity and are not averse to openly advising them to use quite unfair methods to gain advantage in any situation. Some of them even bully their children into this attitude to life.

Too much bullying at home will probably result in the child becoming a bully outside his own home and later in life this could show itself in spasms of over-aggression, particularly so in physical competitions.

Children are very good at imitating their elders and are some-times affected by what they see on films and television. They are good at 'playing to the gallery' hence the pantomime which usually takes place after a goal has been scored or when a penalty is awarded against their team.

You are bound to come across the parent who becomes a regular nuisance to the play area. This type is not easily recognized at first because usually he makes an effort to get acquainted with and accepted by the playleader before he starts his 'I know my rights' business. Such people have to be handled with extreme diplomacy otherwise they are apt to upset the play area staff which in turn could have serious repercussions throughout the scheme.

It will be found that some parents have a genuine interest in the scheme because they recognize its communal value. These people can usually be persuaded to give some little help in one way or the other, depending of course on the background of their commitments in other ways.

As a general rule it is practically impossible to persuade people to relinquish their spare time consistently without remuneration to work as voluntary playleaders. But some parents who are really interested in major sports activities such as soccer, netball, basketball or gymnastics because their own child is showing potential in one of these activities will help.

Some parents, who are few and far between, will offer all manner of help even if their efforts do not benefit their own children at all.

One section of a playleadership scheme which usually derives some help from parents is the playclub for under-fives: this is because each child must be accompanied by an adult. Once they are present, a good leader can persuade them to give a hand.

This association between parents and playleaders is somewhat different from that which exists between teacher and parents. Such association, with intelligent guidance, can prove most beneficial to a play unit.

TRAINING THE PART-TIME PLAYLEADER

Elsewhere in this book I say that 'experience is the best teacher'; indeed my service in the work has taught me that it is the only teacher.

Academic ability is way down on my list of attributes of a playleader, and no amount of training can put 'natural flair' into a person's characteristic make-up. Training will not create in the student:

An unsentimental liking for the young
The right personality
Sufficient enthusiasm to combat disappointment
Confidence in his ability
A sense of humour
A positive attitude or the will to succeed
The ability to guard against over-confidence
The knack of leading 'just enough'
The virtue of patience
A sense of diplomacy
A sense of responsibility
A sense of fair play.

Training will broaden his outlook in many respects, but I feel – and here lies the difficulty – that he should receive all his practical training, which should be in excess of 90% of the course, within the actual district where he is eventually going to be employed. The theoretical part of the course can be taken anywhere because it is purely incidental. No doubt this outlook will invite criticism, but not from really experienced 'all round' playleaders, who will realize the advantages of such training.

A local short-term course will benefit a playleader much more than one which is run in another area and which makes attempt to cram too much into too little time and places much emphasis on the least relevant aspects.

Too much time may be spent on lectures and discussions and insufficient time on practical work with children, equipment, and materials.

The National Playing Fields Association course which takes place annually does make an attempt to provide a degree of practical work and caters for as many aspects of playleadership as possible within a one-week period. Quite obviously certain aspects of the work do not receive sufficient time to do them justice.

The syllabus for this particular course is fairly all-embracing in its concept except that, in my own opinion, it could provide for more practical work than it does.

After experimenting for a number of years with a local course for playleaders I find that the best results are achieved with a very simple form of syllabus which provides for a practical activity at each session in addition to a talk or discussion. For example:

Session I	The Mechanics of Playleadership
	Illustrated with colour slides
	Practical session – Bounceball – Shinty
Session II	a. The Year's Work
	b. Organizing your Annual Festival
	Practical session – Ring Stick – Three-a-side
	football – Art
Session III	Constructions and Decorations
	Practical session – Elementary Gymnastics
Session IV	Public relations – Poster making –
	Handicrafts
	Practical session – Dodge Ball (various)
Session V	Music and Playleadership
	Practical session – Rounders – Baseball –
	Relay Events
Session VI	Equipment and Improvisation
	Practical session – Games with improvised
	equipment – Ideas for adventure play
Session VII	Organizing Special Events
	Practical session – Skipping routines –
	Movement routines – Dancing
Session VIII	Discussion and Summing up
	Practical session – Batinton and Net Games

The actual talks at these local courses are broken up with the object of giving playleader students, who are all part-time, an insight into the complexities which exist in a Local Authority Play Scheme. The following topics should be covered.

An introduction to playleadership

A brief account of the emergence of Playleadership after the war and how it was first introduced into the area.

The mechanics of a playleadership scheme

1. Responsibility
2. Different types of schemes
3. Definitions
4. Activities (free play and organized play)
5. Staffing

Public relations

1. Senior staff and committee
2. Committee and public
3. Organizer and playleaders
4. Playleaders and public
5. The Press
6. Playleaders and children
7. Playleaders and other council employees

Organization of special events

A comprehensive guide to help students understand the complexities of organizing a special event.

Equipment and materials

1. Expenditure
2. Storage and marking
3. Priorities
4. First aid equipment
5. Donated equipment
6. Purchased equipment
7. Equipment manufactured by the Authority
8. Improvised equipment

The use of music in a playleadership scheme

1. What the Leader needs to know
2. Powers of attraction
3. Making full use of the record player
4. Making music
5. Musical activities

Competition

1. Organization
2. Danger of over-organization
3. Knock-out competitions
4. One against all
5. League competitions
6. Effect of competition attendance

Discussion and summing up

Experience has shown that in order to get good results with new student playleaders – including a chance to assess their potential and to gain an insight into how they may get on with their associates – it is necessary that children and young people are invited to take part in each practical session. In this respect it is well to bear in mind that those who are invited should not be an organized party from one particular school or other institution but should preferably be recruited from local play-scheme units. School groups are more or less under instruction to 'watch their step' on such excursions which quite often defeats the object of the exercise. Playleaders who are known to such groups of children should not take an active part in these sessions.

The most comprehensive course yet devised for part-time playleaders to my knowledge was that which took place at the Harlow Technical College in 1966-67.

SYLLABUS OUTLINE OF THE HARLOW COURSE

The duration of the course is 18 months. There is one $2\frac{1}{2}$ hour class each week during term and one at one of the many playcentres in Harlow during the vacation periods.

The course aims to provide a means of training responsible people for the job of organizing and supervising the activities at play scheme centres which are springing up all over the country.

It is planned to help the future playleader gain an understanding of children's patterns of behaviour, and to provide him with a range of suitable and healthy activities which will stimulate and interest the children in his care.

The hours to be spent on each activity given here are approximate and will vary slightly according to the ability of the class and the number of students.

I. ATHLETICS.   Four $2\frac{1}{2}$ hour periods

An understanding is given of the relevant A.A.A. laws and an elementary knowledge of coaching in Sprints and Relays, Jumps, Discus and Shot Put.

2. ART.   Four $2\frac{1}{2}$ hour periods

The course will include printing, design and creative work for children between the ages of 6 and 16 and a knowledge of basic materials.

3. CHILD PSYCHOLOGY. Six 1 hour periods

The subjects discussed are the basic impulse of play, innate/acquired fears, motivation and environmental influences and social development.

4. DANCING. Six 1 hour periods

This course is designed to provide an interesting and simple method of introducing children to folk dancing. The playleaders will experience this practically themselves before progressing to learning suitable folk dances for children.

1. Basic steps to teach children
2. The 'calls' used in folk dancing
3. General progressions
4. Examples of suitable folk dances for children

5. FIRST AID. Six 2½ hour periods

Students will attend lectures by a doctor before obtaining practical training under the guidance of St. John Ambulance Instructors.

6. GYMNASTICS. Six 1½ hour periods

The students will be given an understanding of the necessary supporting techniques for the following vaults and agilities:

a. Vaults
Astride, Thief, Through, Neckspring, Short-arm overswing, long-arm overswing.

b. Agilities
Cartwheel, handstand, headstand, headspring, back spring, crab, flick-flack.

c. Trampoline
Erection and dismantling
Safety precautions
Teaching of basic movements

7. LIFE SAVING. Five 2½ hour periods

'Syllabus for Bronze Medallion Award'
Students will be given a practical test at the completion of this

45

course in which the minimum requirement will be that they are capable of towing a subject to the side of the pool from 15 yards, landing him on the side and starting artificial respiration. In the case of disability the student must show the ability to direct rescue operations. The course will aim at preparing students for the Bronze Medallion examination and it is hoped that the majority will obtain this qualification.

8. REFEREEING AND UMPIRING.   Fourteen 1 hour periods

Every student studies each of the following five games to a standard which is sufficient to enable him to referee or umpire children's games adequately.

1. Soccer
2. Cricket
3. Rounders
4. Netball
5. Tennis

And four of the following games to the same level:

1. Table-tennis
2. Hockey
3. Rugby
4. Basketball
5. Badminton
6. Korfball
7. Volleyball
8. Quoits

9. SMALL GAMES AND USES.   Five 1½ hour periods

There are hundreds of recognized small games. For the purpose of this course twenty have been selected and will be demonstrated and practised throughout the course.

10. YOUTH HOSTELLING, CAMPING AND HIKING
Four 1 hour periods

1. Map reading
2. Pitching and striking a tent (Choice of site)
3. Hiking (provisions and equipment)
4. Youth Hostels and camping sites

11. DISCUSSION GROUPS. Fourteen 1 hour periods

Subjects include playleaders' problems, activities for particular playgroups and upkeep of equipment.

12. PRACTICAL EXPERIENCE

Each student must complete a minimum of 40 hours practical work assisting experienced playleaders during evenings and school vacations. The successful completion of the course will entitle the student to hold *The Recreational Playleaders' Diploma.*

It would appear that a great deal of research was done before this excellent syllabus was devised; it is first-rate and I applaud the efforts of the college and their foresight.

I found disappointment on one count only, this being the omission of what I consider to be one of the greatest attractions to young people in this day and age: – the importance of music in a playleadership scheme.

TRAINING THE FULL-TIME PLAYLEADER OR ORGANIZER

The training of potential full-time playleaders and organizers, although closely related in many respects to that of part-time playleaders must be much deeper in content. Training need not be on the student's local site. Mr. E. J. Sidebottom, B.Sc., Principal of the National College for the Training of Youth Leaders at the first Annual Conference of the Youth Service Association said: 'As those of us who are older in the service move on, we ought to ensure that those who come into it are given all the help and support they need in their early years and the further training they should have before progressing to higher posts. We ought to be helping some of the leaders of today to be the organizers and trainers of tomorrow.'

I would say that this statement, although not intentionally, applies equally to those of us in playleadership which is one of the reasons why this book has been written.

Before setting out to train a professional playleader it should be established that the would-be student possesses all the necessary

47

attributes and that he has at least three full years' playleading experience which is backed by positive proof of success from his employers. I would clarify this by saying that 'three full years' means all school holidays and every weekend throughout winter, spring, summer and autumn, except of course for his annual holiday and during illness. To my way of thinking he need not be a specialist in any one particular sport or recreational activity but rather a 'Jack of all trades' in a number of interesting recreational pursuits. If he does happen to be a specialist, great care must be taken to see that he is not a fanatic otherwise other activities within his scheme may suffer because of concentration on his own interest.

I am of the opinion that his academic ability does not necessarily have to be in any way outstanding but his English needs to be average in order that he can submit reasonable written reports to his senior officers.

As I have mentioned elsewhere in this book, he needs to have his fair share of common sense – or average intelligence – and the higher his academic background the better, but all the other attributes mentioned earlier in this chapter are more important.

His appearance needs to be clean and presentable and in no way unusual or 'way out'; he should be of a pleasant disposition.

THE THURROCK COURSE

The first-ever full-time course for playleaders has been set up at Thurrock Technical College, Essex, by the National Playing Fields Association and the National Association of Recreation Leaders. It is a two-year course leading after nine months' probation to the Certificate of the National Institute of Playleadership and the status of Qualified Playleader.

ADMISSION

Applicants need to be 18 and unless over 23 must have four passes in the General Certificate of Education, one at Advanced level.

EXPERIENCE OF WORKING WITH YOUNG PEOPLE

They must show evidence of having worked successfully with young people. A report from a Playleadership Organizer, a Youth Officer, or playleader with similar responsibilities is normally required.

Applicants without such experience will be advised how they may best obtain it before the time set for interviews.

This is to ensure that applicants have the aptitude for the work for which they will be preparing themselves.

The course

Part 1 will be largely academic or theoretical, providing background study for an understanding of the role of the playleader in the community. The main subjects will be:

1. Psychology – with an emphasis on Human Growth and Development
2. Sociology
3. Local Government and the Social Services

Part 2 will be concerned with principles and techniques of Playleadership, and with organization and administration. There will be work in movement and drama and lectures in First Aid and Hygiene.

Part 3 will be *practical*. Each student does between eight and twelve weeks' full-time work in play areas, mainly in the Easter and Summer vacations. They probably receive payment for this. In addition, during term-time, half of one day each week is spent in schools, youth clubs or nursery groups. There are visits of observation to social work agencies.

I consider that the course is an excellent one and should result in a flow of first-class manpower into the profession. I would express reserve on two points only on the course, these being that I feel that the minimum age should be 23 years for students and that the course could be much longer, but no doubt this will come in time.

Several years before the Thurrock Course was instituted, the National Association of Recreation Leaders drew up a suggested syllabus of training which is now nearly all incorporated in the college course. Members of the Association were invited to submit their observations and suggestions for consideration and possible inclusion in the final document.

My contribution at that time – and I feel that it is all the more relevant now – was a good break-down of what I consider a course

49

should really consist of. The emphasis is on practical activities which take place in an organized games scheme and operating in a play park. It does not touch on the work of an Adventure Playground Leader, or a leader concerned solely with the 'under-fives' because I feel that the training of these people is somewhat different in many respects and requires a completely different approach.

A SUGGESTED COURSE

I. THE NEED FOR PLAYLEADERSHIP

A. Social Development through recreational pursuits
B. The basic impulse to play

2. PLANNING FOR PLAY

A. Taking stock of facilities available. Making the best use of them
B. Early preparations
C. Layout for play and games areas, including indoor facilities
D. Seasonal programme
E. Monthly programme
F. Weekly programme
G. Daily programme. Morning/Afternoon/Evening
H. Sessional programme
I. Initial provision of equipment
    (a) Type
    (b) Quantity
    (c) Quality
J. Training your own part-time playleaders

3. REPORTS AND STATISTICS

A. Attendance figures/Assessments
B. Weather/Effect on activities and attendance
C. Activities in order of popularity
D. Making out reports/Incidents/Accidents/Progress

4. PUBLICITY AND COMMUNITY RELATIONS

A. Variety of relations
    Senior Staff and Committee

Committee and General Public
Organizer and Playleaders
Playleaders and Public
Playleaders and Local School Staff
Playleaders and Parents
Playleaders and Children
The Press
Playleaders and Park Staff
Organizers and Council's P.R.O.
B. Activities evolved from publicity
C. Dangers of insufficient publicity
D. Wrong type of publicity

5. MUSIC AND ITS IMPORTANCE IN PLAYLEADERSHIP

A. The Playleader and what he should know about music
B. Powers of attraction/listening to music
C. Using the record player/radio/tape recorder
D. Music for tiny tots
E. Music and dressing up
F. Music making/percussion band
G. Singing/competitions/choir/carols, etc.
H. Music and movement/musical skipping/marching
I. Musical games
J. How to organize a musical quiz
K. Music and mime. Choreography
L. Pantomime production
M. Music and rhyme
N. Making musical instruments

6. ORGANIZATION OF SPECIAL EVENTS

A. Suggestions and ideas
B. Procedure/Bye-laws/Cost/Research/Laws of association/
    Publicity/Chief Officer/Committee
C. How to organize the following events:
    Handicrafts and flower arranging exhibition
    Sports meeting (Novelty)
    Gymnastic competition
    Candy sports
    Dancing competition
    Inter-park friendly games competitions

Children's pet shows
May Queen festivals
Mammoth treasure trail
Scavenger hunt
Rebound tumbling (Trampoline) competition
Concert parties
Kite-flying competition
Fancy dress competition
Bits and pieces (Collecting) scramble
Inter-parks games leagues
Table games competition
Road safety displays
First aid demonstrations
Annual finals day
Fishing competition (if relevant)

D. How to organize a league and trophy competition on a large scale
E. How to compile league tables
F. How to organize a games rally

7. PRACTICAL GAMES SESSIONS

A. Rounders games
B. Tag and Tug games
C. Ball games
D. Romp and remainder games such as
   battle for the banner, bonnets, bull in the ring
E. Dancing
F. Handicrafts
G. Table games

8. FULL-DRESS GAMES

Films and talks by qualified officials followed by discussion periods. Students to pre-study rules.

A. *Boys*
   Association Football
   Five-a-Side Football
   Cricket
   Basket Ball
   Volley Ball

Korfball
Rugby Union
Rugby League
Shinty
Hurling
Gaelic Football

B. *Girls*
Netball (A.E.N.A. Rules)
Rounders (N.R.A. Rules)
Hockey
Lacrosse

C. *Miscellaneous*
Batinton
Quisling
Deck Quoits or Teni Quoits
Catch Ball
Fencing
Judo
Boxing
Swimming and Diving

D. *Street games* such as
Have All (Lamp post)
Fag Card a Look
Winter Warmers
Hoops

THE TRAINEE PLAYLEADER

Next in line and most important is the trainee playleader, I say
'most important' because usually they are far more physically fit
because of their youth and are able to obtain a closer relationship
with the children than can the older leaders.

Many of their duties will include actual participation in activities
provided for the children. The girl trainees will be expected to help
train and organize netball teams and to umpire games, sometimes
amongst the children of the parks where they are employed and
sometimes involving children from other parks. They will, if they

53

are able, help to teach various forms of dance to the younger children. They will be encouraged to create and help to make costumes for the dancing troupe, to organize items for shows that the children put on. They may be asked to assist in the 'Under-five Playgroup Areas' with painting and other activities specially provided for the little ones. Boy trainees will be asked to help referee some of the many football matches that take place in the parks, to help keep records of the league tables, and most important to help look after the equipment. Both boy and girl trainees could be in charge of representative teams, and children making visits to other parks for friendly games. These items are only a very few of the many duties they will be expected to undertake during their employment as trainees.

In one respect a trainee has a slight advantage over a playleader in that he is able to judge a scheme from both sides of the fence as it were. It is more likely that he has gained lots of experience as a participant of the scheme, and progressed to the position of trainee through a prefectship. Before he gets any fixed ideas – it is surprising how many of them change overnight – he must be guided in a manner which will not only be beneficial to the scheme but to the trainee himself, bearing in mind that this is probably his very first paid employment. What is instilled into him now may stand him in good stead for the rest of his working life.

3 · Relations with the Community

THE PLAYLEADER AND THE LOCAL AUTHORITY

Committee members always like to be in a position to explain to their constituents exactly what is happening in their locality. Therefore it is the responsibility and duty of the organizer to make sure that all relevant information is given in the reports he submits to his senior officers.

Local Authorities desire the best possible public relations at all levels and in order to achieve this many of them appoint a Public Relations Officer. If an authority employs a P.R.O. it would be advisable for the playleader to liaise with him on all matters appertaining to publicity. He will have many contacts and can be most helpful to you, so be most careful always to keep him well informed.

Relationships

a. *Senior staff and committee*
   The Chief Officer will keep the Committee well informed at all times but obviously he must be supplied with the information to pass on and details of this must come from the playleader.

b. *Committee and the public*
   On request, the P.R.O. will release a 'Press Notice' for the playleader on the occasion of a major event. In order to do this he will require full details giving information about What, Where, When, Why and Whom? Usually he will liaise with the Chairman of the Committee during the preparation of the press release.

55

Chairman of controlling committee and organizer

Apart from meeting the Chairman in Committee, the playleader will obviously invite him to attend various playleadership scheme functions during his term of office. On these occasions there will probably be discussion about the progress and future projects of the scheme. As he is the Council's representative and one who holds a great deal of authority, it will be his business to know more about the scheme than his fellow councillors and it will be found that he will be very knowledgeable and interested in all aspects of control and progress. This relationship should form part of a united effort to provide a more efficient service to the community, therefore the organizer should school himself to give information and ideas with this end in view.

Immediate superior officer and organizer

The functions of a playscheme most probably form only a very minor part of a senior officer's responsibility unless of course it is a large all-embracing scheme. Minor and petty problems will not be welcomed by him but he should be informed about major trends in the work, not only in his own authority's scheme but in others throughout the country and abroad. Unless he is well informed he will be unable to make effective decisions for the benefit of the scheme. The relationship between leader and immediately superior officer should be based on regular discussions and informative reports.

OTHER CONTACTS

In carrying out his duties the organizer of a scheme will at some time or another come into contact with officers and servants of other departments. To have the ability to converse with people at different 'status' levels without feeling inferior (or bearing an air of superiority) is essential. Although experience shows that the old maxim 'It's not what you know, it's who you know' can be applicable in most walks of life, it is very important for the playleader to feel that what he knows and what he is doing is sufficiently important to give him the right to meet and know anybody on any level.

In many respects an organizer's work outside the play area is of paramount importance. Much of this work will be done in conjunction with other people who are not directly concerned with children's play. Some of these will be fellow employees of the Council and other public bodies and some will be from other walks of life in the local community. The organizer must endeavour to enlist their co-operation, for on this will depend much of the successful running of the play area.

Parks Superintendent and his staff

If a scheme operates mainly in parks it is important to bear in mind that it is imperative that a healthy relationship exists between the head of the scheme and the parks superintendent. Poor planning on one side can make life very difficult for the other. The play organizer should be aware that parks are meant to cater for others apart from children and that noise and mess are just as offensive to some people as restrictive play notices are to others.

A park superintendent has the difficult task of trying to please all people who use the parks and to maintain a happy balance of provisions for them all. Quite often his task is made all the more difficult by vandalism and staffing problems. Therefore the last thing he wants is an element of young people who can create just as much havoc as vandals under the protective umbrella of a council-backed scheme.

The head of a scheme can help in many ways to ease the superintendent's unenviable task by consulting with him on all matters of programme planning, particularly those where organized games will involve the park staff in any way.

Too much should not be taken for granted when working in council parks and it should be borne in mind that situations can change in a matter of minutes. What one park keeper feels is permissible may not be allowed by another. so if an activity commences whilst one park keeper is on duty it may be stopped by another keeper just starting his shift. Such situations can and have in the past caused unnecessary trouble and only a good relationship between the parks superintendent and the play organizer, based on a sound understanding of each other's responsibilities and the desire to work together as a team and back each other up will overcome the many difficulties which are sure to arise.

It may well be that a park keeper who takes immense pride in 'his' park fears damage to 'his' turf etc., and so is unsympathetic to the scheme. If a park keeper also feels that playleaders receive a higher remuneration for 'playing' it can make the relationship rather strained and in such a case it is as well for the playleader to leave all dealings to the organizer.

Playleaders can be faced with a difficult situation when a decision has to be made on the condition of the ground. When at the time of play the ground appears to be in good playing condition, a group of disappointed youngsters may find it difficult to understand a foreman's ruling that the ground is not fit, not realizing that the ruling is made on a decision possibly made earlier in the day. The final word must rest with the foreman and the playleader must do all he can to maintain a good relationship with and between both parties.

Workshops Superintendent

It will be found that in a council's sponsored scheme the keyword to success is co-operation. No officer can expect to 'go it alone' and succeed because the work requires experts and 'know how' from many different angles. Games furniture will have to be designed, manufactured and regularly maintained and this task will no doubt come within the orbit of the workshops superintendent's responsibilities. He will no doubt seek your advice from time to time in order to instruct his tradesmen on exactly what is required. Quite often, because of vandalism you will need to seek his assistance at very short notice: therefore a close relationship must exist bearing in mind that at no time will he need the play organizer to make his job a success but the play organizer will at times need him.

Transport Supervisor

On many occasions for a multitude of reasons transport will be required involving the use of different types of vehicles from mini-vans to articulated lorries. In a large authority it is sometimes difficult to acquire a vehicle exactly when it is required. Sometimes a vehicle is available but not a driver. At certain times of the year the main problem is shortage of drivers and on occasion the demand for vehicles exceeds the supply. Playleadership must be well down on the list and certain disappointments should be expected. It always helps the transport supervisor a great deal if notification of requirements is given well in advance. Organizers should be in sympathy with the fluctuating pressures of demand on the transport supervisor and make allowances in their relationship accordingly.

Stores Superintendent

Organizers and stores superintendents will be in constant liaison with each other on various aspects of equipment provision for the scheme. The organizer should know exactly which equipment and the amount he needs and the stores superintendent should know where to procure it. The stores superintendent as well as the transport supervisor has a great deal to contend with, much of it connected with items of more importance than play equipment or materials. He also is usually under pressure from other officers in practically every department of the authority. The relationship between organizers and stores superintendents should be based on respect for each other's problems of demand and supply; the relationship will be helpful if the stores superintendent appreciates that some children won't (easily) take 'No' for an answer and that the organizer doesn't like to let them down, and if, on the other hand, the organizer and children accept that the stores superintendent cannot guarantee to get equipment and have it delivered at the organizer's whim and fancy at a certain place by a certain time.

Printing Shop Officer

Contact should be established with the officer who is responsible for printing. A well-organized scheme will have a constant stream of memoranda, instructions, pamphlets, application forms and requests going through the pipeline.

The success of any such venture depends a great deal on the kind of impact which is made on the general public. Much of the responsibility for creating a good image will rest on the shoulders of the people responsible for lay-out and printing. Such officers will require as much information as possible about the project – and lots of time to work on it – and then they should be left to get on with it without undue interference. Colour schemes and sketches will be asked for on the odd occasion, but generally speaking these people are more than capable of handling everything to attract youngsters.

Highways Superintendents

Quite frequently these people are in a position to dispose of unwanted but quite useful materials which can prove invaluable to adventure playground users. Old shoring timbers, trestles, rope,

59

sand and sometimes small huts can be had for the asking. Picks, shovels and old wheelbarrows are sometimes written off as being unserviceable to council employees, but children will make use of them if given the opportunity. Old handcarts, pulleys and lifting tackle have been obtained in the past and on one adventure playground a fish pond was created by using an old tarpaulin which had been obtained from the highways department. Unserviceable braziers and lamps can make fire play more interesting for children; for example, one can roast potatoes better on a brazier and a lamp is 'better than an electric light' in a den built by oneself.

Refuse Superintendent

It is absolutely amazing what some people throw away and a visit to the refuse sorting yard can prove well worthwhile.

Of course before such visits are made it will be necessary to seek the co-operation of the officer in charge of the department. It must be borne in mind that anything collected by the council's refuse workers automatically becomes the property of the council, and its sorting and disposal is the responsibility of the refuse superintendent.

Predominant on the metal scrap heap will be found parts of scooters, tricycles and fairy cycles. The majority of these are in need of very minor repairs. Usually a wheel is loose or missing. Some of these are comparatively new and sometimes several parts of the same model are to be found, so it becomes a simple job to put these various sections together.

As refuse is brought to the yard each working day it is highly unlikely that time can be found to check all of it.

On the other hand if a good relationship exists between the play organizer and the refuse superintendent, a system could be adopted whereby he will arrange for such items to be placed on one side to be viewed when convenient.

Old People's Welfare Officer

Opportunity should be made available for children and young people to take part in playwork which will benefit older members of the community. Projects to achieve this could keep the children busy to provide live entertainment for the old folks, and to raise money for the benefit of the adopted club. One such play unit I know raises cash which is used to take a coach load of elderly people to the coast each year. Money is raised during the Christmas period by groups of children who tour the estates singing Christmas carols. In return for this the old people have presented the play unit with an 'Award of Merit' inscribed 'To the young people of Chinbrook, from the elderly of St. Swithins'. This award is presented each year to the boy or girl who has worked hardest for the play unit. Judgement is made by a panel of children from the play unit itself.

The Old People's Welfare Officer can be instrumental in circulating information to the elderly, about such things as concert parties and displays which the children are willing to give during school holidays and on special occasions.

Sometimes the Old People's Welfare Officer can arrange for old people to act as judges in such things as fancy dress or May Queen competitions.

Civic Entertainments Officer

Increasing numbers of Local Authorities are appointing officers to be responsible for the provision of various forms of entertainment. Concerts and variety shows, dances, quiz competitions, fêtes and open-air entertainment in the parks are part of the responsibilities of these people. Some entertainment officers organize indoor five-a-side football, tennis and other forms of physical recreation but generally speaking these functions should be the responsibility of a physical recreation officer, if one exists. Co-operation with entertainments officers therefore is a necessity. On occasions when he organizes fêtes and gala days he can provide opportunities for children of a play scheme to take part in displays and competitions which will act as an incentive to them to become proficient in whatever the activity may be.

An entertainments officer can be most useful to a play scheme if it produces plays or concerts. His expertise on stage management, lighting and sound-effects etc., can be a very helpful factor.

Librarian

Advertising forthcoming events is a serious business to a playleader and one of the council's officers who can be most helpful to him in this and other ways is the Borough Librarian. A library is an excellent place to display posters and distribute pamphlets to school children, especially during the long summer holidays when it is not possible to use schools for advertising purposes. Arrangements to

61

use libraries for the purpose should be made with the children's librarian, giving plenty of time before the proposed event is due to take place.

Librarians are usually able to put on film shows at play centres during school holidays and termtime evenings. Most librarians have their own ciné projector and many library assistants are capable of operating one. These people have contacts with advertising agents from major industrial concerns and are able to obtain the loan of many interesting films free of charge. Lots of these films have an educational value and are much in demand from borrowers. Quite often it is found that they are not obtainable when required, so it would be wise to give the librarian as much time as possible to book these films for your shows. As much as six months may be needed to secure a particular film.

Lecturers may be booked by the Borough Librarian to give talks at local playleadership courses on subjects ranging from child psychology to the work of local sports councils.

The Music Librarian

I feel quite sure that any well-experienced playleader will agree that music in almost any form is a most powerful attraction.

The subject of music is covered more fully in its own chapter and my only concern at this point is to bring to your attention the importance of striking a good relationship with the Council's music librarian.

He will be able to place at your disposal the use of a record library from which you can choose music that is suitable for almost any occasion ranging from recorded pop concerts to the classics. Many music librarians are pleased to arrange recitals and sound illustrated lectures covering a variety of musical tastes. He will probably be able to arrange for qualified adjudicators to officiate at any competitions being organized or to obtain the services of professional instrumental demonstrators who can make a lecture on music very interesting and entertaining.

It is also possible for him to provide musical scores for percussion band work and he may be able to provide accommodation at the library for such a band to rehearse or practice in.

Baths Manager

Being a specialized activity, swimming is not catered for in every play scheme in the country, although in my opinion it should be. Various reasons exist why it is not included, for example:

a. Lack of pools adjacent to play areas
b. Difficulty of finding playleaders qualified in life saving and so able to accept responsibility
c. Reluctance of Local Authorities to introduce specially reduced prices of admission for parties from play schemes
d. Congestion of popular pools during peak holiday periods

If swimming becomes part of the programme, good purpose will be served if an understanding is fostered with the Baths Manager. In all probability he will be able to create an interest in life saving with some of the older children. He will be able to have them coached and examined in this subject and could be instrumental in introducing youngsters with potential into local swimming clubs.

A co-operative Baths Manager will assist and advise on occasions when you are organizing a swimming gala. He will probably be able to help recruit specialized or experienced officials from amongst his many contacts. It is doubtful if you will have sufficient personnel of your own staff to run a gala.

Housing Manager

Another very good method of contacting young people, especially those who have left school, is with the help of caretakers of blocks of flats. Vandalism is rife in blocks of flats in some areas and usually caretakers realize the value of playleadership or any other form of recreation which will occupy children and young people. Many caretakers will co-operate on the issue but permission must first be obtained from chief officers of housing departments before such approach is made. Caretakers will distribute pamphlets, etc., giving information about programmes and activities. They will also display posters on notice boards. Some caretakers will even undertake to form five-a-side football teams and act as team managers for groups of youngsters from their estates.

In some authorities housing managers have powers to provide play facilities and leaders. Approaches are sometimes made to playleadership organizers by housing managers seeking information and advice on the types of provision which suit certain circumstances.

Co-operation is essential between heads of housing departments

63

and play scheme organizers if the local authority in question is making an attempt to find a solution to this problem of vandalism on housing estates.

Borough Architects

An increasing interest in designing playgrounds is evident amongst architects, in particular landscape architects. During recent years they have contributed a great deal to the design of playgrounds and major pieces of play furniture and some are known to have given serious study to children's play patterns and needs before making their contribution. Not all architects are of the same mind (thank goodness) because one or two attempts have been made to create play sculptures with very little degree of practical success, except from a visual point of view.

In the past the majority of creations have tended to be built upwards in order to cater for a child's natural instinct to climb. Some are now being created whereby the child must go down first into a cavity and then climb up to get out. Underground tunnels are being incorporated in designs of static play complexes on the continent, which we are told help to combat claustrophobic tendencies. The last such experiment that I heard about had to be closed, because water seeped in when it rained. No doubt this effect was not designed by an architect.

It would appear to me that in the near future architects and planners are going to play a major part in the provision and development of playgrounds, particularly adventure playgrounds. The result of their efforts may be partly based on information supplied by you, therefore if your assistance is requested by the Borough Architect it might serve the future child community of your area well if your answer were given after very carefully studying all aspects of the points in question.

Architects are a particular breed of meticulous thinkers who endeavour to cater for every conceivable need of people who use their creations, but they must be fully aware of what these needs are.

They will be concerned about such things as safety, durability, degrees of attraction of specific activities and they will probably seek information as to whether any other similar type of playground is situated in the same area, and if so which type of activity is most popular.

64

Ultimately the finished playground may reflect some of your ideas and once it is constructed it may be too late to make major changes. With regard to buildings in playgrounds, many different concepts exist and no doubt many more designs will emerge. One major problem at the present time is the amount of vandalism directed at such buildings. This is the architect's problem, but you should endeavour to help in any way you can.

Blue Cross

One of a playleader's responsibilities is to encourage children to care for their pets properly. It is quite amazing how attached some children are to their pets and yet are unaware that they are not looking after them properly.

The Blue Cross Society, which is affiliated to Our Dumb Friends League, is always ready to help children with advice and to care for their sick animals.

If a children's dog or pet show is organized, the Blue Cross will be found to be most helpful, so I would suggest that contact be made with your local branch.

St. John Ambulance Brigade

This organization can be of benefit in a number of ways to a play leadership scheme.

For example they will be only too pleased to assist in providing first aid training for playleaders. They will provide an attendant at events and on occasion they will accept, on the playleader's recommendation, young people to train as St. John Ambulance Cadets. On organizing a playleaders' course it will be found that they will be most helpful in providing lectures on hygiene, first aid, water safety and artificial respiration.

Youth officer

As playleadership and the youth service have much in common it stands to reason that a close relationship should exist between the two officers responsible for these public amenities. In some ways their duties tend to overlap especially where a play scheme caters for a higher age group than normal.

The playleadership organizer should encourage a system whereby it becomes the done thing for his children to join the local youth club when they become old enough.

At the time of writing, the youth service is already beginning to lower its age limits, so naturally a much closer liaison will become a necessity.

A senior youth officer will be able to assist the play scheme in many ways, chiefly with the loan of equipment, the use of school buildings and in some cases the secondment of specialist instructors if they are ever required; he will also be useful from a public relations point of view in that he will distribute your literature and application forms to all his clubs. He will undoubtedly be able to obtain some voluntary help for the scheme by involving some of his young people who are taking their 'Duke of Edinburgh Award' and who must do some voluntary work as part of the syllabus.

Area Education Officer

No approach may be made to any schools for any reason whatsoever unless permission has first been obtained from the Area Education Officer. If such approach is made, headmasters invariably will ask if the permission has been granted. By obtaining this co-operation it is possible to get through to every child in the district which of course is what you must endeavour to do. This officer will distribute information about coming events and projects to every school in the district. Of course he will vet everything very carefully and in some cases he will probably refuse permission, especially if he feels that no educational value is attached to the project. Contact with his department can be most beneficial to a play scheme.

Playleaders and staff of local schools

Seldom, if ever, does any difficulty exist between local school teachers and playleaders; indeed, many teachers work as part-time playleaders but awkward situations do occur sometimes. One of the most common happens when a school teacher is employed as a part-time leader at a play area frequented by the children whom he teaches at school.

Fortunately this does not happen a great deal but friction usually occurs when a playleader who is not a qualified teacher gets involved in discussions on academic subjects when the teacher is present. Relationships also suffer when games rules are altered for reasons peculiar to the playground, especially if the teacher is involved with taking the same games at school under a different set of rules.

Perhaps the most serious threat to good relations between play-leaders and teachers is the situation in which young people are encouraged, and sometimes ordered, to address their playleaders in a formal manner. But this is mentioned under the subheading Playleaders and Children, on p. 76.

Officers in charge of neighbouring schemes

Children living on the borderline between two boroughs which both have play schemes quite often make use of facilities in both areas and are usually known to both organizers.

Scheme organizers will find that a close liaison with their counter-parts in neighbouring authorities can prove an asset in more ways than one. Inter-unit events can be organized jointly to create an extra incentive for more children to participate in play amenities in both areas.

Experience and ideas should be encouraged and in cases of doubt advice should be sought from neighbouring officers. Information about successful projects and about failures should be freely given to your associates if you think such information will be beneficial to them.

In adopting this policy of co-operation with your associates opportunities will be created for children from your own units to take part in dancing and gymnastic displays, etc., at galas and special events sponsored by other authorities.

Occasions may arise when you want to borrow extra equipment for a special event or when you can be of assistance to one of your associates in a similar manner.

During your local course on playleadership it sometimes helps to call on the services of another play organizer to speak on a particular subject in which he is well experienced and you may reciprocate in a like manner.

Road Safety Officer

Co-operation with the road safety officer in promoting facilities for instruction and examination in cycling proficiency should naturally rank as a must in the work of a playleader. It must be borne in mind that although the responsibility is his the concern should be yours and you should assist him as much as possible. On the other hand he may not need your assistance, especially if he works in conjunction with schools.

67

Residents' Associations

These bodies usually are very much aware of what is going on in their locality. Some are known to be actively involved in some play schemes and give considerable help in one way or another. Others are known to be opposed to play schemes for various reasons, mainly because of the element of noise, which is inevitable where large numbers of children congregate. Whatever the attitude of a residents' association to a play scheme may be, the organizer should keep in close contact either to engineer help for his scheme on the one hand, or to co-operate and help to alleviate their grievances on the other.

Local sports council

An endeavour should be made to obtain representation on local sports councils for playleadership schemes. One of the aims of sports councils is to seek and obtain provision of dual purpose educational buildings and other undertakings to enable sports clubs and organizations to use them outside school hours.

The Department of Education and Science has issued a circular (No: 11/64 'Provision of facilities for sport'), which draws attention to the possibility of combining with other local authorities or voluntary bodies to provide sports facilities for use not only by pupils and students but also by the *general public*.

Representation on the local sports council will provide an opportunity for the needs of a play scheme to be put forward for consideration.

It will be found that much pressure will be exerted by the administrative bodies of local sports clubs and, in particular, organizers of those sports which are recognized as 'indoor activities'. Once these clubs establish and obtain their needs they are more than reluctant to share facilities with others, especially members of the public who do not belong to any particular club. Some sports clubs are very far from 'sporting' in their outlook when it comes to co-operation, and as a general rule playleadership schemes are way out on a limb when such considerations are being made. In new ventures it would be as well to get your requests in early.

Social Worker (formerly called Children's Officer)

A Social Worker is responsible for children who are resident in homes belonging to the authority. Housemothers and fathers are always pleased to be advised about activities and special events which take place in a play scheme, so they should be kept well informed.

Young deprived children who attend under-fives play schemes derive a great deal of benefit from their visits and from the integration between themselves and children from normal homes.

Older children from homes are usually brought to the play area to take part in organized games competitions, and a good relationship between houseparents of the homes and playleaders is essential. This is nearly a foregone conclusion because people of both these professions have many things in common and basically they are all fond of children.

A Social Worker will sometimes make contact with a play organizer if he is involved with a problem child or a difficult young person to see if the youngster can be catered for in some way and thus may be helped to overcome his problems.

In making an approach to houseparents about events and activities, it must be stressed that protocol decrees that permission must be granted by the Social Worker before such approach is made.

VOLUNTARY ASSOCIATIONS

Pre-school Playgroups Association

This association makes a splendid effort to encourage the provision of under-fives playgroups all over the country. One of its most important functions is to establish training courses for playgroup assistants and supervisors. Although a difference exists in their concepts, play-clubs and playgroups have one thing in common – activities provided for the children. Therefore much of the training which is given to playgroup assistants is also relevant to play-club leaders. Opportunity should be afforded to playleaders who will be working in a play-club to attend one of these courses.

Contact should be made with the local branch of the P.P.A. in order that literature can be obtained from them. Their magazine and pamphlets give some extremely useful information about all manner of play provision. Visits to other under-fives play units can be arranged which in turn should result in a much broader understanding of the whole question of provision.

Council for Children's Welfare

The Council for Children's Welfare, founded by the late Dr. Simon Yudkin, is a voluntary organization concerned with every aspect of children's lives. Its aim is to see that all children are given the opportunity to develop their full potential. Thus the range of the Council's activities is wider than that of more specialized organizations with which it often co-operates. It keeps a watchful eye on any current issue to do with children and by means of meetings, conferences and publications it presses for any necessary action to be taken.

The Council also undertakes special studies and research and makes recommendations for legislation and other means of reform. For years the Council has been deeply worried about the lack of play provision for children in an urban environment. A study of the subject, financed by a generous grant from the Calouste Gulbenkian Foundation, has resulted in the publication of *Children's Play – A Study of Needs and Opportunities* by Anthea Holme and Peter Massie (Council for Children's Welfare, Michael Joseph). This book provides information and guidance for local authorities, architects, planners and voluntary organizations.

The work of the Council is neither static nor limited. It remains constantly watchful of any problems or social change which may affect children in any way, and it welcomes suggestions from members about possible new areas of action. If you are interested in any of the past, present or future activities of the Council for Children's Welfare, please join and make your views known.

The Save the Children Fund

The Save the Children Fund works for children, irrespective of race, colour or creed – the only criterion is need. In many countries of Europe, Asia and Africa – including Italy, Korea, Hong Kong, Algeria and Kenya – SCF administrators, doctors and nurses are working to free children from hunger, disease and poverty. Today, in the United Kingdom, Fund Playgroups, Clubs and Homes are all helping to give tomorrow's citizens a foundation of health and happiness.

National Playing Fields Association

The National Playing Fields Association is a voluntary organization which aims to give everyone an opportunity to participate in the activity of their choice by encouraging the provision of adequate playing fields and recreational facilities for the whole population.

The Association was founded on 8th July 1925. The first President was H.R.H. The Duke of York, later H.M. King George VI. From its inception the Association has been keenly supported by allied sporting bodies, local authorities, industry and individuals from every walk of life, whose devoted work to the Association is outstanding in the annals of voluntary service.

Before 1925 the supply of public recreational facilities was a local matter; provision was spasmodic and held back by the lack of central direction. The foundation of the National Playing Fields Association steadily established recognition of the vital importance of playing fields to the physical, moral and mental welfare of the youth of the country.

The Association was incorporated by Royal Charter on 18th January 1933. As a National Charity the Association was entered on 26th April 1963 in the Register of Charities established by the Charities Act 1960. There are six sub-committees:

Appeals, Grants, Finance, Grounds and Layout, General Purposes and Children's Playgrounds and Playleadership.

The Headquarters staff under the General Secretary perform the day-to-day work and evolve the groundwork of policy and development for consideration by the sub-committees, and the Association has affiliated County and City Associations and County Representatives which cover the whole country.

THE NATIONAL PLAYING FIELDS ASSOCIATION'S AIMS AND
OBJECTS

1. To secure adequate playing fields available to the public and facilities for open air and indoor recreation.
2. To assist in the development of existing recreational facilities where needed.
3. To co-operate with Local Authorities in making the fullest use of their powers when preparing Town Planning Schemes to ensure that ample playing space is secured.
4. To secure properly equipped playgrounds for the use of children and press for facilities to be made available where required.
5. To encourage the training and appointment of Playleaders for children's playgrounds.
6. To co-operate in saving threatened recreational facilities.

71

7. To act as a centre for advice and assistance for local authorities, sports clubs and other interested organizations on all matters connected with the acquisition, layout and use of grounds and buildings for recreation.
8. To provide and maintain a Technical Service of high standard to form the complete counterpart in the Counties of the National Sports Council Technical Service.
9. To raise money so that financial assistance, by way of grants and loans, may be given where needed for recreational facilities.

With the continuing development of land for housing, roads and other purposes, the provision of adequate recreational facilities is increasingly important to the life of the country.

The National Association works through the County Associations, on whom it relies for information and guidance. Most County Associations depend almost entirely on the voluntary service of their members, even those administered and staffed by Local Education Authorities and by Community Councils.

With their many years of experience, the County Associations are in a position to be extremely useful to their own Local Authorities, sports associations, youth and sports clubs.

National Association of Recreation Leaders

The National Association of Recreation Leaders was founded in September 1960. For three or four years several Local Government officers employed in the London area as chief playleaders had felt that a need existed for the creation of a professional body of people so employed.

At a meeting in Wandsworth it was decided to draw up a draft constitution and to invite all who were employed on a part-time basis. The first full meeting of the Association was held in Playfield House, London and it may be of interest to note that its founder members were:

Bill Fry	Senior Games Warden	Beckenham
George Green	Chief Playleader	Dagenham
Bernard McGovern	Games Organizer	Lewisham
Charlie Parker	Chief Games Warden	Tottenham
Harry Pearce	Games Organizer	Wandsworth

After two years the Association became affiliated to the International Recreation Association whose headquarters are in New York, and to the National Playing Fields Association, London.

The main objects of the Association are:

(a) to advance provision of recreation and play facilities especially for children and young people
(b) to promote training facilities and to obtain official recognition of its examinations

It aims too to 'act as a clearing-house for the exchange of progressive ideas relevant to Play and Recreation' and to publish and circulate books and papers.

The Association provides speakers for playleadership courses throughout the country, and, with other bodies, was instrumental in creating the first full-time course in playleadership at Thurrock College. It created National Play Day.

An offshoot of the Association – albeit entirely separate – is the National Association of Recreational Administrators which is concerned mainly with the welfare of its members.

International Playground Association

This association was represented on the international panel which drew up the International Charter for Leisure. It is an extremely active body which contains members from all over the world. Its News Letter which is regularly published in a number of different languages is very informative and enlightening.

The association holds valuable conferences in different countries. Reports are received from different countries and results of research studies are published in the News Letter. A large number of other organizations are affiliated to the International Playground Association, in addition to many individual authorities on play. Its membership includes teachers, educational psychologists, youth workers, architects and planners, careers advisers, social workers, playleaders, play organizers, adventure playground leaders and community Play Centre workers.

Adventure Playground Workers' Association

At the time of writing this body has only just been formed. It is represented on the Constitutional Sub-committee of the Institute of Playleadership together with the National Playing Fields Association and National Association of Recreation Leaders. Its aims are obviously directed to the further provision of adventure playgrounds throughout the country and to the specialist training of adventure playground leaders.

Other public bodies

Your co-operation may be sought by other public bodies such as the Probation Service or the Police; I emphasize the word 'may' because from personal experience I was approached on only two occasions during my first fifteen years as a playleader and on both counts I was unable to be of assistance to these officers because I did not know the children about whom they were concerned. Much depends on the type of area where you are employed and I am given to understand that in certain depressed areas this function supersedes many others, and that some leaders spend much of their time attending 'Children's Courts'.

After discussing this subject with the Local Probation Officer I find that different courts have different attitudes and where one court may welcome evidence – if this is the right word – from school teachers and other close acquaintances of the youngster in trouble another court may only admit parents or guardians. During this particular discussion the phrase 'delinquency is a spare-time occupation for bored youngsters' was voiced which may be a pointer to the fact that the majority of the young people who make use of play scheme facilities never see the inside of a juvenile court because they are seldom if ever bored, depending again on where the scheme is situated. The same phrase brought to my mind the definition of a delinquent given by a social worker doing research into child behaviour as being 'one who had appeared before a juvenile court'. From experience I should think that a more realistic definition – albeit just as foolishly incorrect – would be 'one who was unlucky enough to have been caught scrumping apples'. How many of my readers have been guilty of a crime such as a well-planned, well-organized 'Operation Garden Wall' where all the gang acquired stomach-ache from eating crab apples and possibly were belted on the backside with a broom handle as they climbed back over the wall and dropped some of their apples back into the orchard? Very few of us who consider ourselves as being normal have not been involved in escapades such as this.

My own working area of London – the south eastern – has a

population of 350,000 plus and embraces districts of contrasting social status from suburban Bromley on the fringe of the stockbroker belt to the docklands of the Thames and Greenwich. Within the bounds of places like these can be found practically every kind of social environment in the book of the sociologist. It might be reasonable to assume a close liaison between playleader and these bodies, but this is not so. I doubt very much if more than six or so playleaders have ever been asked for their co-operation since the scheme commenced fourteen years ago.

If such co-operation is requested of you it is your duty as a responsible person and as a public servant to assist as best you can. As far as making initial contact with these bodies is concerned, it should go without saying that as a responsible member of society you are duty bound to make known to those in authority any case or incident which warrants their attention. If it should happen to be a suspected case of neglect for example it should be brought to the notice of the Social Worker (formerly Children's Officer). No attempt should be made to deal with the case personally (unless of course it is of an urgent nature) or to interfere in the work of specially trained professional people. Your actions although intended for the best may do more harm than good. In such cases you must be very discreet and in many instances it would serve a better purpose if you notified the child's headmaster at school as he probably has a better knowledge of the child's home conditions.

Co-operation with the police is a different matter. If the case involves crime your first concern is to make absolutely certain that your suspicions or accusations are correct; this could prove difficult particularly if information had been given to you by other children of the play community. When you are sure it might be as well to inform parents as well as police. You must of course give much thought to each case and judge it on several aspects because, if the crime is not of a serious nature, for example stealing a bar of chocolate, with one type of child you could do irreparable harm by going to the police and with another you could with the help of an understanding policeman give the youngster the fright of his life which could have a lasting effect on his future. If the case is of a serious nature you should consider the interests of society and do your duty as a member of the community.

PLAYLEADERS AND CHILDREN

This book has been written with the knowledge that all professions have basic principles, and that no progress is possible without some knowledge of these principles. It is also written with the knowledge, gained during years of practical pioneering experience, that the very mainspring of success is a good relationship between playleaders and children. To foster a good relationship a leader must possess the right personality plus likeability and versatility. I have produced this book first and foremost after many requests from my colleagues and contemporaries with the object of giving the inexperienced organizer and playleader some ideas on which to build their schemes. I sincerely ask any young leader reading this book to give serious thought to that which follows.

Your playleading interest; what is its object, will you work for amusement or for gain? Whatever the reason you must like children for their own sake, or you will fail.

To the inexperienced playleader I would say that from the very beginning you must cultivate tolerance and remember that a little kindness and unselfishness will gain you lots of respect but, above all, you must be modest and friendly.

To the newly-appointed organizer, remember that now the time has come and you have the responsibility of administration on your hands, make sure you have really cultivated that tolerance, kindness and friendliness plus the power to look at things impersonally.

Whether you are a playleader or organizer, your mind will probably be full of theory at first but, after commencing your duties, it will not take long for you to realize that theory is all very well but it seldom, if ever, works out. You are completely on your own as a leader and your first task will be your most important; that is, to sell yourself to the children for whom you will be working. They will either accept you for what you are or they will reject you and that will be that. No theory exists giving the answer as to how children, particularly a mixed age group of both sexes, can be persuaded to accept an adult.

Usually the theorist will begin by trying to enter by the back door, in other words, striving to create a system whereby the children are indoctrinated (for want of a better word) to respect him. This type of leader, who could be described as the 'dominant type', adopts the attitude 'I know best, so things will be done my way. If you don't like it get out of the playground', and in so doing immediately creates a barrier between himself and some of the youngsters, thus creating bad Public Relations.

He will soon discover that already he has created problems for himself by dividing the children into two groups, those for him and those against. There will be no neutrals except the very young. He will also have unwittingly organized his first game, and made himself the 'bait', because bait him they will!

Experience has shown that a new leader must be the first to indicate openly to the youngsters that *he* respects *them* and this from the very beginning. To expel young people from the playground is a sure sign of the leader's inability to cope. The people you send out are probably more in need of your guidance than those who remain.

Strong-arm methods are absolutely taboo, except of course in self-defence; attempting to impose any degree of force or even adopting a threatening attitude to inhabitants of the playground indicates that a playleader is obviously in the wrong job. In attempting to act tough he creates the worst possible public relations, which could take months to re-establish.

It is of course possible to demonstrate your toughness, if you think this is important, in more subtle ways. For instance, you could prove your ability by participating in robust physical activities with the older age group. If you can take what eighteen-year-olds can give and hold your own in rugby or any similar body contact game, it will not be necessary for you to tell them how tough you are. Your relationship with this age group will stand according to your degree of sportsmanship and likeability. If you are unable to take their jibes, sarcasm and abuse you will never make a good all-round playleader but, after a short time, providing you do not retaliate, the jibes and sarcasm will cease and your relationship with these youngsters will improve tremendously and you will realize that in nine cases out of ten, you were being 'tested'.

One very experienced organizer has stated that a good playleader will keep his hands behind his back when an eleven-year-old boy calls him a bastard!

Playleaders must give friendship, especially to those whose home life is suspected of being insecure. These children will be far happier through a friendly relationship with a leader to whom they can speak freely, which indicates that a good playleader should get to know the children, their parents, their home life and environment. This may take time and you must not go out of your way to pry. You will find that the youngsters will disclose a great deal of information during normal conversation *with each other*.

In his efforts to establish a good relationship with the users of his play area it is advantageous for the playleader to develop his versatility. Being expert at one activity without some knowledge of others, will prove a tremendous drawback after a short time.

Difficulties sometimes arise when a leader is unable to cope with an activity that is popular with the opposite sex. Most men playleaders know little, if anything, about country or national dancing just as women leaders know very little about the laws of, or administration of football. In establishing relations between two parties the first requirement is that they should both have something in common otherwise they will look elsewhere to find other interests.

Having the ability to converse with the opposite party in their own language is a tremendous asset when attempting to cement a good relationship; the playleader should therefore endeavour to learn as much as possible about the everyday interests of the average child or teenager. If the playleader is not in touch with whatever 'vogue' is in trend he will find himself at a disadvantage during discussions with youngsters and in danger of becoming labelled an 'oldy' and this he can ill afford, especially in the early stages. I am not suggesting that he must be in sympathy with all new trends but he should know something about them. To be in a position where he can make a contribution to the formation of good public relations the leader should also have a good working knowledge of most popular games. He must be able to handle and maintain many items of equipment used in a play scheme and must possess the initiative to improvise both activities and equipment if the need arises.

Opinion is divided as to the best method of personal communication between leaders and children. One school of thought advocates that children should be encouraged to address their leader as Mr. —— and some extremists of this group even press for the use of 'Sir'. Attempting to analyze why, it appears that this group favours the opinion, amongst others, that this particular form of address automatically tends to form a foundation of respect for the leader thus indicating that some form of psychological union exists between playleaders and school teachers and that by having the children use a means of address similar to that used with their school teachers a degree of the teacher's authority will be transferred to the leader.

The other school of thought advocates complete freedom of personal address, be it Mr. Jones, Sir, or John and that no attempt should be made to influence one way or the other. I am of the opinion that if the intention of the leader is to establish a 'friendly relationship', which it should be, the second approach is by far the most effective.

Whatever the method you choose to adopt you will probably be given a nickname. For example, if your name should be Mr. Jones – or Sir to the children – a nickname will be bestowed on you according to your popularity, so you will become Jonesy (with affection) or Jonah (with reference to our friend the sailor who can do nothing right!) but if you indicate your name is John, well, John they will probably call you.

At all costs you should endeavour to accept whatever name is bestowed on you in a good spirit because it is unlikely that you will be able to change it for the asking.

The practice by children of using nicknames or Christian names is evident between the ages of about nine or ten up to the age of fourteen or fifteen when it then falls into a definite pattern with leaders being addressed as Mr. ———. Occasionally a youngster will come along using the term 'Sir', which to me would be an indication that he was new to the play area.

Playleaders will find it difficult to remember the individual Christian names of every boy and girl who frequent the play area but in the interest of his public relations he would be advised to adopt an expression that can be applied to all and sundry. Personally I have known no boy who has registered disapproval when being addressed as 'Son' and no girl has ever complained of being called 'Dear'. This method will also help to alleviate the risk of giving the impression that favourites exist.

Great care should also be exercised when selecting prefects, or helpers, for special occasions. Possibly the safest method is to choose more than you need, then select, by open lottery, the number you actually require. The leader first and foremost must possess a more than average amount of good sound common-sense. His policy of relationship with the youngsters should be based on friendship, not fear; on what is right and not who is right.

Children as publicity agents

A playleader's primary objective as far as public relations are concerned is to 'get the message across' to the youngsters in order that they may take advantage of the amenities provided for them. This can be achieved in many different ways, and the very mechanics of getting the message across can in itself create play work for some youngsters.

For example a basic poster which could be used for any event can be designed and distributed to playleaders who in turn would delegate responsibility for its completion to one or more children. Better still several posters could be given out and a competition organized to see who produces the best efforts. Very striking results can be achieved in this way with water colours, chalk, crayons, and cut-out pictures or lettering from magazines or used posters.

It is important to advertise the daily programme of activities for the benefit of the public and for those children who prefer to watch others take part. This can be done in about five minutes flat and exhibited in a place where the public usually congregate, for example the café or the play building. The method is simply to obtain pieces of paper of quarto or foolscap size and have the information written on it with coloured pencil. (See Fig. 3/1 which is not reproduced in colour but gives an idea of a poster which can be completed at short notice.)

PLAYLEADERSHIP CLUBS

The N.P.F.A. voice their opinion that playleadership should cater for the recreational needs of the whole family and for people between the ages of $2\frac{1}{2}$ years to 90 years. And yet indications – whether well founded or not – point to a situation where 70% of our younger population are not members of any kind of club. Some of my readers may consider this to be a very unhealthy social situation while others may think it to be a very good state of affairs. A fairly large number of young people volunteered the following information which may explain why so many young people stay outside playleadership scheme clubs.

The question put to the young people was:

Have you been a member of any kind of club, or are you still an active member of one? If not, why not and if you were, why did you leave?

Some answers were rather startling, and some rather ridiculous, but nevertheless, they tell a story. They may be of value to any play-leader who is hoping to set up various clubs in his area.

1. FINANCIAL REASONS

'Subscriptions much too high'
'Café prices too expensive'
'Too many raffles on club nights'
'Public transport fares too high'

2. SITUATION OF CLUB HOUSE AND AMENITIES

'Too far distant'
'Last bus or train leaves too early for return journey'
'No television at the Club'
'Club's musical group of very low standard'
'They have a juke box instead of a record player, and I don't see why we should have to pay to hear pop music'

3. POLITICAL OR RELIGIOUS REASONS

'Club has good netball team, I would like to be in it, but only church members can join. I'm of a different religion'
'The nearest good club is the Young Liberals, and that is not my party'
'It is more of a church service than a club meeting'

4. CLUB RULES AND REGULATIONS

'The application form is ridiculous, it is too searching'
'I don't like the Club Leader or his mate'
'Too many rules for comfort'
'It is nearly like being back at School'
'I don't know anybody in the club who will sponsor me'
'My nearest club is only interested in one activity. They are fanatics'

5. LACK OF PARENTAL PERMISSION

'Mum says it is too expensive, because there are three of us'
'Dad thinks it is too rough, and that gangs meet there'
'My parents insist that I am home by 7.30 p.m. and the club only opens at 7.00 p.m. so it is not much use my joining'

6. CLUB MEETINGS

'I would like to join, but they meet on Tuesdays and Thursdays and I go to Evening Classes on those evenings'

'The instructors are only interested in the potentials or the experts. The others don't get a look in'

'They are a very clannish lot, seem to be snooty'

Personally I am of the opinion that a well-run club creates a healthy leisure-time environment for young people, but care must be exercised not to duplicate the work of other organizations. In some instances one is compelled to run activities on club lines and in certain cases only bona-fide members of such clubs are permitted entry into premises where these clubs meet. It becomes necessary to have these clubs properly constituted and to have Council representatives on its committees. This situation prevails in my own area and adds much to the success of one of the local Council's large indoor play centres. Each club has its own allotted meeting period which results in a large number of young people being able to belong to a group of their own choice. This particular centre is open from 10.30 a.m. until 10.00 p.m. on four days each week and used exclusively by playleadership clubs. On other days it is used by physically handicapped groups. Morning and afternoon sessions are reserved for the playleadership scheme under-fives play-club.

Its advertised timetable of activities is as follows:

Batinton	Boys & Girls	Tuesday 8.00 p.m.
Trampoline	Girls	Tuesdays 6.00 p.m.
Table Tennis	Boys & Girls	Tuesdays 8.00 p.m.
National Dancing	Girls	Wednesdays 6.00 p.m.
Basketball	Boys	Wednesdays 6.00 p.m.
Five-a-side Football	Boys	Friday 6.00 p.m. (Winter)
Play Centre		Saturdays 10.30 a.m.–6.00 p.m. School Holidays excluding Monday and Thursday
Under-Fives Play Club	Tuesday Wednesday Friday Saturday	10.30 a.m.–12.30 p.m. 2.00 p.m.–4.00 p.m.

It will become necessary to keep a register of attendance and to run the various clubs on as few rules as possible. Club members should have a big say in the affairs of their club and where possible a junior committee should be formed. They in turn will elect the club captain and vice-captain. The only role which the playleader should exercise is that of being an unobtrusive adviser.

Figs. 3/1 to 3/5 show some playleadership programmes.

PLAY LEADERSHIP SCHEME

WHAT'S ON TODAY

SPECIAL EVENTS

10-45	5-A-SIDE FOOTBALL Semi-Final DIVISION IV MAC's TROUBLES v L.C's UNITED
11-45	TRAMPOLINING FOR ALL BRING YOUR GYM SHOES
2-45	SCAVENGER HUNT PRIZES! PRIZES. PRIZES! (YOU WILL NEED A PENCIL)
6-0	ITS A KNOCKOUT — TRIALS BOYS AND GIRLS Under 13 years
7-0	Dance Troupe Practice FOR OLD FOLKS SHOW

COMING EVENTS
SATURDAY NEXT

Netball Rally
at Chinbrook Meadows

Fig. 3/1

BOROUGH OF LEWISHAM

PLAY LEADERSHIP SCHEME

Entry FREE

UNDER 5 YEAR OLDS

FANCY DRESS COMPETITION

Prizes

2:15 pm Saturday, 20th JUNE 1970

LUXMORE GARDENS MALPAS ROAD BROCKLEY

FOR CHILDREN RESIDING IN THE BOROUGH OF LEWISHAM

Fig. 3/2

Fig. 3/3

PLAY LEADERSHIP SCHEME

FINALS DAY '69

FORSTER PARK

PARENTS,

Make it a family day out and take your children to the colourful and enjoyable

FINALS DAY at Forster Memorial Park, Whitefoot Lane, Catford, where they can take part in some of the activities organised especially for them.

They will be able to see the many floral decorated floats depicting "Tune Titles" including the "Diddymen", "The Sound of Music", "The Indian Wedding", "Swan Lake" and many others that will appeal to all age groups.

Dad will enjoy the many various games finals including Five-a-Side Football, Copstick, Shinty and Volleyball etc.,
Mum will enjoy the competitions for selecting the Queen and Princess's of the Parks and of course all the family will enjoy "Its a Knockout" and the Pets Corner.

SATURDAY 2.30pm
6th SEPTEMBER

Fig. 3/4

87

ORGANISED GAMES

for children and young people take place in

FORSTER MEMORIAL PARK
HOME PARK (Sydenham)
CHINBROOK MEADOWS (Grove Park)
SOUTHEND PARK

under the guidance of Play Leaders

FROM 26th MARCH to 1st OCTOBER
EVERY EVENING (EXCEPT SUNDAYS)
FROM 5.30 p.m.

Additional Sessions:—
SATURDAYS AND ALL SCHOOL HOLIDAYS
10.30 a.m. to 12.30 p.m. — 2.30 p.m. to 4.30 p.m.

FOOTBALL - VOLLEYBALL - CRICKET - BOXING
SHINTY - TUG-OF-WAR - BASKETBALL - JUMPING
NETBALL - HOCKEY - ROUNDERS - FOLK DANCING
COUNTRY DANCING - PET SHOW - "SCAVENGER" HUNTS
TREASURE TRAILS - FANCY DRESS COMPETITIONS

IT IS SAFER AND BETTER

TO

PLAY IN THE PARKS

Games Organizer:
Bernard S. McGovern

Alan Milner Smith
Town Clerk.

OBELISK PRESS & SIGNS, LTD., LEWISHAM, S.E.13

Fig. 3/5

4 · Basic Essentials

EQUIPMENT AND ACCOMMODATION

Timing

The month of April is a very good time to make an impact on the younger community. This time, or better still the actual Easter school holidays, is a very good occasion for the activities of a new scheme to begin. Record charts of attendance show that during this period, figures are higher than at any other time of the year. Possibly this can be attributed to the fact that very few families go away from home at this time of the year and that the extra hours of daylight tend to draw youngsters outdoors after the long winter period. Atmospheric temperatures are noticeably higher and the general feeling of all and sundry is to get out and about.

Of course it will be essential to carry out a great deal of preliminary work before the scheme really gets under way, therefore the playleader will need to be on the spot making his preparations some weeks before activities commence.

This preliminary work will include a certain amount of public relations, planning, negotiating with fellow officers, local research, preparation of application forms and the provision of equipment.

Expenditure

When considering the amount of equipment required for a new scheme the first aspect to be considered will be that priorities may be governed by the amount of money available in the current estimates. As these were probably prepared before the new organizer's appointment it is highly unlikely that they will coincide with what he considers to be a reasonable figure. It should be assumed that a certain amount of research has been undertaken by the committees concerned and that their findings will more or less determine the amount available in the current year's estimates. Much will depend on what their concept of such a scheme is and whether they intend to make provision for an all-embracing scheme or just one particular pattern of playleadership.

As a general rule less money is allocated to provide an adventure playground than an organized games scheme simply because an impression has been created over the years that a great deal of improvisation should take place in an adventure playground and that a good playleader can manage on next to nothing. This is of course not the case because all schemes irrespective of their character require certain basic materials and equipment.

During the early stages of any new project local authorities are apt to be very cautious with expenditure, particularly so if the scheme concerned makes no financial contribution in the way of charges etc. It therefore follows that priority must be given to the absolute essentials.

A base to work from

It will be to the new organizer's advantage to make sure that satis-factory provision has been made for him in the way of office accom-modation. This should include a telephone and other necessary office equipment plus the services of a typist when the need arises. Instances have been known where the newly appointed officer has been left completely uncatered for during the all-important first three or four weeks after taking up his appointment.

The play area building

Arrangements should be made as soon as the organizer takes up his duties, if they have not already been made, to provide a suitable building on the site of the first play area. Ideally this should contain storage space for miscellaneous equipment with an ample supply of lock-up cupboards. It should be served with mains water, heating, lighting (which should be grill-protected), toilet and ablution facilities, cooking facilities, a first aid room, separate staff changing rooms for males and females and a telephone. Its windows should be well protected by removable shields and locks for its doors should be of the five-lever pattern. Extra keys should be provided in order that playleaders and park staff can gain access without unnecessary delay. The building should also contain refuse disposal units. Leaders should be able to survey all the play area from it. The ideal position for such a building would be on the perimeter of the play area. It should have access from the road and another one from the play area. This would enable the building to be used at times when the play area is closed. The size of the building should be as large as financial resources allow, the larger it is the better. Buildings for this purpose should be as strong as possible with an internal matt finish only, with little interior decoration. Decorating a play building should be an activity for its users. Furnishing such a building is difficult when little or no knowledge exists as to the interests of local children even when there is no language barrier. A primary condition is that all children like to listen to music of one form or other and they like to bring their own records along to be played. Therefore it would seem sensible to obtain a record player which can be used from mains or batteries. This of course would be an asset when the instrument is required outside during the fine weather. It should be a good strong model capable of standing up to abuse and should always be securely locked away after each session. Record players are known to be the primary reason why many such buildings are broken into. They seem to hold an attraction for petty thieves everywhere. Experienced playleaders usually take their record players home with them each evening or leave them in the home of a reliable parent for safekeeping.

Actual furniture should consist of a number of very strong chairs and tables, but great care must be taken to leave as large an open space as possible in the centre of the room in order that games may be played.

FIRST AID EQUIPMENT

It would be advisable to provide a folding stretcher, two blankets and a well stocked portable first aid kit containing, as a minimum, the following:

Elastoplast (all sizes)
Dettol (must be used diluted)
Cotton wool
Bandages (all sizes)
Triangular bandages (only used by qualified first aiders)
Scissors
Safety pins
White lint
Small enamel bowl

PLANNING FOR INDOOR PLAY CENTRES

In England the provision of indoor play facilities for playleadership schemes is given comparatively little thought when one considers the complexities of our climate.

In many cases where provision is made the accommodation is inadequate, or else too much emphasis is placed on providing an elaborate semi-useless show-piece.

I should first of all make it clear that I am referring to a purpose-built play-centre which is intended to provide amenities for children from a fairly large district, and not one usually associated with play parks whose main purpose is to store equipment and serve the needs of a toddlers' play-club or at the most 25 or so youngsters.

The main drawback in most instances is lack of money, and I would strongly advise playleader organizers not to press for a temporary type of play-centre building if they feel that sufficient cash is not available for a really adequate one. If they accept a temporary – and not really adequate – building they may find themselves stuck with it for years, particularly so if they build up a successful play scheme.

An authority may take the view that a better building is not an essential part of the formula for success. It is much better to wait, even if the project is done in stages over a long period of time. To my knowledge, prefabricated buildings are not very successful except where they are used exclusively for infants; even so such buildings seem to present a challenge for older children to break into.

To those who become involved with the planning of a new purpose-built play-centre which is intended for the exclusive use of a playleadership scheme and to cater for the needs of a wide age-range I would strongly recommend that consideration be given to the following points. To my way of thinking this may result in the eventual creation of what may well be an ideal play building.

    1. Do not waste money on elaborate external design or internal decoration. Expect it to get knocked about.

    2. Procure a building as large as finances will allow. It cannot possibly be too large, but it can be too small. Aim for one that will comfortably seat about 200 children for shows, etc.

    3. Try to make your fellow planners 'vandal-proof conscious'. Whether there is such a thing as a vandal-proof structure or

not is open to question, but it should become your objective to prove that there is.

4. Fire regulations for all buildings are now very stringent. These must be allowed for in the budget. Means of escape must be considered. If an old building is to be used for play, organizers must seek advice on all safety aspects, including fire precautions. The major fire disaster in France recently in which many young people died at a youth centre dance is a warning. No amount of money is too much to provide a safeguard against such a happening in a children's play centre.

5. Heating and ventilation are naturally of great importance if the scheme is intended to operate throughout the whole year. Heating may come from under the floor, or overhead.

6. All internal playhall walls should be free from protrusions except for such things as basketball back-boards etc.

7. The goal ends of the main hall – assuming of course that it is oblong shaped – should contain no doorways.

8. All doorways should open outwards, away from the main playhall.

9. Electric plugs should be set into the wall behind a protective cover.

10. Tables should be constructed so that they fold into the wall leaving a flat surface. This is even possible with table tennis tables. The system provides a solution to storage problems.

11. If the roof is high – which it obviously should be – and contains many windows, consideration should be given as to how such windows can be easily cleaned. One such building is known to have a scaffolding structure erected inside the main hall at periodic intervals in order that its roof windows can be cleaned.

12. All forms of internal lighting inside the main playhall should be protected by safety grills.

13. Floors should contain a sufficient number of metal sockets – with covers – to allow for the erection of games and play furniture.

14. Metal games-furniture such as mini-football goal posts or jumping-stand uprights should be constructed to a telescopic pattern to facilitate storage. Netball, badminton and certain types of gymnastic equipment can be erected in the same way. When it is not being used it could be conveniently

93

stored underneath adjacent tight-fitting removable floor-boards.

15. A large pair of trapdoors could be installed in the centre of the playhall in order that equipment may be stored under the floor.

16. Various forms of gymnasium-type climbing apparatus can be suspended from the ceiling; for example, ropes, climbing nets, and rings.

17. Wall windows should be protected by wire or plastic mesh or made of unbreakable glass.

18. The floor should be of sufficient quality to allow roller skating and should contain markings for as many games courts as possible, from hopscotch to roller hockey. It is permissible and practicable to extend the markings of some courts up the wall if space is not available. One such game is batinton.

19. Some of the walls could be specially prepared to facilitate chalking and painting on them.

20. Wherever possible small communal rooms should be provided (without doors).

21. Netting should be installed on gliding rails to partition the main playhall into smaller sections for multiple use.

22. A removable barrier (in sections) should be provided which will allow for a number of spectators to watch competitive events from one end of the playhall.

23. Clocks and notice boards should be set into the wall with appropriate protective covers which should be used when ball games are in progress, or else unbreakable glass should be used.

24. An amplification system with record player facilities should also be installed with its speakers set into the wall or ceiling, and these should be protected with grills.

25. Observation windows, also of unbreakable glass, should be provided so that people in charge may see into the main playhall from adjoining rooms and passages.

PRIORITIES

It should be noted that so far equipment and accommodation priorities are as follows:

A. Office accommodation and materials with telephone for leader or organizer
B. Play area building (A and B could of course be combined)
C. First aid equipment (as recommended)
D. A mains or battery-operated portable record player
E. A quantity of tables and chairs

If there is no building it is unlikely that a play area building even remotely similar to the one described on p. 90 will be provided in the first instance. It could even take years to acquire one, therefore the new leader should be prepared to improvise on the grand scale, probably in a small wooden hut or even one shared with the park staff. If this situation should arise, further thought of indoor activities should be forgotten for the time being. The leader would be well advised to cater for outside activities only and to make available any necessary equipment for this to be done.

Equipment purchased by the authority

If the authority does not stock sports or handicrafts equipment in its own stores considerable delay could occur before some is purchased. Probably tenders will have to be sent out to different firms, with the result that it could be a month or so before the necessary equipment is obtained. If new equipment was not ordered before the leader took up his duties he should rectify this situation immediately on taking up his appointment. Assuming that no equipment is available in the first instance, it is highly probable that the Chief Officer will liaise with the Committee Chairman to make arrangements to buy a small amount of equipment to get the scheme under way. Quite possibly any delay in providing equipment before the leader took up his appointment may have been made to give him the opportunity to make his own choice. Careful consideration must be given as to which equipment to purchase when working on a tight budget. Several points are worth considering.

a. Provision must be made to cater for children of both sexes, to provide equipment for mixed activities and for a multitude of interests.
b. Certain items of equipment have a wide price-range (i.e. footballs). One may purchase an expensive item intending to make it last but if the inhabitants of a district are notoriously acquisitive of public property this may prove a false economy. The purchase of cheaper equipment may be the best bet until

95

the scheme has settled down and has been accepted by the local population. It will be found that equipment will not disappear as frequently as it did when the scheme was first started. Of course much will depend in this respect on the amount of surveillance employed on the play area and particularly on the exits.

c. Probably children of a wide age-range will make use of the area; therefore one's choice of equipment will be governed accordingly.

d. Purchase of expendable materials, i.e. paint, crayons, chalk, raffia etc., should be severely restricted until a set pattern of use is established whereby the leader knows how much of these materials will be used during a given period of time. Organizers should obviously enlist aid from the stores officer or purchasing officer who besides being able to give advice as to the correct procedure of purchase will probably be able to help in many other ways. His experience will enable the best value for money to be obtained. The following list of equipment is only intended as a guide and is by no means all-embracing of what will eventually be required when the scheme is fully operational but its contents will prove adequate for one play unit during its early stages of existence:

EQUIPMENT (All to be marked)

Purchase

1 Transistor record player (battery or mains operated)
1 Set of batinton with 1 dozen extra shuttlecocks
4 Soccer balls (2 of size 4 and 2 of size 5) with spare bladders
2 Netballs with spare bladders
2 Volley balls
6 'Mouldmaster' plastic footballs (strong)
24 Coloured play balls ($2\frac{1}{2}$ inches)
12 Lawn tennis balls
$\frac{1}{2}$ gross table tennis balls (hard good quality)
1 Football repair outfit (complete with pump and set of adapters), spare laces
4 Frido rugby balls (plastic)
4 Rounders clubs

12 Table tennis bats

12 Shinty sticks

4 Cricket bats (vellum covered), size 3 to 6 (3 of size 4 will probably be required)

2 Springback wicket units for cricket

6 Composition balls (English make)

10 Cricket leg guards (boys) plastic

1 pair of wicket keeper's gauntlets

6 pairs batting gloves

6 Table tennis nets

1 Volley ball net

1 Vaulting box (5 sections)

1 Spring board or reuther board

4 Coir fibre gym mats (or Recticel)

1 pair of jumping stands with laths

1 pair of adjustable netball posts with rings and nets giving 8 ft. to 10 ft. heights

1 Transistor 'loud hailer' (battery operated) megaphone

4 Rolls of coloured team braid, red, green, blue, yellow

1 First aid box (fully stocked)

2 Blankets

1 Folding stretcher

12 Hoola hoops (cane)

100 yards coloured bunting (plastic)

12 Country dancing records

4 Tennis rackets

6 Whistles (for games officials)

6 Coloured Magic Markers

24 yards of cheap gingham material, different colours

1 Box of sewing needles

12 reels of thread (colours)

Equipment manufactured in the authority's own workshops

If an authority maintains its own workshops it may prove more economical to have certain items of equipment manufactured therein. Such equipment is usually much more robust in its construction and will give better service than cheaper items purchased elsewhere.

Schemes administered from within a borough surveyor and engineer's department are fortunate in that he usually administers

97

the authority's workshops. In this respect it is quite often possible to obtain material which is of no further use to the section, but can be utilized in a number of ways in a play scheme. Adventure playgrounds can be supplied with all manner of unwanted materials which when used by the children often prove to be of more value than they were in their original use. Experiments in the design of play furniture and games equipment can be carried out to advantage in such a department but great care should be exercised to ensure that no copyright design is used during experiments.

The following list gives a good idea of what can be manufactured in or obtained from the authority's workshops but again this is only a rough guide.

Skipping ropes (8 ft. lengths), ordinary hemp
Stilts (can be made adjustable)
Play bats
Small cricket bats (8 ply) for tiny children
Wooden swords
Table tennis tables
Corner flags
Giant draught boards (plywood)
Draughtsmen (square and coloured)
Volley ball posts
Rounder baseball bases (plywood discs painted white)
Notice boards
Five-a-side football goalposts
Eleven-a-side football goalposts
Blackboards and easels
Sand bins on low wooden stands
Trestle tables (collapsible)
Stool ball stands
Old car tyres
Wooden offcuts from carpenter's shop (painted)

Mention is made at this stage of the time factor in relation to equipment manufactured in the authority's workshops. It should be realized that after an order has been placed for work to be carried out such work will have to be executed in its turn and that other jobs of work may have to be carried out at short notice. Priority is given accordingly to urgency of work and the need for maintaining and manufacturing public property. This being the case it is difficult to surmise correctly just how long it would take to procure equipment ordered from the workshops. Usually the practice is to order it at least four to six months before it is actually required for use.

Equipment donated to the scheme

From time to time various items of equipment are presented to the council's playleaders by parents and children who no longer have any use for them. Equipment acquired in this way should be carefully inspected for any defects, particularly mechanical vehicles such as tricycles and scooters.

Items of clothing should be thoroughly cleaned before being given to the children to use; this also applies to soft toys and dolls.

No play centre can have too much small equipment for individual use and the variety is endless. This being a proved fact, every playleader should constantly be on the lookout for such equipment which would otherwise be thrown on the rubbish dump. It is really surprising what people will give away just to make a little extra space at home and equally surprising how children will suddenly reject a favourite piece of play equipment when they leave the junior school to start their first term at senior school.

Therefore leaders should be on the lookout for such discarded equipment round about the month of September and again, just after Christmas, another turn-out of the toy cupboard takes place at home to house newly acquired Christmas toys. Comics, books and magazines become available at regular intervals but the acquisition of these will depend upon the amount of effort which the playleader uses to get the system operating. In particular, comics, all of which should be scrutinized by the playleader to safeguard against horror and violence, are read during the weekends and then thrown in the dustbin early the following week. A wise playleader will make arrangements for children to bring their unwanted literature to the games hut at a certain time each week to be collected by the prefect responsible for equipment or, alternatively, a 'swop shop' for comics could be organized once during each week. A similar system could be organized to cater for young people who are collectors of gramophone records. The fact that some item of useful equipment is probably available is sometimes disclosed unintentionally by children in chance remarks to the playleader or to one of their friends. 'My Dad is painting the bathroom' should convey to the playleader that some paint and maybe a paint-brush or two might soon be going spare. 'We are getting a new record player' should make the playleader ask about the old one especially if another child's father is helpful and handy with repairs to electrical equipment. In one centre where I worked in my early days as a playleader we acquired a television set and a radiogram just by being asked to remove them from a parent's home and by having some small repairs done to them by another interested parent. In another centre which had the use of a miniature dirt track we acquired a dozen or so bicycles from different sources, had them repaired, tested by the police and placed at the disposal of youngsters who had no bicycles of their own. On another occasion we discovered that one of our regular families was moving to another district: by offering to get one or two of our older boys to help with the packing we acquired a tricycle, a scooter, a doll's pram, a large quantity of used clothing and a large box of table games.

One very enterprising playleader acquired a hut which was in excellent condition complete with windows, two doors, cupboards and shelves. He obtained it from a building contractor whose employers were completing the final stages of a project near the park. It was overheard that a new and larger hut was being purchased for use on the site of their next contract and that the present one was about to be dismantled and burnt. The contractor even delivered the hut together with a selection of equipment including shovels, ropes, lengths of chain link, broken pick-axe handles, an old but serviceable wheelbarrow and an enormous quantity of timber and corrugated iron sheeting. Needless to say this kind of windfall does not come one's way very often but I mention it to illustrate the initiative of the playleader in going to see the contractor personally and his tactful approach.

Another way in which equipment can be obtained is by offering to clear away surplus goods after jumble sales. Usually a condition is attached that it will be necessary to clear the hall completely of everything which has not been sold, irrespective of whether it is any use to you or anybody else. Sometimes it will be found that quite heavy and bulky objects are left for you to dispose of. Pianos for example or antique washing machines. After one such jumble sale a quite excellent electric sewing machine was left there for the taking. About the best piece of equipment obtained in this manner was a really beautiful television set. Apparently a family had just moved into the district and on finding that their television set would not work took it to a dealer who said it was not worth repairing but that he would sell them another set. They bought a new set and left the old one in the local church jumble sale with a notice 'Bargain – needs repairing': of course nobody bought it. Having obtained the set a child's father just changed the voltage indicator and the set was perfect. The voltage needed in the family's new house was different from that in the house from which they had moved.

Very useful materials can be obtained from shops and stores when they redress their display windows and stands. Such material is invaluable for use in the handicrafts activities, especially coloured felt and display curtaining which can be used for the manufacture of soft toys. Old display stands, papier maché figures, artificial flowers, pieces of hardboard, Perspex, linoleum, window models, wigs, crêpe paper, out-dated wallpaper, catalogues, sometimes electrical fittings and clockwork motors can be obtained depending of course on the line of approach made by the playleader to the stores manager. It is a fact that at certain times of the year these stores are in desperate need of space and are only too pleased to dispose of quite valuable materials to make way for that which is coming in. The leader should make his contact early and promise to be of 'help and assistance' in clearing away any unwanted materials as soon as he is asked. This he should go out of his way to accomplish making sure he never lets anybody down otherwise he will lose his contact and once this happens he will not be able to get it back so easily and will stand to lose a great deal of free material.

Factories, especially those producing clothing, always have quantities of waste material they wish to dispose of and in some cases misfit garments can be had for the asking.

Various sports clubs sometimes give away items of used equipment and clothing particularly at the end of the season; again the enterprising playleader will keep in close contact with secretaries of local sports organizations.

Improvised equipment

One school of thought is that improvised equipment should never be used because the cost of manufactured equipment is negligible to a Local Authority. To a certain degree I am inclined to go along with this because some committees play a little too much on the improvisation aspect and expect playleaders to work miracles.

Improvising should be encouraged as much as possible because this is an activity in itself but equipment should not be improvised in an attempt to eliminate the governing body's need to purchase manufactured equipment.

Improvised equipment never compares favourably with that manufactured by craftsmen except in cost and in some cases durability and of course in not having to enter it on the inventory.

Of course there are occasions when it becomes necessary to improvise particularly when a play unit is in its early stages or when a consignment of equipment or materials has not been delivered. It is not unknown for keys to be misplaced or broken in the lock. When such situations do arise the playleader must be able to cope both equipment-wise and activity-wise.

DOING WITHOUT EQUIPMENT

It is not absolutely essential to have equipment in order to run an enjoyable play session. Evidence of this is found when one considers the type of activities and games children have created for themselves over the years and often referred to as 'street games'; many of these games alas are said to be dying out. No doubt television has contributed a great deal to this state of affairs but on the other hand it has created interest in other activities which are becoming extremely popular, some good, some not so good.

A large variety of games can be played with small objects usually on one's person, for example coins, or a hat or even a handkerchief: other simple items which can be utilized include a box of matches, a ring or a comb and other objects quite easily obtained such as stones, twigs or various other natural items.

Some games which can be played with coins

Guessing the dates or guessing the *combined value* of a hidden coin or coins.

Heads or Tails An elimination game.

Circle Elimination The one at whom Britannia points or is nearest is out.

102

Monarchs   Guessing the name of the monarch whose head is shown on the coin.

Pitching   (1) Pitching the coin to a wall or other object. (The thrower whose coin lands farthest away from the object is out.)

   (2) A coin or coins are thrown into a shoe or a hat or other container.

Balancing   A race to balance a set number of coins on their edge (the last to finish is out).

   Balancing a coin on its edge on top of a pencil (which is stuck in the ground, into a piece of clay, or a potato or other suitable object). The competitor must also stick the pencil in by himself as this is part of the feat.

Penny and Pencil Race   Place a penny on its face side on top of a pencil or piece of stick like an umbrella and traverse from A to B as in the egg and spoon race.

Some games which can be played with a hat or cap

Catchball, *Quoits*, *Dodge ball* and *Rugby Touch* can all be played with a hat instead of a ball. It can be a *missile*, for throwing at or onto something, a *baton*, to be used in various ways when improvising relay races, or a *discus* in distance throwing. It can be *the bone* in Dog and Bone. It can also be a *container* or target for articles pitched at it from various distances.

Games which can be played with matches

These are of course innumerable. Quite a large number are really puzzles, but in an emergency it is quite easy to keep a group of children occupied for a reasonable length of time with these 'parlour tricks'.

Games which can be played with stones

It is always possible to obtain a selection of different-sized stones or pebbles which can be used in a variety of ways to keep a group of children occupied in one way or another. Stones must surely have been the sole 'equipment' used by primitive man for some amusement purposes. If one studies groups of children playing in an adventure playground where only a small amount of conventional equipment is available it will be seen that stones are used in all manner of ways to create pastimes. I know they are used by some youngsters in attempts to maim their 'enemies' and sometimes to see how far they will 'bounce' off windows, but as a general rule they are used as improvised equipment to play games.

Some examples:

Juggling   With two or three stones

Five Stones (Alley Gobs)   A series of balancing, lifting and catching movements effected by one hand and using five small stones.

Missile   Used for throwing at or into something.

Baton   As a baton for use in relay races.

Target Building   Used for building small pyramids which are in turn knocked down by stones thrown at them by 'crack marksmen'.

Discus   A fairly large stone for casting great distances by little boys.

Water Skimming   Flat stones for bounce skimming on a surface of water.

Hopscotch   For marking a hopscotch court on the pavement and then using as a counter.

A game which can be played with a handkerchief

Donkey   Two teams each of equal numbers whose members each form a crocodile line. The last boy has a handkerchief tucked into his neckband or collar and hanging down behind him to represent the donkey's tail. The object is for the front boy in each team to try to get the handkerchief from the opposing team. At no time must the line of the team be broken.

More improvised equipment

A QUOIT MADE FROM NEWSPAPER AND STRING OR SOME UNFORTUNATE YOUNGSTER'S LACES

It is possible to play the following games with an improvised quoit:

Dog and bone
Tennis quoits
Ring the stick or copstick
Tunnel ball
Catch quoits
Paper discus

A HOME-MADE BALL

This piece of equipment can be made with old paper or cloth, and bound together with string. One can organize the following activities:

Rugby touch
Tunnel ball
Pass ball
Catch ball
Putting the weight
Missile
Various types of dodge ball
Bean bag jump etc.

AN OLD PICK-AXE HANDLE CUT SHORT (17 inches)

For use in place of a rounders club

AN OLD PICK-AXE HANDLE (30 inches or so)

For use as a baseball club

PIECES OF CHESTNUT FENCING

For use as cricket stumps, corner flags or markers

A PIECE OF STRING (in lieu of a net)

In an emergency a single strand of string may be used if a net is not available, or even a piece of white tape may be used in place of a football post crossbar. The following games have been played successfully in this way.

Tennis quoits
Catch ball
Volley ball
Quizling
Heading tennis
High jumping
Jumping the bean bag (paper ball on end)
Paper and string sling
Word game (writing with string)
Glide ball (with curtain ring and burst Frido ball)
Marking out small courts
Skipping (with a small weight in the centre to aid momentum)

IMPROVISED SKITTLES

Pieces of wood

Piled up stones
Rolled up coils of newspaper

BURST FRIDO BALLS

Usually these are discarded but really they can be utilized for many games, some of which are as follows:

Three-legged football
Dodge ball
Shinty
Circle games
Football rounders
Rounders polo

CARDBOARD BOXES

Many opportunities can be found to improvise activities using a large cardboard box, for example:

As a target receptacle for missiles cast from various distances (for example the shoes of the boy whose laces are wrapped round the improvised quoit).

Can be used in lieu of a bucket for such events as potato races etc., or used as cricket stumps or even rounders bases.

Can be used as 'static bases' for basemen to stand in during games of one-legged or 'hopping rounders'.

PAPER QUILLS

These are easily made by rolling up sheets of newspaper very tightly to about pencil thickness. Can be used for the following type of activities:

Sword dancing
Competitive design making
Hopscotch court marking
Treasure trail direction pointers

ROLLED PAPER COSH

Must not be made too hard. Always make them yourself. If you leave it to the youngsters to make you might find yourself 'helping the police with their enquiries' in a murder case.

To be used for various circle chase games, where the laggardly slow are 'walloped' to help them on their way. Walloping on the head is never allowed.

OLD SOCCER AND CRICKET NETS AND DISCARDED VEGETABLE
STRING BAGS

These old nets may be used in a variety of different ways.

Batinton
Volley ball
Five-a-side soccer
Obstacle races
Netball nets
Basketball nets
Table tennis nets (vegetable bags)

It is handy to know that old nets have been used in the past to
tie 'old' playleaders to trees.

OLD CAR TYRES

Many activities are possible with the use of old tyres, for example:

Rolling races
Climbing-through races
Football shooting practice
Ground basketball (piles of five each end)
They can be tied to the ends of ropes and hung from trees (Adventure area)
Fastened together they make a climbing web

Many other forms of improvisation are possible, the most common one being the soccer ball case filled with paper to make a medicine ball. Whether one believes in improvised equipment or not I feel it is just as well to know something about it because keys to games huts often get lost when normal equipment is *inside*.

Maintenance of equipment

Maintenance of equipment is best carried out continuously as and when the needs arise. Major repairs can often be undertaken when bad weather precludes outdoor games and when fewer children are present.

A few suggestions about the care of equipment are as follows:

1. Keep all leather footballs and netballs well oiled or dubbined.
2. Cricket bats should also be carefully oiled with linseed oil.

3. Every item of equipment should be kept in its place, and *not* left lying around the games hut.
4. Costumes and uniforms should be kept in a box or a wardrobe.
5. Special care should be taken with the issue of equipment for 'free play'. It is as well to know who borrows it.
6. Officials should take possession of play balls etc. immediately after each game is finished.

If equipment is slightly damaged, for example if stilts are cracked, they should be completely destroyed to prevent children from attempting to use them, thereby eliminating a risk of accidents happening.

Alphabetical list of suggested items of equipment

Badges, playleader	Flag sticks
Badges, various	Footballs
Badminton bats, extra	Football adaptors
Badminton nets	Football bladders
Ball carriers	Football corner flags
Ball Frido	Football goalposts, eleven-a-side
Basket balls	Football goalposts, five-a-side
Basket ball stands	Football inflators
Batinton nets	Football laces
Bean bags	Football lacers
Blackboard	Football tighteners
Blanket box	Gymnastic mats
Blankets (First Aid)	Hoops, plastic
Board card games	Jumping stands
Boxes, equipment	Lamps, pressure (Tilley)
Braid, team	Linseed oil
Catchball sets	Magic Markers
Chairs, deck	Maypole and ribbons
Chairs, nursery	Megaphone
Charts and books	Modelling clay
Climbing frame	Modelling tools
Crayons	Motor tyres
Cricket bats	Netballs
Cricket keepers' gloves	Netball bases
Cricket wickets	Netball nets
First Aid kit	Netball posts

Netball rings
Paint brushes
Paint, finger
Paint palettes
Paint powder
Paint water containers
Percussion instruments
Play balls
Play bats
Play bricks
Play shops
Poles, bamboo
Poles, wooden
Raffia
Records
Record player and needles
Rockers, car
Rockers, Gee Gee
Rounder bases
Rounder bats
Rugby balls
Sand bins
Scooters
See-saw
Shinty balls
Shinty sticks
Shuttlecocks
Skipping ropes
Slide
Springboard
Stilts
Stoolball stands
Stretcher, folding

Swords, wooden
Table tennis balls
Table tennis bats
Table tennis nets
Table tennis posts
Table tennis tables
Tables, nursery
Tennis bats
Tennis racquets
Track suit
Trampette
Trampoline
Tricycles
Tools (carpentry, etc.)
Tug-of-war rope
Uniforms, country dancing
Uniforms, Highland
Uniforms, miscellaneous
Uniforms, netball
Uniforms, vaulting
Vaulting box
Volley balls
Volley guy ropes
Volley nets
Volley posts
Weaving looms
Weaving string
Webbing braid (Maypole)
Wendy house
Wheelbarrows
Whistles, plastic
Wooden beads

5 · Special Playgrounds and Playwork

ADVENTURE PLAYGROUNDS

Some adventure playgrounds of today present a different image from those of a few years ago. One reason for this would appear to be that as in other spheres of children's recreation adults have taken over completely. Many of these playgrounds now consist of mammoth man-made constructions such as forts, towers, giant slides, tunnels, tree houses, buildings with all modern conveniences and in some cases as many as four or five playleaders on the staff. We have now reached the stage where adventure playground equipment is being commercially manufactured with the accent on safety. Designs are changing and adventure playgrounds are in danger of becoming new-look conventional playgrounds with little to stimulate the imagination of children who frequent them.

The adventure playground once had the more accurate title of junk playground. It was subject to heavy criticism, particularly from local authorities and today's adventure playgrounds still do not enjoy full acceptance.

Peter and Iona Opie in their book *Children's Games in Street and Playground* make reference to adventure playgrounds and playleaders and, quoting advertisements in *The Times Educational Supplement* for salaried playleaders, observe that 'the provision of playmates for the young has become an item of public expenditure'; they also give the impression that local authority adventure playgrounds do not satisfy the needs of children for secrecy and wild places and say that our authorities 'exploit our wealth to make improvements for the worse'. Their observations have point, no doubt, but of course we must also give credit where credit is due, and when a police authority states that 'vandalism is on the increase everywhere, except in the immediate vicinity of where playleadership schemes operate', we should accept that their observations are well founded too. Good adventure playgrounds exist as do poor ones and efficient playleaders are employed as well as inefficient ones.

Nevertheless, in spite of all criticism directed towards it the adventure playground and its leaders have proved to be of immense value when all is taken into consideration. Not only do its users derive pleasure from its existence but the surrounding community enjoys many hidden benefits. As a general rule it is not until the playground has closed down that these benefits are realized.

It would be extremely difficult to make an accurate assessment of the more important values of an adventure playground because the concept differs from place to place. Much will depend on the outlook of the person in charge and the calibre of its management committee. I think its most important value lies in the opportunity it gives to children to become involved with projects of their own choice within a community of young human beings with problems and interests similar to their own.

When planning the actual site of an adventure playground consideration must be given to the proximity of other attractions and public amenities. For example it may prove fruitless to site one adjacent to a public swimming pool as it would never prove to be a stronger attraction to the majority of children.

Adventure playgrounds are a strong attraction when they are single units, especially in depressed areas where little alternative recreational amenity is provided.

Where an adventure playground is part of an all-embracing scheme it does not enjoy the success – so far as attendances are concerned – of a single unit playground.

Very few comprehensive schemes are in existence at this particular time and therefore only a little research has been done in this respect. On such play areas as these an interchange of attendance occurs quite regularly where children wander from one section to another as the mood takes them or as their own group leader directs. One such excellent enquiry, which was extremely searching, was carried out in Ulm, Germany, and reported by Heinrich Rupprecht the Director of Parks and Gardens. He tells us of its findings as follows:[1]

'When creating this type of children's playground, we must *not* start from adult concepts of what a playground should be but we

[1] *International Playground Association Newsletter*, Vol. II, No. 7, April 1966.

must consider purely and exclusively the child's viewpoint. Too often those who plan playgrounds are influenced by their own very subjectively-coloured ideas which are weighted with rather splendid concessions to modern phenomena, e.g. fantastic prefabricated concrete blocks. They forget that the world of the child, hardly altered for thousands of years, is formed from his psychospiritual development, which is so strong that environment influences it very little. These needs have remained amazingly constant over the years, paying little attention to all the changes in the outside world, and they will probably remain the same always because they are the expression of the basic laws of nature.

'As we wanted to discover what is the child's concept of his ideal playground and to gain insight into his play habits and his favourite games, an enquiry was eventually organized which was directed towards:

(a) The women workers in kindergartens who are in close touch with children and who can, through questioning, establish:

   (i) Which games or play activities are mostly used by the children, and then arrange these in order of the child's preference.

  (ii) How many (what percentage) of the kindergarten children can readily play at home, i.e. have a playground near their home.

 (iii) What the child's ideal playground near his home should contain (through a sketch or drawing done by the child) – (and then work with the children to establish it).

(b) School children aged 7 to 14 who were asked to answer the following questions:

   (i) What is your favourite game? Place the other games in order of preference.

  (ii) Have you a playground near your home?

 (iii) Which playground do you use?

 (iv) How far is it to the next playground?

  (v) Draw a simple ground plan of your ideal playground and describe it.

This enquiry, which covered both towns and rural areas had replies from:

(a) 105 kindergarten teachers and 6094 children;

(b) 4572 primary school children.'

Some of the results are very interesting and are worth recording: 'Mechanical apparatus (roundabouts, big slides etc.) do not appeal to children at all and they have no real need of them. The child much prefers doing for himself and being active rather than passively sitting on a piece of equipment. From the children's drawings, it was very clear that they had been influenced by the adult conception of a playground with slides and see-saws, roundabouts and swings – or maybe they found these things easier to draw. When one considers and reflects on what the children really like and judge this from their answers to the questions, and when one looks at the order of their favourite activities, these adult concepts are of much less importance. We adults give children, and particularly small children, a great deal of happiness when we allow them to play freely with sand and at circle and ball games. These activities give the child release and relaxation and offer little danger.

'So often when one has levelled a play area and equipped it with the usual swings, roundabouts etc., the sex differences in play between boys and girls are obliterated. Girls like to bake and cook in sand. They want to play with and care for dolls. They like dramatic activities. They like playing circle and team games and they want to dream a lot. We should take cognizance of these desires when setting up playgrounds. If we build little secluded cosy corners by planting shrubs and hedges, we facilitate the development of their world of imagination.

'Differences in play characteristics as demanded by the different sexes must also be fostered in active play because these help to develop individual personality. Furthermore it must be recognized that only through the co-operation of older people, and their joining in play on the children's playground can the high quality of play be passed on from one generation to the next. It was not surprising to notice this lack of contact in the towns where the communal catching and hiding games were less developed and in some cases almost non-existent, whereas in the remoter rural areas a rich and varied play profile, including nursery rhymes and children's songs was often evident.

'It will be necessary in the future to get grown-ups not only to take an active interest in children's play but also to get them to play *with* the children.'[1]

[1] This observation made by Heinrich Rupprecht is an interesting one, because it would appear that in England the very opposite situation exists where chasing games are very popular in town districts.

What is also evident is that the idea of sharp age group divisions in play so often expected by adults and incorporated in the design of the playgrounds is quite false. On these playgrounds near the homes, old and young children and adults must be able to meet.

The play repertoire of rural children was in many ways wider than that of the town child. Nearly everywhere in the country were found games of hiding and catching which the town children hardly knew. The older boys placed football at the head of all their games: handball, badminton and table tennis came next.

Nearly all the children drew water and sand on their ideal playground. These basic elements are the favourite play materials, not only for small children, but are also liked by older boys and girls who build towers and tunnels and make waterfalls.

Another worthwhile result of the enquiry was the demand made by many of the children and by almost all the kindergarten teachers for a covered space to be used as shelter in rain and bad weather. The enquiry further showed the need to carry this sort of research further, and really to establish and maintain playground advisory centres. This does not involve much money or more space, but it is of paramount importance that the concept of new standards and new visions should be planned for at the present time.

Results of the enquiry from kindergarten teachers and school children

(a) FROM THE KINDERGARTEN TEACHERS

Question 1. Which play activity was most popular and what kind of games were played?

Leaders and children named 637 different games which fell into the following 22 types of play:

TYPES OF PLAY OBSERVED BY LEADERS OF KINDERGARTEN CHILDREN

Type of play	Times played	% of total
1. Sand play	81	12.72
2. Round games	62	9.73
3. Swinging	52	8.16
4. Ball play	49	7.69
5. Gymnsatic apparatus	48	7.54
6. Sliding	44	6.91

7. Climbing	40	6.28
8. Singing games	37	5.81
9. Catching	32	5.02
10. Paddling	28	4.39
11. Roundabouts	24	3.77
12. Punch and Judy and puppets	19	2.98
13. Shops	16	2.51
14. Hiding	15	2.36
15. Railways, cars, tractors	15	2.36
16. Running	14	2.20
17. Improvised play	14	2.20
18. Rhythmic play	13	2.04
19. Scooters, tricycles	13	2.04
20. Skipping	10	1.57
21. Jumping and hopping	6	0.94
22. Throwing	5	0.78

Question 2. How many of the kindergarten children could also play at home?

105 leaders and 6094 children participated. Of these 1783 or 29.26% had a playground near their homes. The playground needs of toddlers are not the same as those for school children.

(b) FROM THE SCHOOL CHILDREN AGED 7 TO 14

4572 primary school children took part in this enquiry, that is they answered the four set questions and drew their ideal playground according to their own ideas.

Of these 4572 entries, 1747 or 38.21% were from boys and 2825 (or 61.79%) were from girls. In addition 33 children only sent in a drawing.

Question 1. What is your favourite game?

The 4572 children named 14,179 favourite games which represented 22 different types of play.

The children's favourite games

Type of play	*Occasions preferred*	*% of total games*
1. Handball, volley ball	2627	18.53
2. Badminton	2114	14.91

Type of play	Occasions preferred	% of total games
3. Football	1341	9.46
4. Hiding	1001	7.08
5. Swinging	965	6.80
6. Paddling, swimming, water polo	818	5.77
7. Table tennis	671	4.73
8. Chasing and catching	577	4.07
9. Agilities and apparatus	563	3.97
10. Puppets and Punch and Judy	551	3.89
11. Sliding	540	3.81
12. Climbing	411	2.90
13. Long jumping	368	2.59
14. Sand play	274	1.93
15. Roller skating	272	1.92
16. Racing	244	1.72
17. Roundabouts	226	1.59
18. Scooters and bicycles	181	1.28
19. Basket ball	172	1.21
20. Railways, cars, tractors	132	0.93
21. Throwing skills	71	0.50
22. Shops	60	0.42

BOYS' PREFERENCE

Type of play	Occasions	% of total games
1. Football	1287	24.35
2. Handball, volley ball	924	17.48
3. Badminton	598	11.31
4. Table tennis	414	7.83
5. Paddling, swimming, water polo	314	5.94
6. Hiding	242	4.58
7. Climbing	179	3.39
8. Agilities with apparatus	154	2.91
9. Swinging	146	2.76
10. Chasing and catching	135	2.55
11. Long jumping	132	2.50
12. Basketball	125	2.37
13. Running	114	2.16
14. Sliding	111	2.10

15. Railways, cars, tractors	110	2.08
16. Sandplay	98	1.85
17. Bicycle and scooter	72	1.36
18. Roundabouts	42	0.79
19. Throwing skills	39	0.74
20. Roller skating	37	0.70
21. Puppets, Punch and Judy	12	0.23

GIRLS' PREFERENCE

Type of play	Occasions	% of total games
1. Handball, volley ball	1703	19.15
2. Badminton	1516	17.05
3. Swinging	819	9.21
4. Hiding	759	8.52
5. Puppets, Punch and Judy	539	6.06
6. Paddling, swimming, water polo	504	5.57
7. Chasing and catching	442	4.97
8. Agilities with apparatus	409	4.60
9. Sliding	429	4.82
10. Table tennis	257	2.89
11. Jumping	236	2.65
12. Roller skating	235	2.64
13. Climbing	232	2.61
14. Roundabouts	184	2.07
15. Sandplay	176	1.98
16. Running	130	1.46
17. Cycling and scootering	109	1.23
18. Shops	60	0.67
19. Football	54	0.63
20. Basket ball	47	0.53
21. Throwing skills	32	0.36
22. Railways, cars, tractors	22	0.25

General findings about Question 1. Ball games were favourite among the 11 to 14-year-olds, whereas the 7 to 10-year-olds preferred the other games.

Question 2. Have you a playground near your home?

This was answered by 4429 children out of a total of 4572. 1733 boys and 2692 girls replied.

762 or 17.20% answered 'yes'.
3667 or 82.80% said 'no'.

Question 3. Where do you play now?
Of the 4572 children taking part in the inquiry, 4651 places where they played were named. These were divided as follows:

Place of play	Replies	% of total places
Own yard, garden or house	2229	47.91
Street	888	19.09
Woods or fields	705	15.15
Sports grounds	359	7.71
Proper children's playgrounds	191	4.10
House, yard or garden of a friend	145	3.12
House, yard or garden of a neighbour	98	2.11
School playground	37	0.80

Question 4. How far must you go to a playground?
The children named 3824 different distances which ranged as follows:

Distance to playground	Occasions	% of all distances
More than 1000 m.	1809	47.30
between 500 and 1000 m.	656	17.15
between 100 and 500 m.	854	22.33
less than 100 m.	505	13.21

It is interesting to compare these results with a survey made on a smaller scale in South London in 1971.

John James, a teacher at Bolingbroke School, Battersea, interviewed 100 children aged between 7 and 11. They came from the neighbourhood of Clapham Common, which is a wide expanse of open ground containing games pitches, Redgra area, and conventional playgrounds.

The environmental area itself is a mixture of old properties, high blocks of flats, a large new estate and another section undergoing demolition and re-building. The local population includes a large number of immigrants of whom the younger age groups seem to outnumber those of local family origin.

The children were distributed as follows:

1. 25 7 to 8-year-olds   (18 boys and 7 girls)
2. 25 8 to 9-year-olds   (12 boys and 13 girls)
3. 25 9 to 10-year-olds (13 boys and 12 girls)
4. 25 10 to 11-year-olds (12 boys and 13 girls)

                     TOTAL   55 boys   45 girls

Questionnaire:

1. Do you play any games when you go home after school? If so, what?
2. Where do you play your games?

7 TO 8-YEAR-OLDS

18 Boys

1. Do you play any games when you go home after school? If so, what?

	Yes	No
	100%	—
	(18)	

Football	38.8% (7)
Running	22.2% (4)
Indoor games (cards etc.)	22.2% (4)
Ball games (other than football)	5.6% (1)
Ride bike	5.6% (1)
Play on concrete shapes (on Estate)	5.6% (1)

2. Where do you play your games?

On Estate	33.2% (6)
At home	27.8% (5)
In Park	22.2% (4)
Garden	5.6% (1)
Flats	5.6% (1)
School playground	5.6% (1)

7 Girls

1. Do you play any games when you go home after school? If so, what?

	Yes	No
	100%	—
	(7)	

Hide and seek	28.5% (2)
Skipping	28.5% (2)
Play Schools	28.5% (2)
Running	14.5% (1)

2. Where do you play your games?

On the Estate	71.5% (5)
At home	28.5% (2)

Reasons given

43.5% (3) We play on the Estate because we live there.

14.5% (1) I play at home mostly with my sister, and sometimes I go out to play.

8 TO 9-YEAR-OLDS

12 Boys

1. Do you play any game when you go home after school? If so, what?

Yes	No
66.7%	33.3%
(8)	(4)

Football	62.5% (7)
Various	37.5% (5)

(includes riding bikes, ice-skating, boxing, running)

Reasons

8.4% (1) I play football because I want to be a footballer when I'm older.

2. Where do you play your games?

On the Estate	50% (6)
In the Park	12.5% (1)
In the Street	12.5% (1)
At a Club	25% (2)

Reasons given

16.6% (2) We play on the Estate, because it's good for football.

13 Girls

1. Do you play any games when you go home after school? If so, what?

Yes	No
92.3%	7.7%
(12)	(1)

Indoor games	30.8% (4)
Hide and seek	15.4% (2)

Nothing	7.7% (1)
Netball	23% (3)
Climbing frame	7.7% (1)
Run-outs	15.4% (2)

2. Where do you play your games?

On the Estate	53.9% (7)
At home	30.7% (4)
In the Park	7.7% (1)
In the Street	7.7% (1)

Reasons given

7.7% (1) I play at home with my brother at schools. I can't go to the park because I'm not allowed.

9 TO 10-YEAR OLDS

13 Boys

1. Do you play any games when you go home after school? If so, what?

Yes	No
100%	—
(13)	

Football	69.2% (1)
Indoor Games (chess, ludo, cards, etc.)	15.4% (2)
Swimming	7.7% (1)
Squash	7.7% (1)

2. Where do you play your games?

On the Estate grounds (includes indoor games)	46.2% (6)
In Battersea Park	30.8% (4)
In the Street	23% (3)

12 Girls

1. Do you play any games when you go home after school? If so, what?

Yes	No
91.6%	8.4%
(11)	(1)

Indoor games	58.3% (7)
Running and ball games	33.3% (4)
Helped at home	8.4% (1)

Reasons given

8.4% (1) I help at home, because my Mum is pleased if I do.

2. Where do you play your games?

At home	58.5% (7)
In the Street	16.6% (2)
On Estate grounds	16.6% (2)
At a play centre	8.3% (1)

Reason

8.3% (1) I play indoors because there is nothing to do outside.

10 TO 11-YEAR-OLDS

12 Boys

1. Do you play any games when you go home after school? If so, what?

Yes	No
100%	—
(12)	

Football	66.6% (8)
Swimming	16.6% (2)
Tennis	8.4% (1)
Run-outs	8.4% (1)

2. Where do you play your games?

On the Estate	33.3% (4)
In the Park	33.3% (4)
Local Swimming Bath	16.6% (2)
On the Common	8.4% (1)
At Scouts	8.4% (1)

13 Girls

1. Do you play any games when you go home after school? If so, what?

Yes	No
92.3%	7.7%
(12)	(1)

Running	30.8% (4)
Football	23% (3)
Indoor games	15.4% (2)
Rounders	7.7% (1)
Shapes on Estate	7.7% (1)
Television	7.7% (1)
Netball	7.7% (1)

2. Where do you play your games?

On the Estate	46.1% (6)
In the Street	23.1% (3)
Indoors	15.4% (2)
Gardens	7.7% (1)
In the Park	7.7% (1)

Some reasons given

The Estate grounds are really the only place to go except the Park, but the Estate is nearer, the boys go to the park for football.

Summary of all groups

1. Do you play any games when you go home after school? If so, what?

	Yes	No	
	93%	7%	
Football			34%
Running			18%
Indoor games			17%
Hide and Seek			4%
Swimming (including Squash)			6%
Various			21%

2. Where do you play your games?

On the Estate	43%
At home	20%
In the Park (Battersea)	15%
In the Street	11%
In the Garden	2%
In School Playground	1%
At Local Club	2%
Local Swimming Bath	2%
Boy Scouts	1%
Clapham Common	1%
Play Centre	1%

The investigation carried out by John James contains much of interest to people involved in playleadership although as he points out one has to remember the limitations inherent in a small study of this kind. I give here his main findings.

Children are adventurous and have what seems an inexhaustible supply of energy when school finishes for the day. The majority of the children took part in a number of games, playing either football, running games, (hide and seek) and swimming, while only 7% said they went home to watch television or help in the home, playing no games at all.

The most likely place where he found the children playing their games was on the housing estate on which the majority of them lived. A fairly large number, 20%, played their games at home, while the rest played either in the local park, in the neighbouring streets or at clubs.

He found that 42% of the children selected the rope as a favourite apparatus for the thrill and excitement that it provided; as one child said, 'I like the rope best, because I jump from a bar onto the rope and swing about, I get a funny feeling in my tummy'.

For some children, 23%, who were perhaps more exploratory and daring, the box provided the most opportunity to experiment. This seemed to be more of a favourite with the boys than with the girls, for it appeared to capture the adventurous spirit of them. As one boy put it, 'The box is something that you can do most on, like jumping, climbing, rolling'.

The horizontal bars, too, proved a favourite, for 14% of the children interpreted the apparatus as a challenge to strength, balance, co-ordination and having scope to arouse the inborn desire for excitement as was said by one child of 9 years, 'I like to do exciting things, I can do them on the bars'.

A child, it would appear, has a never-ending supply of energy, and at the end of a school day, one can see children busily involved in some game either in the street, park or near their home.

Of the children questioned for the study, 93% of them played some form of game after school. It was hardly surprising to find that a large number of the children, 34%, played football, while running games too proved popular with 22% of the children playing games such as hide-and-seek, catch, leap-frog and run-outs. (Run-outs is a team game, where one team finds another, similar to hide-and-seek).

Some children, 6%, often visited the local swimming baths and enjoyed a riotous splash about, before they went home to a more relaxing occupation of watching television or, in a few cases, reading a book.

Only a small percentage of children, 7%, said they did not play any games after school; instead, they watched television or as one nine-year-old said, 'I help at home, because my mum is pleased if I do'.

He found that the majority of the children, 43%, played their games on their housing estates, not that its provision was good for games, just that it was virtually the only place to play for a majority of the children. Some, 15%, who were lucky enough to be near Battersea Park, had available possibly better play facilities than those children who lived further away. Near them lay a large ground of football pitches, an adventure playground, and an open space where they could run about freely, able to forget for a short while the restrictions and limitations that an urban area presents to them.

For some, 20%, home provided the ideal play situation where they could play with brothers and sisters with dolls, toy cars, cards, ludo and chess. For others home was the only safe place, as one child said, 'I play at home with my brothers, we play schools. I can't go to the park because I'm not allowed.'

In a few cases he found children belonging to clubs, such as scouts or swimming club, and these children were able to break regular habits of playing in the same place, by going weekly to their club.

Of course many children do not like to be organized in any way at all; they prefer to look after their own leisure-time interests without interference from other people, especially adults. Probably when Professor Sorensen first noticed that children spent a good deal of their time playing amidst the rubble of bomb sites he realized they did so partly as a means of escape from adults who generally kept themselves well away from the dangers of these debris-strewn places.

In some areas playgrounds are provided but no playleaders are employed. These have proved successful in some cases simply because children will always find some activity and are not really dependent on adults to do all their planning for them. As far as incidental equipment is concerned children are past masters at improvisation and can manage quite well without it as many of their games and activities need only the participants. The true value of such playgrounds can be summed up in a few words. 'They are places where children can be exactly as they want to be and where they can get away from it all and this, in effect, means away from the world of the adults.'

Present-day architecture is in one way responsible, to a degree, for eliminating facilities which in the past provided children with an alternative to playing on the streets.

A few years ago the average town child would have been able to play in his own back yard or garden with one or two of his close friends. In all probability he would have had his own den or a couple of trees and, more important, a certain amount of privacy. But in this present day and age things have changed drastically for the average town child.

The building of large blocks of flats has created the necessity for playgrounds to be set aside to provide children with the opportunity of going somewhere to do the things they probably would do if they had a private garden or a backyard, but many children still spend some of their leisure time playing on the streets because unless the playground is situated within easy reach of their homes – three to four hundred yards – they will not go there, unless a special attraction exists.

A misconceived impression exists that traditional street and play-ground games are passing into obscurity, but I feel that this is not so. At least school playground games with all their excitement and noise are played just as much in the primary school playground as they ever were. New games emerge almost daily but the old ones are still with us and are played with much exuberance and imagination in those playgrounds and play parks where no playleader is employed, but one noticeable difference is that no one game seems to hold the interest of its participants for as long as it used to do a few years ago. Another noticeable difference is that disagreements occur more frequently between participants, which is one of the reasons why games do not last. Street games are still extremely popular on large housing estates, particularly where families are lucky enough to live in houses as against blocks of flats and where play patterns change slightly according to surroundings but not a great deal.

Local schools are really the workshops of games creation where the rules of countless thousands of them must be stored in the minds of children. These are games which have been passed on from parent to child and brother to brother for generations. The mechanics of most of these games seldom change but words, rhyme and title do. Such minor changes are influenced by current events in the adult world or by television but they are seldom long-lasting in popularity.

Adventure playgrounds do provide opportunities for children to adapt some of these games more realistically and this they do, always providing the playleader leaves them to do so without any interference.

Small schools in close-knit communities are places where traditional games are fostered and kept alive and adventure playgrounds situated in such areas are used by children for the adaptation of new forms of these games which can be played under unusual conditions.

It would appear that a need has been shown for the provision of adventure playgrounds especially in depressed areas where little or no land is available for play park conversion, but whether a playleader is necessary on all playgrounds is debatable and from personal observation in my own working part of London I would think not. Yet on the other hand some playgrounds would not be the success they undoubtedly are without their playleaders.

Playleaders who work on adventure playgrounds in England originally carried the designation of 'warden'. Their main function was to obtain industrial waste materials for the playground population to utilize; for example, timber, nails, tools, paint and remnant soft furnishings. Also they were responsible for creating and maintaining the interest of local inhabitants and for obtaining as much voluntary help as possible. But the rôle of the adventure playground leader is gradually changing and many see theirs as being a mixture of playleader-cum-community general adviser: some even keep a dossier on all children who use the playground and are not adverse to incorporating old people's welfare in their orbit of responsibility.

I am inclined to disagree with playleaders who hold this view and I think that in order to implement a full and interesting programme of play activities it is fairly obvious that the adventure playground leader should occupy himself fully with this end in mind. He should not be expected to concern himself with matters not directly relevant to play or to become involved in matters which are the responsibility of other people: his very title indicates this.

Playleaders employed in organized games schemes are advised not to specialize in any one particular sport and that any youngster who shows promise should be helped to improve his game by being passed on to an appropriate club, where specialists can help him. This system should apply in other matters also and where a youngster needs help of any kind he should be referred to the appropriate specialist.

The playleader's working life in his adventure playground will be hard enough without his having any other community needs to worry about. Indeed it would appear to be questionable whether a leader could become involved in other community matters and still provide an efficient play service to those children who use his playground. The only solution in this situation would be to employ extra staff and this could prove an obstacle, especially so if money is hard to come by, not to mention the difficulty of recruiting suitable staff.

A major concern of the present day adventure playground leader – and indeed all playleaders wherever they may work – is the infiltration into his playground of troublemakers. I have been asked on numerous occasions, 'What would you do if . . . ?' followed by some of the most absurd 'situation stories' imaginable. The blame for most of these situations can usually be attributed to the Management Committee for expecting a new leader to effect miracles overnight. Quite simply the reason is that they provide a playground, give it the wrong kind of publicity and throw it wide open for all and sundry to use, *without any programming or restrictions*. Attracting the wrong element into a playground is very easy, but once it is there it will prove to be a heartbreaking task to re-educate or overcome it. It then falls to the unfortunate playleader's lot to do something constructive about the situation. Some committees are impatient for overnight success and in too much of a hurry to solve all the social problems of the children at once.

Good adventure playgrounds happen, they are not made, but emerge slowly, and only gradually do they become accepted by the local community – usually after a period of open hostility.

It is quite obvious to the experienced leader that one must restrict entry during the early period of a playground's existence to younger children in order to establish a longterm policy of acceptance by its users later on. For example, during the morning and afternoon sessions, exclusive use could be given to under-fives who are accompanied by adults. During termtime evenings, Saturdays and school holidays, children of primary school age could be catered for. As these children go on to secondary school they should still be allowed to come to the playground and even when they start work they should not be barred. In this way they will more or less grow up in the environment of the playground.

A playground always attracts a large number of children when it is first opened because of the novelty, but eventually the numbers will drop until it reaches a bearable play population which is governed by environment, facilities and space. One factor which quite drastically reduces attendances of young children is the admittance of teenagers when the playground is first opened.

When planning a new playground it might be a good idea to read the words of Linda Cottam of *The Phoenix Gazette* who tells us of a talk by Madame Tanon, 'Junk Playgrounds are in'. She quotes:[1]

'Children like most to experiment, to build things, tear things down, make things, destroy them.'

'Then what good, really, is a playground full of swings and slides?'

' "In Europe, we have little money for playgrounds," says Madame Claude Tanon of Paris, President of the International Playground Association. "So we studied to see what children are really interested in." '

'Madame Tanon, heading a conference on playgrounds at Arizona State University said that children are interested in activities which they do themselves, not those already prepared for them.'

'She told teachers and recreation leaders the merits of a playground system now spreading across Europe – the "junk" playground.'

' "Children play in the street because the street is more interesting than a structured playground," she says, "We have built playgrounds so that they are more interesting than streets." '

'Materials used in these playgrounds are "just common junk", ropes, water hoses, shallow ponds, holes and hills.'

' "They look somewhat messy," Madame Tanon admits. "But if grown-ups complain that they don't like to look at them, we build hedges and fences to block their view."

"This makes the place very secret," she adds, "and children love places that are secret from grown-ups." '

'Although the playgrounds look dangerous to the child and therefore very enticing, they are actually very safe.'

' "Playground leaders (a type of chaperon) test the equipment and tools every morning," said Madame Tanon. "Children are taught to use hammers and saws properly, and few accidents occur." '

'Some of the principal materials found in most of these playgrounds are ropes strung from towers to slide down or stretched from trees to walk across, sand and water for boats or mudpies.'

' "There are also few fights at these playgrounds," Madame Tanon says, "children fight when they have nothing better to do." '

[1] *International Playground Association Newsletter*, Vol. III, No. 4, September 1968.

'She explained that at a certain age every child goes through a stage of wanting to do things which are antisocial. "On these playgrounds," she said, "children can build or destroy as they wish, and they have no need to participate in vandalism." '

'The delinquency rate was lessened tremendously due to these areas, according to Madam Tanon. This type of playground has proved to be an effective deterrent to juvenile delinquency. Lady Allen of Hurtwood in England experimented with this when she introduced what she called the "adventure playground" to the poorer parts of London after the war, utilizing bombed holes for the children to play in.'

'The playgrounds are now widespread in England, Scandinavia and Holland. One of the problems with introducing the "junk" playground to America is that Americans are very fussy about keeping their children clean and neat. '

' "But when parents are persuaded that this playground is better for their children's development, they will overlook the messiness," says Madame Tanon. "American mothers will realize this just as have European mothers." '

It must of course be realized that a distinct difference exists in the management of a playground which is governed by a voluntary committee and one which is controlled by a Local Authority.

I think that much more freedom of action is available to the playleader who works for the voluntary playground in that he is not subject to so many rules and regulations as is his counterpart in the Local Authority. In the Local Authority Scheme, no need exists for a playground committee to worry about such things as appeals and fund raising. As far as contracts and the acquisition of materials are concerned this is more or less covered by the officer in charge of the playleadership scheme (not by the playleader) as they are part of his duty.

The two distinct approaches to the job mean that playleaders working under different conditions of service sometimes find it hard to understand the methods employed by their counterparts. The fact is that both playgrounds create some situations which are relevant only to their own type. For example a voluntary playground situated in a built-up area may remain open until 22.00 hours whereas the Local Authority playground situated in a park may close at 19.30 hours because the park itself closes at that time. Entry into the playground may be restricted to a certain age group because of a bye-law in the park, whereas the voluntary playground may admit whom they like. One outstanding difference which exists is that in some Local Authority schemes playleaders are not allowed to take children out of the play area under any circumstances at all, which means that no outside activities can be organized, yet some voluntary playgrounds have outings and trips organized regularly.

Playleaders in voluntary schemes become involved with other sections of the community, but the Local Authority playleader, with very few exceptions, stays within the confines of his playground and leaves the outside community work to those specially trained for it. He usually welcomes work which is brought into his playground if it can help the community in any way, but his job is in the playground, and that is where he is usually requested to stay by his employers.

Adventure playgrounds outside the local authority

For those who are interested in the voluntary aspect of adventure playground work, some valuable information which I give below about the setting up of a Management Committee and buildings has been collated by Mr. W. D. Abernethy, Secretary to the Children's Playground and Play Leadership Committee of the N.P.F.A. I am indebted to him for the advice given below. Those who are working for a local authority will not of course be concerned with the fund-raising aspects outlined here.

I. MANAGEMENT COMMITTEE

The following points apply to the Committee of Management of the Playground. I would suggest that there should be three people in addition to the normal Chairman, Secretary and Treasurer.

(a) *Appeals Secretary.* This person should be other than the Treasurer and should be prepared to spend a lot of time working on the affairs of the Committee. However much money comes in grant-aid from other sources towards the salaries and from the Borough Council towards running and maintenance, the Committee will always need more and it should be prepared to have in hand enough to carry it through for one year, in case the sources of grant-aid suddenly dry up. The Committee should seek charitable status so that it can invest money. It is essential to keep appeals constantly going.

(b) *Contacts Secretary.* The leader should obviously make a number of contacts with people in the authority himself and I give below the people he should deal with directly, but he will need frequently to know people in all walks of life with varying professions and skills. These people should be looked after and cultivated by the Contacts Secretary. They are people who will have some knowledge, skill or money to give to the playground and whose advice may frequently be needed at a moment's notice by the leader when for instance he is confronted with a situation which perhaps only a psychiatrist can deal with. The leader has not the time to do all this himself. It must be done for him and he must have permanent communication with the Contacts Secretary so that he knows exactly what services and help are obtainable.

(c) *Materials Secretary.* This person should also contact everybody in the Borough who has or may have some kind of material which might be useful on the playground; namely contractors for wood, tools etc., Local Authority for scouring the depots, divisional education office for old desks, chairs, books etc., British Rail for old sleepers, wine merchants for wood, builders' merchants for paper, paints etc. A constant flow of materials like this is necessary. It is no good the person going to find something when the leader asks for it. They must have their contacts known and warned that they may be asked, long before the demand occurs on the playground. Children rapidly become disgruntled if there is a lack of materials with which they can work. To get the best out of any ideas the collecting of materials has to happen very closely after the ideas flow, otherwise the ideas stultify. It does not matter how difficult the collection is – in fact the more complication the better because this is all part of the exercise. The children have to know and see that things are moving directly the ideas begin.

All these three secretaries will make many contacts in the community for their specific purposes. They should all take occasions to invite their contacts to the playground so that a large number of adults become interested in the site and getting to know the children. This makes the opening of other playgrounds very much more assured so that they are not likely to collapse after the opening.

2. THE LEADER

The procedure for the leader should be as follows – before opening the playground:

(a) Contact teachers, police, probation officers, social workers, pre-school playgroups and youth clubs. He should of course liaise throughout this time with the Contacts Secretary. He should tell them what he is doing and explain the help that he needs from them, namely arranging for pre-school playgroups to use the hut; police, probation officers and social workers to tell him who are the most difficult and likely gang who will break up the site. The moment he realizes who the likely marauders are he must get to know them so that he may obtain their help and so avoid their ultimately burning the hut down.

(b) As soon as building starts on the site, he should go to the nearest school and briefly tell the children what is happening and let the children in half a dozen at a time. Never start off with too many. The gang of course should be encouraged to come in at this stage because it is then that they can be tamed so that they do not worry the younger children. By the time the crowds begin to come in there will be a reasonable number of children of all ages who have grasped the kind of tradition and pattern of work which the leader wants.

3. OPENING

The playground should not be officially opened until it has been in operation for twelve months. It is most important to get it growing steadily and gradually with the least possible publicity until a reasonable behaviour pattern has been assured. Once this is done a great gala fête can be run. It should be opened by the Mayor and the children can make a mass of money for the playground by the sideshows that they run. Everybody will be involved. The 'yobs' can give people motorbike rides on the pillion at 10 to 15p a time!

Hut for adventure playground

Siting the hut is dependent on a number of factors which arise:

(a) It should be as near the services and sewers as possible so that heating, lighting, washing and lavatory arrangements can be suitably set up. Tying into the services etc. is a very expensive business.

(b) The leader, from the hut, should be able to have a fairly good view of everything that is going on.

(c) The main entrance to the hut and any balcony or verandah should face south so that one side of the hut can be set up for the under-fives and their play in the open can be near the hut and in the maximum amount of sun. At the same time, the building can be used to separate the under-fives outdoor area from the play area used by the older children and young people. This should not be considered a separation, but built in such a way that the children are not separated by rule or regulation. They should obviously be allowed to work through the building or around it, but it just happens to be an obstacle in the way.

(d) If money will stretch, the hut should have a flat roof with a strong balustrade so that this can be an additional play area. This is commonly used for playing records and generally talking quietly away from the rush of normal life in the playground. Access can be by a formal stairway, if you like, but a ladder or even a kind of climbing mound up one side of the hut could be useful.

(e) A slide could be made to come down from the roof to ground level, but this should not be set up in the way slides normally are – it should not come out from the top of the ladder into space and downwards. It should be on whatever mound you put as a climbing access to the roof.

(f) Do not decorate the inside of the hut. This should be left to the children to do, because probably even twice yearly, they will want to redecorate it and each group that does this work becomes deeply involved in the building. If they go in the normal educational system to a superbly built and expensively finished palace, they do not care about the place at all. They have no sense of belonging – indeed quite the reverse.

(g) In all cases, you will find that access to the lavatories is on the inside. This is another important factor.

(h) I don't know of any site at the moment that has more than one lavatory for boys and one for girls, but our technical adviser says that there ought to be a minimum of one W.C. and urinal for boys and two W.C.'s for girls – each section having two wash-basins. This is something that will have to be cleared when planning permission is obtained. Of course in many ways the less you have the easier it is to keep clean, but as long as they are kept in good working order and the Health and Education Authorities are not worried from the under-five point of view, all should be well.

As regards the type of building, brick has generally been considered best if it can be afforded but our Technical Adviser says that there are several cheaper buildings which might be suitable. He suggests that for the kind of use an Adventure Playground hut is likely to get, a concrete floor with perhaps a latex screed to act as insulator would be suitable, or slightly cheaper, asphalt could be laid over the concrete with a damp course between. These are the main points made by Mr. Abernethy.

At the time of writing it is true to say that no serious accidents have occurred in any adventure playground in England. I most sincerely hope that this situation prevails, but the law of averages being what it is, the time always comes when a local authority is taken to court for negligence. In an effort to obtain an insight into the views of one who could very well become involved in such a case, I asked an associate officer in the employ of my Authority to give a few observations on some research he had done into this aspect of provision for children's play. Mr. S. J. Fraser is a Member of the Institute of Municipal Safety Officers and has kindly made these comments:

SAFETY IN ADVENTURELAND

With the increase in the number of adventure playgrounds it is certain that controversy will arise regarding Local Authority liability and responsibility with regard to the safety of young people using the playgrounds.

It will be argued that few serious accidents occur to children in adventure playgrounds and that children are sufficiently resilient to withstand the kind of knocks and falls that might disable an adult. Moreover, that the thrill of 'living dangerously' is the very essence of the adventurous play that appeals most to the young mind.

Nevertheless, care can be exercised to ensure that unnecessary risks are avoided.

There have been numerous claims in the courts for compensation, charging Local Authorities with negligence in Municipal Playgrounds of the conventional type. Such cases show very clearly where those authorities stand with regard to their responsibilities when they invite children onto their premises.

The adventure playground, however, presents a very different picture in this context. Litigation arising from an accident to a child in one of these playgrounds might conceivably give rise to the question of what could reasonably be regarded as safe in consideration of the nature of the playground and whether the Local Authority owners had been negligent in their surveillance. Very careful consideration should be given, therefore, to the composition and condition of an adventure playground and especially to the quality of its supervision. Zeal for allowing children to 'do their own thing' and free themselves of inhibitions must not obscure the need for the supervisor to be able to discriminate between what is reasonably safe and what is downright dangerous. I use the word 'reasonably' as one cannot lay down rules for the same degree of safety that one can expect in a place of work, otherwise the creativeness of the lively-minded child would be so severely restricted that the very purpose of the adventure playground would be mutilated. This would be a retrograde step since there is an ever-pressing need for facilities to capture the imagination of children – particularly in densely populated conurbations.

Whilst building adventure playgrounds is not the panacea for vandalism there is a distinct correlation between the absence of adequate play facilities and vandalism.

However, without attempting to dampen down the great enthusiasm shown by organizers in this field and without lessening the undoubted appeal of adventure playgrounds, one should attempt to lay down safety guidelines in order to preclude serious accident.

The Playleader

The quality of the leadership of any group is of primary importance and this especially so with the leader of an adventure playground. Many qualities are required of such a person and I will not enumerate them here fully since they will be obvious. Suffice it to say that with regard to the safe running of the playground he or she must be able to guide play along constructive lines rather than allowing it to drift along in a destructive fashion that can be dangerous, mainly to the less adventurous and the young children. The playleader must be a person who can be turned to in critical situations and strong enough to ensure that the bully is not able to rule the roost. Albeit, he or she must not be looked upon as a policeman, or as a teacher, but as the means of conducting a free-and-easy atmosphere within the group.

Condition and composition of the adventure playground

Inanimate objects such as old boats, motor cars and parts of old aircraft are always of interest to children but as with all old discarded materials, they should be removed as soon as their condition becomes dangerous. Many organizers will exclude old cars as they are so quickly reduced to a condition where the rusting metal is of danger to young limbs. Petrol tanks have been responsible for a number of tragic accidents when children have introduced lighted matches to the filler plugs. This can be avoided by removing petrol tanks before the cars are used in play.

Loose materials placed in the playground to serve the imaginative child's creative drive should be watched carefully and as with objects mentioned above, discarded when they have outlived their usefulness in constructive play. Previously-used timber should have old nails drawn before further use.

Although the adventure playground can never be expected to look as tidy as the conventional playground it must be prevented from deteriorating into a rubbish heap. Whilst it is true that new attention-attracting property will, for a while, attract vandalism, badly maintained and run down and dirty property will always be fair game for destruction.

Structure building

This will probably be the most popular pursuit in the playground. Most children are eager to build 'dens' and a whole range of structures recognizable perhaps by only the children themselves. This is the type of play environment where guidance can be useful. Obviously the structures erected will, for the most part, be rickety affairs and the possibility of collapse from too great a height must be considered. Tree houses and platforms need special attention and if they are such that children can easily fall or get knocked off, then a safety net should be judiciously placed.

Tools supplied for building will come in for much hard wear so they should be well maintained.

Aerial runways and ropes

All materials for runways, and climbing nets must be frequently examined and be such as will withstand hard usage. Broken pulleys or those previously thrown out as worn and unserviceable should not be utilized. Due regard must be paid to the height of aerial runways and the speed at which the block is likely to travel. Although some will want to build the very highest and fastest possible, the guiding playleader should allow common sense to rule rather than allow himself to get carried away by the more ambitious youngsters.

Rope can be used in the playground for a variety of purposes and should always be looked at with a critical eye. I am sceptical of all old materials begged from industrial firms, particularly rope. Short lengths may be useful for lashing structures and for purposes where their condition (within reason) and load-bearing properties are of no great importance. But long lengths must be *carefully* examined as industrial use may have brought them into contact with chemicals that have caused deterioration of the fibres. This may not be patently discernible but testing the rope before use and examination by twisting open the lay will reveal whether the fibres are in good condition.

If wire ropes are used the danger to hands is seen by close examination. Those with 'soldiers' (protruding broken strands) should be discarded. It should also be remembered that wire ropes are not so easy to make fast as ropes of fibre which, if used for an aerial runway or to suspend a climbing net are simply made fast to the support by a couple of round turns and half hitches. Wire rope ends should be finally lashed to their main part otherwise the hitches will ride back, causing slackening. Wire ends must also be firmly bound as an unravelled end can mean a scratched face or possibly the loss of an eye.

The use of ropes and the various knots employed for different purposes can be shown by the playleader when he is assisting the children in the creation of the play environment. If the playleader has a knowledge of rope-splicing, so much the better as lively young minds will respond to this instruction.

Fire

Fire has always held a fascination for children and most will experiment with it at some time, often by playing with a box of matches.

Just as a family will gather round a fire in a home, so a fire in an adventure playground will provide a focal point for children. There they will experiment with various types of materials for flammability. The fire area can provide knowledge with minimum risk unlike knowledge gained by experiments in the home, possibly by bitter experience.

The fire area in the playground must be separated from the general play area and needless to say, the fire must be kept within certain limits. This is easier if the fire is contained within a metal drum. On no account should a fire be allowed within the 'dens' that are built.

Quieter pastimes

Not all children will want to indulge in the energetic activities for which the adventure playground is noted, so a separate section should be provided for quieter pursuits such as painting and other forms of handiwork. It may be said that these are not really the activities of the adventure playgrounds but most children including the small ones, will want to identify with the playground which with the right leadership quickly becomes a club where all tastes can be catered for.

The quieter corner also serves the purpose of preventing smaller children from coming to harm as a result of the strenuous activities of the older ones.

Finally, I cannot emphasize too strongly the need to prevent adventure playgrounds from becoming decrepit rubbish tips.

Articles have appeared in periodicals dealing with places that are little more than dumps. Journalists have approached the subject with the notion that adventure playgrounds are for the express purpose of smashing things up with no harm done and the more dangerous it all is the better the children like it.

The adventure playground concept is worthy of deeper study as it has already proved of great value in the provision of healthy outlets for youthful energies. Possibly future statistics may show a decrease in the delinquency rate as a direct result of such playgroups where natural aggression may be safely channelled.

UNDER-FIVES PLAY CLUB

Tiny Tot play areas existed in Wandsworth as long ago as 1947 as part of its playleadership scheme. No specific playleader was employed solely for the Tiny Tots play area. Its fenced playing area contained a quantity of toys and equipment which was placed at the disposal of parents, who encouraged their children to use it.

No indoor accommodation was provided for use during inclement weather. The thought behind this fact was that children should be at home during unsuitable weather and that sensible parents would not bring them out. But to compensate for the uncertainties of the English climate the play area was only about ten yards away from the park restaurant which had a seating capacity for about eighty and where cooked meals could be had at any time of the day. This restaurant remained open all day and every day. If it suddenly rained parents would take their children into the restaurant for refreshments where they could carry on chatting – which is the reason why many of them came in the first place.

Toilets were adjacent to the restaurant which in turn was situated near the park entrance.

The initial reason why the Tiny Tots area was introduced was to cater for very young children who were brought to the park by their elder brothers or sisters who had themselves been attracted by the facilities provided in the scheme. The fenced area was already in existence around the bandstand, and the original intention was to keep the older children out rather than to keep the younger ones in.

At first no toys or equipment were provided and many of the youngsters brought their own favourite toys with them.

About fifty yards from the bandstand was a conventional playground containing a slide, swings, see-saws and roundabouts. Naturally this proved a tremendous attraction to the little ones, most of whom had paid a visit to it at one time or another with those who were looking after them. Occasionally one of them would wander from the Tiny Tot area to the conventional playground by himself, with the result that a number of accidents occurred and several little ones became lost. To prevent such occurrences the organizer delegated responsibility to one or two senior girls whose duty it was to keep the little ones inside the area and to let them out only when they were called for by the person who brought them.

This situation naturally created problems. Firstly, it was found that children who deposited their very young charges at the Tiny Tot area disappeared for hours on end and on one occasion I remember, one eight-year-old completely forgot to collect her four-year-old sister. Secondly, it was found that at times the young girl on duty in the Tiny Tot area found herself trying to cope with situations which would test the patience of a saint.

To counteract the attraction of the conventional playground it was decided to provide items of play equipment for the tiny tots. These included collapsible climbing apparatus, see-saws, doll's prams, small chairs and tables and rocking toys. Later it was found necessary to provide small blackboards, painting and chalking materials – incidentally chalk was quickly withdrawn after one child stuck a small piece in his ear which required a minor operation to remove it. Next came Plasticine and dressing-up clothes, tents, pots and pans, toy cups and saucers and cutlery.

Even at this stage it became apparent that another strong attraction existed in the conventional playground; this was the sand pit, and so a large sand tray on short legs was introduced into the Tiny Tots area with great success.

Finally it became necessary to introduce a large water container because the little ones had acquired the habit of climbing on to a stage and playing with the water in fire buckets. Both sand and water have a magnetic attraction for young children; they are more attractive than anything else in the play area.

Very little difference exists between these schemes and present day Under-Fives Play Clubs or play groups.

Of course a great deal of experience has been gained since the early days, and a great many surveys have been carried out. Here are examples taken from one particularly searching working party questionnaire in the early sixties. Are there adequate play facilities for young children both in and outside the home, are young children's educational needs being met – were questions asked. Information and opinions were asked for about provision for children with special problems – immigrant children, children of unsupported mothers and working mothers.

PLAY-CLUB ASSOCIATION

Where play clubs exist for under-fives in a playleadership scheme
it would be wise to consider the possibility of forming a play-club
association. Such an association, comprising parents, councillors,
senior officers and staff can benefit the club in many ways. Responsibility can be delegated to parents on the Executive Committee
for many functions which such a body can institute. Money-raising
ventures can be organized by the association with intent to provide
extra equipment and consumable materials such as paint and
play dough, etc. Outings and parties can be organized with cash
which comes from the proceeds of jumble sales, sales of work and
sponsored walks. Organizers and playleaders in charge of play
groups should strive to create and maintain a happy relationship
between themselves and the rest of the committee, and in particular
the parent members. Experience has shown that such committees
are comprised of people, especially women, whose personalities are
apt to clash and that the best deterrent to this is a strong character
as Chairman.

A danger exists in clubs like this that some committee members
are apt to be overambitious. They take on projects which are
sometimes beyond their capabilities. The problem is not so much
in inability but in not having time to carry out the work. It should
be remembered that they all have a child under the age of five to
look after, so organizers would be wise to keep a wary eye on the
programme, and make propositions which are especially designed
not to offend. I say this after the experience of being unintentionally
guilty of offending mothers by the most insignificant remarks.
Some women who are overstrained by the demands of a spoilt child
are emotionally unstable and quite often they accept extra club
responsibilities in an endeavour to counteract this often unrealized
state. When these club responsibilities build up, the effect on a
young mother is evident in a number of ways, some of which could
have rather disturbing effects on the whole play community. These
occurrences are quite infrequent but very unpleasant to all and
sundry when they do happen.

A pleasant atmosphere produces good results as a rule, and an
efficient committee can do no end of good for a play club. But
here lies another danger in that a super-efficient, ex-business type

of mother on the committee can cause just as much upset and is sometimes secretly resented by some members of the committee. To strike a happy medium and elect a group of happy mothers who are interested in the welfare of the club as well as in their own children is not always possible each year. Committees are elected by the usual democratic process which results in the election of differing personalities, some suitable for the work and others who are not really cut out for it. But for all this it will be found that in most cases of dispute – no matter who sits on the committee – common sense prevails in the end.

THE PLAYGROUP

During the 1960's in New Zealand, playgroups for under-fives seemed to be much more experienced than those in England. One of the foremost authorities, Beverley J. Morris, M.A., Dip.Ed., Director of Training, Hutt Valley Play Centres, Wellington, New Zealand, wrote a most useful booklet for the Pre-School Play Groups Association.[1]

She discusses discipline in the playgroup. Must you have discipline? Yes, but it must not be a fear-orientated discipline imposed by adults. Rather, discipline should stem from the limits set by the equipment. For example, bricks will not balance unless properly stacked, jig-saw pieces pushed around haphazardly will not complete a puzzle. Essential rules will concern the safety of children and a playgroup should aim at a permissive atmosphere. There is no need in the playgroup to prepare children for 'the discipline of the infant school'. A child who has had satisfactory play experience between the years of three and five will have little difficulty in adjusting to school life.

Playgroup work is exacting but rewarding. One sees a tense child relax at play. One watches the unselfconscious way in which a small child is completely absorbed in a painting. One is contributing towards the development of well-adjusted personalities.

A playgroup supervisor needs to understand the value of play and know its different stages. Creative play, for instance, starts with the sampling stage, when a child handles and tastes his material.

[1] *A Guide for Pre-School Supervisors.*

There must be 'free activity'. Without direction from an adult a child should choose what he is going to play with at a play session. There should be group activities, singing, dancing and story-telling, but it is up to the individual child whether he joins the group or not.

Free activity implies a widespread choice and this means that the Supervisor must ensure that there is working equipment for a varied programme. Scissors must cut. Paint must be thick enough not to dribble. A jig-saw with missing pieces, or a truck without wheels only causes unnecessary frustration. It is the Supervisor's task to check equipment and see that a wide choice of play is available to children at every play session.

THE PLAY CLUB

A distinct difference exists between playgroups and play clubs. In the former, children are left in the care of a supervisor and her staff, whereas in play clubs it is usually a condition of entry that each child is accompanied by its mother or guardian who is re-sponsible for it. In fact the mother is the member. The play club is staffed by playleaders who are there mainly in an advisory capacity, but who try to create a situation whereby the mothers play with the children. Another important difference between these two concepts of provision is that a charge is made for each attendance at the playgroup whereas the play club is more often a public amenity.

The value of playgroups, so far as adults are concerned, lies in the fact that they make it possible for the mother, if she is financially able, to have a temporary break from the vigilant responsibility of caring for her child: this practice is strongly supported by the Pre-school Play Groups Association who say that the temporary break does them both good. Without acrimony I would here observe that it also appears to do local Bingo halls a lot of good during their morning and afternoon 'quicky' sessions. Even some mothers who can ill afford to gamble are guilty of dumping their offspring in the playgroup and toddling off, with their pencils behind their ears, to their own recreation at the 'Casino'.

The most obvious benefit derived by mothers and children who attend the play club is that in which they are together and learning a great deal about each other in a different environment from home, and that they are fulfilling the natural requirements of nature which decrees that mother and child should remain constantly together during that period of infancy when the child is still dependent on its mother.

Another benefit derived by mothers who take their children to the play club is that they are able, if they are sufficiently observant to see different characteristic traits emerge in their children which only come out when they are playing with other, and sometimes strange, children.

I am not advocating that separations of a short period should not occur, because they are a necessity in order to prepare the child eventually to 'stand on its own feet', or that the child should constantly be at its mother's side, but that during its play periods mother should be where the child can find her, when those uncomfortable new experiences occur which could have an everlasting effect on the child's future if he is left alone to cope with them. A supervisor is no real consolation or substitute for mother when some of these happenings take place.

A very brief outline of the stages in a young child's development, based on National Playing Fields Association research, may be helpful to those who will be concerned with playgroups or clubs for the under-fives.

0 TO 1 YEARS

This is the time when a baby's whole emotional and social development depends on a loving relationship with his mother (or mother substitute). The relationship with his father is important too. There must be time for the baby to play with his parents each day.

1 TO 2 YEARS

He is learning to talk, walk and explore the world. He wants to put everything in his mouth. He will enjoy playing with solid movable objects which he can push and pull, load and unload.

2 TO 3 YEARS

From the age of two he will enjoy playing with water, sand and earth. Try to give him opportunities for running, climbing and jumping; and 'see-saws'. He will also like short, simple stories.

145

Some Suitable Toys

1. A box with sand – in the yard or garden
2. A wooden spade and bucket
3. A Kiddy-car
4. A doll's pram and dolls
5. Wooden cars and trains on wheels
6. Large wooden blocks (for building 'houses')
7. Fitting-in toys – nests of boxes or 'Russian' dolls that fit into each other
8. A swing

Make sure that he doesn't get sand in his eyes making 'sand-castles' and that any swing is stoutly constructed and safe.

3 TO 4 YEARS

Children at this age like increasingly to copy adults, playing 'mothers and fathers', 'shops' and 'hospitals' etc. Put him in a plastic overall when he wants to play with water in the sink or bath; he will 'measure and pour' water into plastic bowls and jam jars. Spread newspaper on the floor and allow him to have paints, crayons, chalk and lots of drawing paper. He will now love looking at picture books and be increasingly interested in stories.

The following toys are enjoyed by this age group:

1. Coloured crayons and paints. Big sheets of drawing paper or newspaper. Large paint brush
2. Model clay or Plasticine
3. Dough (mix flour, salt and water and colour it with powder paint)
4. A toy telephone
5. Dolls, doll's clothes, toy beds, tea-sets, brushes, etc.
6. Wooden farmyard animals
7. A doll's house
8. Plastic and rubber toys for the bath
9. Roundabout toys: a wheelbarrow or toy wagon to ride
10. Fitting-in toys of geometrical design to build small 'houses', arches, bridges etc.
11. Balls of various sizes

4 TO 5 YEARS

He needs toys with which he can make or do something. The

ability to concentrate matures slowly and even at 5 years, 20 minutes is usually long enough for one occupation. He also needs an increasing outdoor life.

Children of this age love 'dressing up' and make-believe, so keep a box in which to put odds and ends of old material and clothes. With an old felt hat and a toy gun he'll believe he's 'The Lone Ranger'. You can easily make a 'Wendy House' out of an old clothes horse covered in material. Let him have a patch of garden to 'dig and plant'. Cloth hand puppets are also fun. Children will play happily alone for only a time; they need playmates of their own age in order to develop and learn; and for the big lesson of getting on well with other people.

Some suitable toys
1. Toy railways, boats, motor cars and aeroplanes, etc.
2. A tricycle
3. Simple wooden jigsaw puzzles
4. Scissors with *blunt* ends to cut out pictures from old magazines
5. Simple card games such as 'Snap' and 'Happy Families'
6. Old Christmas cards, a tube of paste and a scrapbook
7. A tool set (not a toy set) – real small hammer and flat wire nails, pieces of wood, not splintered
8. Bat and ball

Let him play in his own way, providing he isn't doing harm. Understandably many adults are tempted, for example, to take the paint brush out of his hand and say 'No, you must paint the sky blue, not green' but remember he's the one who is learning and it has been known for artists to paint a green sky.

Finally I would say that wherever possible it would be wise always to employ a mother as the Senior member of staff in a play club.

6 · The Programme

Although 'free play' is the most important aspect of play area activity, it should be realized by playleaders that this in itself is insufficient to create an interesting atmosphere which will help to produce incentives for children to co-operate with each other in group work and which will make for a co-operative existence in the playground. The programme of activities should always be interesting enough to stimulate curiosity and provide an attraction to large groups of young people. Programmes should be devised to provide as wide a choice as possible so that children can choose alternative interests.

The long-term objective of play schemes should be to make provision for an unlimited higher age range starting with under-fives and to extend it gradually to embrace the whole community. Many playgrounds with excellent facilities fail miserably to meet the needs of a young society just at the time when it most needs their support. Playgrounds should provide for the recreational needs of young people up to the time when they leave school, but some only cater for children up to the age of eleven years, when they are still comparatively easy to control and when they have not really developed any anti-authority tendencies. My own Authority has increased its age range for young people up to the age of 24 years. Groups of these young people are known to have taken part in small team games, mainly five-a-side football, and to have kept the same players together for periods of up to eight years. At the time of writing these units are known to be still together and have made application to carry on playing for another season.

Annual and monthly programmes are compiled by the organizers and will comprise major events such as rallies, displays, inter-unit activities, pet shows, exhibitions and all such activities which embrace young people from all the schemes units, and which are approved by the Committee.

The senior playleader will be responsible for compiling weekly

148

and daily programmes which will be based on his own experience and concept of the work and tailored to meet the abilities of his assistants and the programme of organized games fixtures in his unit.

Programming at any level requires a certain amount of know-how and several rules exist which it would be advisable to follow.

For example, if co-operation is necessary with another department or an outside body, one would be well advised to make contact with them as early as possible in order to ascertain whether their services will be available or not. Another important point to bear in mind is that it is quite possible that more spectators than participants will be attracted to the event and one should therefore endeavour to make the affair as interesting as possible for the former. Provision for their possible needs should be seen to, for example the availability of refreshments, background music and visual entertainment during any breaks or intervals which are planned.

Annual events are better programmed on the same day each year if it is at all possible. My own Authority follows this procedure. The annual display day is always held on the first Saturday in September. Each year the children's pet show takes place on the first Saturday in June, and because of this requests for entry forms for this event begin to arrive at the Town Hall early in the month of May. The play scheme's five-a-side football competitions which involve six hundred or so teams representative of players between the age of six years and 24 commences on the first Monday in May. I should imagine that practically every boy footballer in the Borough is aware of this, because many flock to the Town Hall for application forms during the month of February in order not to be left out.

Unless special facilities exist, criticism will be directed at organizers who programme for major events to take place at the same venue each year. It is always best to make a change of venue each time the event is held. When doing this it also pays to work systematically when drawing up long-term plans for programmes. I suggest working to a graph system which is governed numerically and alphabetically. The names of the activities in the left-hand column are in alphabetical order from top to bottom, so are the names of the play parks on the top line reading from left to right. The year and date also are listed in consecutive and numerical order which ensures that the cycle of repetition is absolutely fair and regular.

	BLYTHE	CHINBROOK	FORSTER	HOME PARK	LUXMORE	SOUTHEND	BLYTHE	CHINBROOK	FORSTER	HOME PARK	LUXMORE	SOUTHEND	BLYTHE	CHINBROOK	FORSTER	HOME PARK
ANNUAL DISPLAY	1970	71	72	73	74	75	76	77	78	79	80	81	82	83	84	85
ANNUAL SPORTS		1970	71	72	73	74	75	76	77	78	79	80	81	82	83	84
BASEBALL			1970	71	72	73	74	75	76	77	78	79	80	81	82	83
BASKETBALL				1970	71	72	73	74	75	76	77	78	79	80	81	82
COPSTICK					1970	71	72	73	74	75	76	77	78	79	80	81
ITS-A-KNOCKOUT						1970	71	72	73	74	75	76	77	78	79	80
NETBALL							1970	71	72	73	74	75	76	77	78	79
PET SHOW								1970	71	72	73	74	75	76	77	78
SHINTY									1970	71	72	73	74	75	76	77
SOCCER										1970	71	72	73	74	75	76
VOLLEYBALL											1970	71	72	73	74	75

During the year any programme of activities should be evenly dispersed between all play units in the area and so planned that they will present opportunities to youngsters of all ages to participate occasionally if they so desire.

Inter play-unit competitive events are desirable and absolutely essential up to a point, but those involving inter-areas – Town *v.* Town – are frowned upon by some authorities.

An extract from the annual calender might read:

Special events on Saturdays

DATE		EVENT	VENUE
FEBRUARY	6th	Scottish Highland Dancing Competition	Tower Hamlets
	11th	Playleadership Show	Town Hall
APRIL	10th	Seven-a-side Football (CUP FINALS)	Forster Memorial Park
	11th	Easter Parade	Battersea Park
	21st	Old Folk's Show	St. Swithins
	23rd	Indoor Five-a-side Football (CUP FINALS)	Ladywell Centre
	27th	Show for Handicapped People	Saville Club
MAY	8th	Play Area Open Day	Southend Park
	8th	Batinton Rally	Southend Park
	15th	May Queen Festival	Chinbrook Meadows
	15th	Netball Rally	Chinbrook Meadows
	22nd	Children's Carnival	Forster Memorial Park
	22nd	Rounders Rally	Forster Memorial Park
	29th	Children's Day	Warren Avenue
	29th	Volleyball Rally	Warren Avenue
	31st	Festival of London Stores	West End (London)

DATE		EVENT	VENUE
JUNE	5th	Adventure Playground Open Day	Adventure Playground
	5th	Tug-of-War Rally	Adventure Playground
	5th	Children's Day	Home Park
	5th	Mini Shinty Rally	Home Park
	12th	Play Queen Festival	Municipal Playing Fields
	12th	Copstick Rally	Municipal Playing Fields
	19th	Park Open Day	Northbrook
	19th	Gymnastic Rally	Northbrook
	26th	Children's Carnival	Ladywell Centre
	26th	Dancing Rally	Ladywell Centre
JULY	3rd	Margaret McMillan Park Open Day	Margaret McMillan Park
	3rd	Fancy Dress Competition (Open)	Margaret McMillan Park
	10th	Telegraph Hill Open Day	Telegraph Hill
	10th	It's a Knockout	Telegraph Hill
	17th	Beckenham Place Park Open Day	Beckenham Place Park
	17th	Football Rally Div. I	Chinbrook Meadows
	17th	Football Rally Div. II	Northbrook
	17th	Football Rally Div. III	Beckenham Place Park
	17th	Football Rally Div. IV	Warren Avenue Playing Fields
	17th	Football Rally Div. V	Blackheath
SEPTEMBER	4th	DISPLAY DAY	Forster Memorial Park
To be decided		PET SHOW	Forster Memorial Park
To be decided		SPORTS MEETING	

The weekly programme

It will be found on experiment that certain activities will snowball in popularity if they are held at specific times each week. This applies not only to such things as games, barbecues, painting competitions or record sessions but it is particularly noticeable in specialist pastimes such as dancing, music and movement, trampolining or vaulting. During school holidays in the summer time when play parks and play centres are open for most of the day it is usual in most large play units to split the play period into three two-hour or two and a half-hour sessions. These three sessions I suggest are utilized as follows:

Morning Session – Preparatory and mainly 'free play'
Afternoon Session – Main playleadership activity and special event of the day
Evening Session – Rehearsals – Practices – Organized games for older age groups

Of course once the pattern has been established every effort must be made to see that it is maintained because activities of a specialist nature are apt to attract children who live some distance from the play park and who would not normally come there. It does not do to disappoint children who make the effort to come. The weekly programme which is devised by the playleader in charge of the play park will obviously lean towards his personal interests but he should be careful not to overdo this aspect as it may do more harm than good in the long run. All such programmes should be subject to alteration at short notice and where possible alternative activities should be made available. Although one or two items may have been arranged by the organizer, the rest of the week's programme will require much attention to detail on the part of the senior playleader who must always look well ahead and make his preparations accordingly.

The following example of a week's programme is given as a guide but is based on an actual programme which took place at a play park in my own area. Its composition was due largely to the wishes and interests shown by local children.

MORNING	AFTERNOON	EVENING
MONDAY Prepare the week's programme. Record session. Free play activities	Record session. Poster making session. Circle games for the very young. Free play activities. Cricket or volley ball for the older boys.	Batinton for boys and girls. Dancing troupe practice. Organized league games. All in rounders baseball Boys *v.* Girls. Free play activities.
TUESDAY Music and movement. National and country dancing for Juniors and beginners. Free play activities.	Display practice. Boxing for juniors. Musical games and activities for the young. Wrestling or 'rough and tumble' for the older boys. Free play activities.	Netball sessions (seniors). Boys' trampolining. Organized league games. Copstick for boys and girls. High jumping and long jumping for the young. Free play activities.
WEDNESDAY Practice for dancing troupe. Musical skipping. Percussion band practice. Marching troupe practice. Free play activities.	Music and Movement. Sports practice. Trampoline for young children. Free play activities.	Netball sessions (seniors). Boys trampolining. Dancing practice (learners). Organized league games. Free play activities.
THURSDAY Concert party rehearsal.	Treasure trail for young children.	Boys shinty. Netball (juniors).

MORNING	AFTERNOON	EVENING
THURSDAY (cont.) Handicrafts and dress fitting. Free play activities. Prepare Treasure Trail.	Mixed vaulting. Rounders. Baseball. Free play activities.	Sports training. Organized league games. Free play activities.
FRIDAY Music and movement. Record session. Swop shop (records). Free play activities.	Jousting. Swop shop (comics, stamps). High jumping. Free play activities.	Novelty race events. Boys' vaulting. Girls' vaulting. Record session. Organized league games. Free play activities.
SATURDAY Free play activities. Record session. Make preparations for the afternoon's special event.	Week's special event. Free play activities. Tiny tots' sports. Friendly Inter Park Netball Game.	Play units do not usually operate on Saturday evenings.

Planning and preparing the weekly programme

Session by session preparations are made by the playleadership staff with much care. Preparations for this Monday programme would be on the following lines:

MORNING	AFTERNOON	EVENING
MONDAY Prepare the week's programme. Select helpers or prefects for the week. Have information board brought up to date with posters, news, and league tables etc. Check batteries in portable record player. Contact park foreman for any requirements which are his responsibility. Have games furniture erected. Check first-aid box to see that it has an adequate stock. Mix sufficient paint and get paper ready for afternoon session. Do minor repairs to equipment if necessary. Get the morning's activities under way. Lock up after the equipment has been collected in.	See that everything is ready in good time for the main attraction of the afternoon. Make sure that all games' furniture and equipment is available for use on the play area. Appoint a trainee or one of the older girls to organize circle games for the very young. A senior boy or a trainee should be detailed to organize the volley ball session. Have the information ready as to the content of poster competition. Lock up after the equipment has been collected in.	Appoint official to control the organized games. Make sure that all games' furniture and equipment is available for use on the play areas for free play. Get the batinton and dancing under way as quickly as possible. During the latter part of the evening, organize the boys *v.* girls rounders baseball game. Try to get everybody involved. Get equipment cleared from the field and secure major items of games furniture. Lock up. Leave the keys with a member of the park's staff.

Each Monday the week's organized games' programme could be exhibited to give spectators an opportunity to plan visits to the play area if any particular matches are of interest to them.

ORGANIZATION OF SPECIAL EVENTS

The primary objective of any special event in playleadership is not the success of the event itself – although this should be striven for – but to create a situation in which many young people will busy themselves through their play work in contributing something that personally interests them towards the finished object or activity. The interest of young people, their parents and the council must be stimulated and maintained over a long period of time.

It is immaterial how this contribution of play work involves them, be it physical or mental, as long as they are willing to work with their associates. During the process of this play work they become involved with each other in many ways and, in so doing, they learn to accept or reject certain rules or standards set up by their own natural leaders.

It is with the understanding that all groups of human beings have a leader that the person responsible for organizing special events will endeavour to enlist the co-operation of these group leaders – whether they are all aware that they are being utilized or not – including all relevant branches of society in the district at all levels, from children to councillors.

For a special event to have its full effect on the child community of any particular area, it will not be the one that is organized one day and completed at 5.30 p.m. the following day. A well-organized event requires a great deal of attention to detail and, besides making provision for the playleaders to carry out their duties efficiently, it should provide the children with a steady 'build-up' of activities for a long period of time – possibly a number of weeks – right up to the last minute.

An experienced organizer will understand the value of lengthy preparation for a special event and should always be on the look-out for new ideas, knowing that without these 'specials' certain young people tend to become bored very quickly and can easily present the playleader with problems of a different kind. This refers particularly to the accepted leaders of groups of young people. I firmly believe that when playgroups start flagging it is the playleader's fault, not the children's. If this happens the organizer should quickly appraise the situation and take action. It sometimes helps to introduce a new leader from another area – this very often gives the group a lift – and there are many things you can organize when you sense that interest is dropping.

New organizers will find themselves inundated with all kinds of suggestions from many sources. Parents and relations of children will ask you to organize certain events at which their offspring are probably very proficient.

Councillors who are personally interested in a particular activity may ask you to experiment by organizing a special event to test the interest for that activity amongst the young people.

Ideas will emerge from people who have read something in a sports' magazine or from children who have seen something in a comic, e.g. 'Let's all make a big wooden horse, Mac, like they had at Troy, then we could see which park makes the best one and then have a smashing bonfire on Guy Fawkes night with a Guy on each horse.'

Your own contacts with other members of your profession from other schemes will result in an exchange of ideas and experiences.

Literature is sometimes distributed at courses and conferences, or sent to you by various National Associations. This literature may tell you about an event that has been tried out in another part of the country.

Sometimes an idea is born because some national event is having lots of publicity or a major business concern has a sales' gimmick operating.

Children get ideas when they are on holiday, especially after coming home from a holiday camp.

Assuming that a particular suggestion has enough appeal and potential, the procedure to be followed is more complex than one with little experience would imagine.

A number of important factors have to be considered by the organizer.

1. *Time-factor*

a. Have you sufficient time in which to organize the event to the satisfaction of all concerned?

b. Have you any other events taking place on that particular date and if so, is there any chance of a clash of interests?

2. *Venue*

a. Is the suggested place or ground available?

b. Is the venue within easy reach by public transport?

c. Can the children get back home by a reasonable hour?

3. *Bye-laws*

Check to see if such an event is permissible according to the Council's Bye-laws and Regulations.

4. *Cost and authorization*

a. Is sufficient money available in the estimates to cover any cost that may have to be incurred?

b. Has authority been granted by your committee for an event of this kind to take place?

5. *Equipment*

Care should be taken about the availability of any special equipment that would be required for the event.

6. *Judges and adjudicators*

Ascertain whether judges and qualified officials or adjudicators will be available if the event warrants their services.

7. *Laws of sports' associations*

Make sure that you would be able to organize the event within the laws of the relevant sports' associations.

8. *Research*

Research into the possibility of similar events taking place on the same day, or other events that could act as a stronger attraction to the children.

9. *Age check*

If the event is organized according to different age groups make absolutely sure that the children are in their correct sections.

10. *Club memberships*

For some sports, i.e. swimming, it is as well to check carefully that you have a sufficient number of first-claim members so that your unit can be represented in each section of the event. It is unwise to rely too much on second-claim members.

11. *The children's outlook*

Consideration must be given to the opinions expressed and to the amount of interest shown by the children. When you have completed your enquiries, when you have received agreement from officials, when the children are keen, and when you yourself feel that you could organize the event successfully, you are ready for the next step.

Before actually committing yourself in any way with officials or before you complete any application forms – that is if the event is sponsored by another organization – it is advisable that you arrange a meeting to discuss the suggestion with your departmental administration officer as early as possible.

This officer will more than likely require the following information:

COST

An estimate of the cost giving a breakdown of the expenditure.

REPORTS

a. He will ask to see any reports about similar events that have taken place previously.
b. The Administration Officer will also want a detailed draft report about the suggested event.

It is important at this stage to mention that a good working relationship should exist between all adults who are in any way connected with the playleadership scheme. In working with a variety of personalities of different temperaments it is normal that problems affecting the scheme will arise. Helpful criticism given in a tactful manner should never be resented. Consideration and kindness are necessary for pleasant relationships and the critic may be trying to do you a good turn. Your attitude towards other officers should be firm but not stubborn; once you have made a decision stick to it but always be wary of the 'super diplomats' in local government.

The administration officer will then decide if the idea is practicable and make alterations to the draft report if he thinks it necessary.

When this has been done the report will be sent to the chief officer of the department to see if he will submit a report to the committee responsible for managing the playleadership scheme.

He will require further information and may call the Organizer or chief playleader for a general discussion about the suggestion before deciding to put a report to the committee for approval.

Local authority committees meet at regular intervals, usually each month but some are known to meet every sixth week and others every third month. This being so, it is obvious that many special events take place as much as six months or even a year after they were first suggested.

Usually committee members are sent a copy of the report a few days before they hold their meeting; this enables them to study reports at their leisure and also gives them a chance to do a little research of their own, if they think it desirable or necessary.

When the committee eventually meets, it will make its decision and is usually guided in this way by its chairman and the recommendations of the chief officer. If the committee wants further information, it could mean that its decision would be deferred until the next meeting when a further report has been submitted. This situation could in certain circumstances have serious repercussions on the proposed event, especially if the organizer has made any arrangements or promises.

Of course provision is sometimes made for the chairman of the committee to give permission to the chief officer to proceed with arrangements for the organization of the event instead of waiting for the next committee meeting.

Committees are usually very helpful and only on extremely rare occasions are they unable to give a favourable decision; if so there is usually a good reason for their declining.

Let us assume that the committee has given its permission and that the proposed event is some kind of annual festival to be held in a local park.

Now that the way is clear so far as official sanction is concerned, the organizer and his staff are more or less free to get down to the actual business of organizing the event. The opportunity has now been created for a great deal of play-work to be organized and much will depend on the foresight and ability of the organizers and playleaders.

The organizer should make the decision of the committee known to the playleaders and members of the park staff where the event is to take place. After this a number of important arrangements have to be made by him:

a. Inform the council's public relations officer so that he will put the necessary advertising in hand.
b. Work out a suitably balanced programme catering for as wide an age range as possible.
c. Compile a rota of duties for the playleaders and any other staff that are required.
d. Discuss the event with the parks' superintendent (that is of

161

course if he is not your chief officer or senior officer) so that he is fully in the picture.

e. If any application forms are required, arrange printing and distribution.

f. Book any transport that may be required to move heavy equipment and the necessary labour to do the moving.

g. Liaise with the Divisional Education Officer so that he will allow you to advertise the event in the local schools.

h. Make arrangements to have posters designed and printed.

i. Arrange for any tentage.

j. Order prizes, having first obtained authority for expenditure.

k. Send invitations to V.I.P's.

l. Contact the Mayor's Secretary to see if he is otherwise engaged. Invite the Mayor and his Lady as early as possible.

m. Arrange for floral decorations and bouquets for female V.I.P's.

n. Make arrangements for catering.

o. Draw cash from Treasurer's department for miscellaneous purchases, e.g. balloons. (See 'j' above.)

p. Keep the Administration officer informed about all your preparations.

The organization of a major 'special event' will involve the playleader staff, particularly those employed at the park where the event is to take place. There must be local preparation and interest must be created amongst the children so that they will also become involved.

A playleader who is wholeheartedly interested in the young people of his unit will use this situation to great advantage. He will make full use of his own talents and interests and if he possesses the right personality and is able to project his ideas to the group it will not be long before evidence of his leadership qualities is seen through the activities of the children.

It is well known in playleadership circles that when a leader is interested in a particular activity that activity is more or less bound to be popular in the area where that leader is operating.

One of the unfortunate situations that prevails in some areas is the fact that some leaders only take an interest in activities that suit their own purpose with the result that many schemes are not all-embracing in their outlook and tend to defeat one of the objectives of playleadership, that is, to provide a wide choice of activities for a large number of people catering for their many interests.

Local preparations made by the playleader are of paramount importance. He will be expected to use his initiative in making the following arrangements, particularly with regard to the sequence in which he does this:

a. Enlist the aid of local voluntary helpers. Some parents are keen to lend a hand, and if any liaison exists with a senior citizens' club, its members are usually pleased to receive an invitation to help.

b. Rehearsals: If the event incorporates any displays or shows this will give the leaders a chance to exploit their versatility. Dance routines or music and movement sequences have to be worked out. Percussion bands and choirs have to practice. Gramophone records have to be checked.

c. If any form of team games competition is on the programme leaders will need to organize trial games to enable them to pick representative teams. Gymnastics teams will need lots of individual and group practice.

d. Liaise with the groundsman or parks' foreman in order that any ground markings can be done in good time.

e. Careful examination of all equipment should be made early in order that any essential repairs can be carried out.

f. Playleaders in charge should arrange the duties of their assistants with great care, making the best use of their capabilities.

g. If necessary extra prefects will have to be appointed for the event. Leaders should make these temporary appointments early.

h. When permission has been granted by the divisional Education Officer visits should be made to local schools to publicize the event.

i. Arrange for costumes or uniforms to be made or borrowed, as necessary.

j. Distribute and recover application forms.

k. Keep the games organizer or chief playleader fully informed about what you are doing.

l.   During the time when these preparations are taking place, normal games' and activities' sessions must be kept operating.

The playleader usually spends many hours working on miscellaneous tasks in order to stimulate and maintain the interest of the children. If interest should decline during this preparatory period for a special event, it is virtually impossible to re-arouse it.

It might seem at this point that the stage is all set for the event to take place but this is not so, only fifty-two of the necessary sixty steps have been taken and the organizer still has much to do!

a.   Arrange for sound amplification if it is required, making sure that the operator is aware of the position of electric points or whether a battery-operated unit is required.

b.   Label all prizes and trophies, etc.

c.   Have posters displayed but make sure they are not displayed more than two weeks before the event is due to take place.

d.   Make the necessary arrangements for a first-aid organization to be present.

e.   If live music is to be performed, make sure you are covered by the council's licence issued by the Performing Rights' Society. Obtain one of their 'returns' forms and make sure it is completed by the person in charge of the musicians.

f.   In the event of gramophone records being played, it would be wise to check with Phonographic Performance Ltd.[1] to see if you are abiding by their rules and regulations. Otherwise very serious repercussions could result.

g.   Retrieve any trophies that are to be competed for from the previous year's winners.

h.   Check and sort out all completed application forms.

i.   Organize a rehearsal if necessary.

The organizer is responsible for co-ordinating all preparations and should be very careful to avoid confusion with the organization of other events he may be working on during the same period.

It is important to remember that no matter what the event is, every single item of preparation is of the greatest importance. One little slip can mean the difference between success and failure. The

[1] Phonographic Performance Ltd., 62 Oxford Street, London W.1.

planning of each special activity or event implies particular advance-programme planning and I give the following as a rough guide for particular activities.

Inter-park netball

Playleaders should make mutual arrangements between themselves about the following points:

1. Where the game is to take place.
2. Ages of competitors.
3. Date of game.
4. Time of commencement.
5. Who the umpires will be.

The playleader of the park where the game is to be played would then need to:

1. Make sure the park foreman knew, so that he could have the court re-marked if necessary.
2. Ascertain that the games' equipment was in order.
3. Choose the team captain, and ask her to select the team, including a reserve player.
4. Have team skirts ready for the players.
5. Make sure the umpire has been appointed.
6. Have a whistle ready, in case the umpire is without one.
7. If possible arrange for changing accommodation for the teams.
8. Arrange for refreshments after the game.

Children's pet shows

A fair amount of preparation is needed for this event, so the following items have to be seen to:

1. Liaison with The Blue Cross to send judges and vets.
2. Arrange refreshments for visiting officials.
3. Have certificates printed, and pre-signed.
4. Have application forms printed and distributed.
5. Hire the necessary pet cages.
6. Hire amplification.
7. Arrange to have marquees and tents erected.
8. Contact local Pet Food firms to obtain free samples and appropriate posters.

9. Order tables to place cages on.
10. Ensure that drinking facilities are available for the children's pets.
11. Arrange for a suitable enclosure to be erected. It should contain lush grass for penned animals to graze.
12. Notify public relations officer (P.R.O.).
13. Prepare completed application forms for the judges.
14. Cordon the area off in sections and erect signboards indicating which area is reserved for each type of animal.

Tiny Tots' sports

The playleader should inform his organizer of certain requirements, which will include the following:

1. Request for miscellaneous prizes as required.
2. The provision of flags, bunting, or balloons for decoration.
3. Blank 'Do it yourself' posters for publicity aimed at parent involvement.
4. Arrangements to have any special marking-out done.
5. Invitations for people to act as judges, etc., if the occasion demands.
6. Other assistance or equipment as necessary.
7. Enlist the aid of voluntary helpers.

Old Folks concerts

These are usually organized because of requests received from club secretaries. Playleaders who are capable of training their own groups of children accept responsibility for the preparation and production with little or no help from the organizer. After the initial approach has been made, these playleaders are left to use their own initiative.

Road safety demonstrations

The police 'road safety' demonstration unit is an extremely efficient organization. Very little preparation is needed. The only stipulation they make is that they do like at least two hundred children to be present if possible. To achieve this object it is usual to have an added attraction during the afternoon such as a novelty sports meeting. The games organizer arranges this, and makes sure there is plenty of publicity.

DOCUMENTATION OF RECORDS

In this present day and age we all seem to be bedevilled with the unsavoury task of having to fill in forms to obtain many of our essential needs. It has become a standing joke that for one to make application to any government department for the slightest need one must complete forms in *triplicate*.

In playleadership the situation is not quite so bad as this, but records do have to be kept and in a well-organized scheme a number of documents relevant to a wide range of different things are always requiring attention.

Time sheets

Quite obviously one of the most important documents will be the weekly or monthly time sheet which is signed by unsalaried staff. In some cases this time sheet or attendance record is signed each day and in others it is signed each session. To some this may seem unnecessary, but I know of part-time teachers (i.e. swimming instructors) who have to have their salary claims signed every half hour.

Accident reports

A supply of accident forms should be kept by each senior playleader who is responsible for seeing that these are correctly filled in and passed on to the organizer or the office. This is extremely important because if it should transpire that a claim for damages should be made, much may depend on the contents of the accident report. If no official accident report form is available it is the responsibility of the senior leader to make out a comprehensive report and to get witnesses to sign it if possible.

Report of Accident

Name of Injured Person.................................Age.............
Postal Address..
Date and Time of Accident..
Place of Accident...
Description..
....

Nature of Injuries...

....

Particulars of any First-Aid Treatment given...........................

....

If Ambulance called, give time called............Time arrived..........
Was Injured Person taken to Hospital.....................................
Name and Address of Witnesses...

....

....

Give particulars of any fault or defect to which accident was due;
and any other information about Accident.................................

....

Signature ....Designation................

Date..............................

Incident reports

These are similar in almost every way to accident reports. They
cover everything of an unusual nature that cannot be classed as an
accident. Wherever possible witnesses should be asked to corroborate
such occurrences and their names and addresses should be contained
in such reports.

Application forms for special events

In an effort to make situations as realistic as possible, children and
young people should be given the opportunity to participate in the
organization of their own affairs from a management aspect as much
as possible. Forms of application for entry of teams or individuals
into events and competitions should be made available for those
young people who wish to take part.

As participation should be made available to a wide age range
the forms of application should be so designed so as not to cause
confusion to very young applicants. Simplicity of layout and
wording is the answer in this respect. If the event involves an outside
organization advice should be sought from them before the application form is drafted so as to ensure conformation to any special
rules or stipulations which they may require.

JUNIOR (under 12 years at time of play)   SENIOR (under 16 years at time of play)

WHICH DIVISION WILL YOU BE PLAYING IN ?...........................

All players will sign their own name on this form.

SIGNATURE	ADDRESS	SCHOOL	AGE

RESERVE PLAYERS (4)	AGE	NEW PLAYERS (4 CHANGES)	AGE	DATE

Team Officials

SECRETARY :...............................   Phone:.................

ASST. SECRETARY :........................   Phone:.................

CAPTAIN : ....   Phone:.................

If possible one of the team officials should have a phone for arranging fixtures.

Equipment inventory

Constant changes are always taking place as far as equipment is concerned so it is up to the senior playleader to make sure that the inventory of equipment is kept up to date. It will be necessary to produce this document on the occasion of an equipment check by audit. As new equipment is issued it should be entered on the inventory, and when equipment is lost or stolen a similar entry should be made. This of course does not apply to acquisition or loss of equipment which was originally obtained from other sources than the employing authority.

7 · Competition

Various schools of thought exist as to whether competition is a good thing or not.

I would be inclined to argue that many aspects point in favour of competition and to agree that others equally balance the argument against it. Much depends on how one analyses the subject for it goes far deeper than games competition.

The first point that should be considered is that children are natural competitors from a very early age. They are competing with something all the time, even themselves occasionally.

On one occasion, to illustrate how children are good psychologists, it was pointed out by a lecturer at a national conference how a baby learned at a very tender age that if it yelled loud enough it would be fed. This is very true; so it would, but what happens when mother wants to remove the empty bottle and baby is not quite satisfied? The baby pits its wits and strength against its mother because it still wants the bottle. Already the child is competing, if the bottle is taken from it the baby will probably yell louder than before. This is temper or aggression. It has pitted its wits against an adversary and lost and does not like the situation. A little later the baby may be competing with older children for the possession of a rattle or a small toy. On most occasions he will win because his opponents will be playing sympathetically, but if another young child attempts to take the object no sympathy will be evident so the competition will be in earnest. This is forced competition.

Life itself and the very world we live in is a competition which on one hand breeds jealousy, hate, greed, contempt and poverty, and on the other pride, riches and affection. Of course many other things could be included but these will suffice as being the roots. All these things, both good and bad, are incubated by or are the by-products of competition in one form or another – competition against our neighbours and associates which should be friendly and fair but very seldom is, the competition of war in which mankind competes to destroy his fellow creatures and the competition of those who stand on the edge of the battlefield and also compete with each other to sell to the antagonists materials with which to do the job.

In many ways competition is forced upon us. We are compelled to play in order to safeguard our very existence and survival both socially and otherwise. Man competes against man, sometimes against his best friend for the hand of a woman, and we are told that 'all is fair in love and war' but does the best man always win? No, we know he doesn't. Many competitions have been lost because the loser was not conversant with the rules of the game or because he played the game too meekly or even because he played too strictly to the rules.

Salesmanship for example is big business in this day and age. It is also big competition where one country competes against another, quite often with no holds barred and where force and strength of muscle means nothing. Rewards come to players who understand the rules and can dovetail them to their type of game. Billy Bremner of Leeds United has published a book entitled *You get now't for coming Second* and he should know; so should Leeds United!

Local Authorities are competition-minded; they like to recruit the best staff they can, and they like to boast that they are the first in the country to start a new project or scheme. Each regiment in the Brigade of Guards is the finest in the British Army according to anybody who has served in one, and no doubt the top brass of these units in brigade headquarters compete with each other to organize the most efficient recruiting campaign to keep their units up to strength.

'Keeping up with the Jones's' is really only an outward sign of an inner endeavour to equal or even better the efforts of neighbours and friends.

Higher grades of competition tend to breed or fuse a more acute degree of aggression in some youngsters and to completely 'freeze' others. It is difficult to predict how particular youngsters will respond to certain competitive situations. Some who are normally well controlled under ordinary conditions lose all sense of self discipline in the early stages of a game and take some time to settle down. For this reason I am not in favour of competition for young people if it involves representation on a high level basis.

When we try to equal the efforts of our opponents as individuals, we stand or fall according to our ability to control our outward image. We nearly all tend to become aggressive when intimidated in certain ways. To some this is serious but it can be overcome.

Competing against each other for equipment, materials or favour

Very few specific activity clubs exist which will accept younger children, apart from swimming and athletic clubs; a younger boy who is particularly interested in soccer and nothing else, and this appertains to eight out of ten – will have to join an organization such as the Cubs in order to get into a team. Even so, when he joins he faces competitions for a place in its team. To join a club at all involves payment of subscriptions and being subject to the laws of association which in turn means that the youngster is being bound by laws which prevent him from participating freely as and when he pleases. In playleadership he can do just this without worrying about such things as whether a qualified referee will be available, etc. He will not have to worry about the ball being the correct size and he can feel as did the Irish footballer who shouted, 'Never mind the ball, lads, let's get on with the game'.

It would therefore seem logical to assume that some form of instruction or advice in the fundamentals of taking part in competition should be accepted as necessary. This is where playleadership comes into the picture, because the boys taking part are not playing for their school or club and are therefore not bound by any laws of association and are not subject to petty restrictions. They can be themselves in their own true colours, and would probably make their teacher's hair stand on end if he could see or hear them. It is by seeing them this way, when the strain of taking part in competition has brought out hidden characteristics, that we can hope to help them. My own experience has shown that children can be persuaded to harness their aggression which is excited under provocation and redeploy their efforts to better advantage. Children should be given an opportunity to cope with competition just as they are given the chance to take part in activities which may be termed dangerous or adventurous. A person must first of all learn to cope with his own emotions before he can compete successfully against an adversary, and by this I do not necessarily mean that he must be the victor. He must also train himself to accept defeat.

Competition and over-organization

If any danger exists in this subject at all it is that of over-organizing competitions or that of over-providing facilities for one activity and neglecting the rest.

Experienced organizers in charge of projects will realize the dangers which will result from being fanatical about one particular activity. It breeds resentment from children who are interested in other pastimes and kills the incentive of staff who have been requested by the youngsters to organize them.

It can also create in those on whom attention is lavished an attitude that the scheme is solely provided for them, thus risking the possibility that some of the children concerned will acquire superiority complexes. This group superiority complex on one side and resentment on the other can eventually lead to a situation that could have a disturbing effect on the whole project.

Another danger lies in the fact that members of staff also compete with each other, albeit on a friendly basis, to produce results for self-satisfaction. If they are denied the opportunity because of a lack of interest from those in charge, they themselves may lose interest and become mere passengers.

Too much of a good thing is bad, so great care must be taken not to overdo the organizational aspect. Children must be given the opportunity to organize their own affairs as much as possible. They should be allowed to choose their own activities and choose where they want to play. They should be given the opportunity to play at a time which is convenient to them, not when it is convenient to the adults involved within reason of course. They should be given the opportunity to persuade their friends to form teams or groups and to take part in competitions strictly segregated in age groups. Competitive fixtures should be made by team representatives, not by playleaders or organizers, except of course during trophy competitions or rallies. Team captains and secretaries should be elected by the team or group and should represent their team on league committee meetings, etc. These teams should be allowed to choose their own name and colours and should be encouraged to arrange meetings in their homes.

Training sessions should be organized by the team captain and visits to play areas to watch the form of the other teams. Opportunity must be provided for these youngsters to arrange friendly games between their teams.

The duty of any playleader or organizer is to provide just enough stimulus to keep interest in these competitions alive but to leave the bulk of the running around to the youngsters. In this way they will feel more independent but, more importantly, those youngsters who take it upon themselves to form teams will take more interest in the scheme as a whole and will – provided the playleader uses the correct approach – make themselves useful in other ways. Children must be given the opportunity to use their own incentive and experience has proved that over-organizing their competitive affairs is probably worse than not organizing anything at all.

COMPETITION AND ITS EFFECT ON ATTENDANCES

It has been mentioned before that one objective of a playleadership scheme is to attract into play areas as many children of the community as possible and to provide a multitude of activities as the basis of this attraction.

It is virtually impossible to provide facilities which will meet the needs of every child, but fortunately most children have more than one hobby or interest. The majority of them will try something they have never done before. It follows therefore that most children attending play units should find something to interest them. This interest will naturally be generated according to the nature of the young person concerned; the influence of his family or close friends may have a bearing on the activity he chooses, or even traditions of his school or club. Nevertheless no matter what the activity is it will be classed as either competitive or non-competitive.

The degree of success of such schemes sponsored by Local Authorities is quite often equated to attendance figures and statistics; this being so it will almost certainly be the responsibility of people in charge of units to keep an attendance record of one description or another. In playleadership this can be a wearisome chore; it can prove time-wasting and frustrating. In 'free play sessions' at outdoor play areas it is nearly an impossibility to keep true and accurate records of session by session attendances because of the fluctuating pattern of playground use. Basically attendance is governed by these factors:

A. Weather conditions
B. Organized events
C. Facilities available

Naturally the situation would be different with indoor play centres.

As far as weather conditions are concerned, nothing can be done to help boost attendance figures except to provide a large building which will be adequate to cater for the recreational needs of large numbers of children during poor weather.

On the other hand attendance figures can be greatly boosted by carefully planned long-term competitive events. A true record of attendance can be kept of organized full-dress games' events.

Organization of competition

Whether one feels that competition is good for children or not, the success or failure of any competition will rest on how it is organized. Activities should be organized in such a way that they will cater for a large number of participants over a long period of time. Preferably such activities should be interesting and popular enough to attract the attention and attendance of other non-participating playground users. Two categories which will have the desired effect are live entertainment and organized competitions.

Automatically this separates the competitive element from the non-competitive and gives the playleader a chance to provide other interesting pastimes for those youngsters who are not inclined to take part in competitions. Some of these non-competing youngsters may have an outside interest in the organization of competitions and may participate in many other ways within the overall organization of the event.

The organizer must endeavour to see that as far as possible all things are equal, so assuming the competition is to involve 'Teams' he must make sure that application forms contain information which can be easily checked in case of dispute.

Competition can take one of three forms:

a. Knockout
b. League
c. One versus the rest

Knock-out competition

The mechanics of a knock-out competition require that a certain number of sections are played in order to cut down on the number of teams each time. These sections are known as rounds.

Luck can play a part in that a team can gain what is termed a 'BYE'. This means that they do not have to play at all in that particular round of the competition and so pass through to the next round. Therefore all teams who win and all teams who have drawn a 'BYE' go through to the next round which will obviously contain only half the number of teams of the preceding round.

Code letters or numbers are always used when first compiling a fixture list, and then when all is in order, the correct names of players or teams are filled in.

For example if eight units are taking part in a knockout competition the code fixture would read:

ROUND I	ROUND 2	ROUND 3
A v B		
	A or B v C or D	
C v D		A B C or D
E v F		v
	E or F v G or H	E F G or H
G v H		

'BYES' are given in a competition when the total number of entries is less than eight or falls short of any number which is a multiple of eight. The number of 'BYES' given will be denoted according to the number of teams being drawn. If for example seven teams are entered one 'BYE' will be placed in the draw to make the total number of eight units. If the number of teams entered is six, two 'BYES' will be placed in the draw but one 'BYE' should never be drawn against another 'BYE' as this would naturally defeat the object of placing another team into the next round.

If six teams are competing the code fixture would read:

ROUND I	ROUND 2 (Semi-Final)	ROUND 3 (Final)

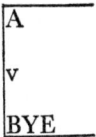

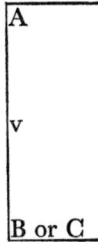

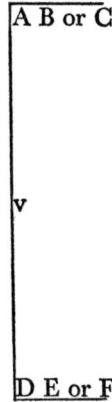

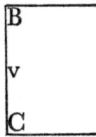

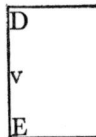

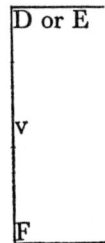

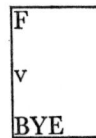

If thirteen units are competing the code fixture would read:

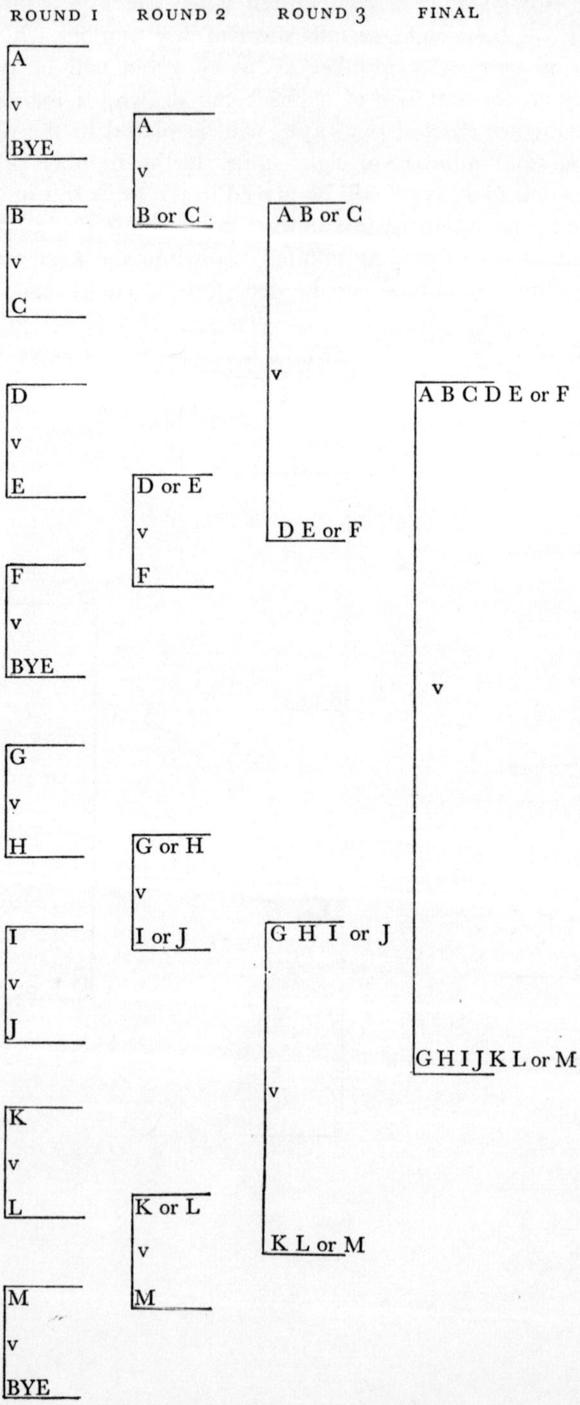

ROUND 1	ROUND 2	ROUND 3	FINAL

A
v
BYE

A
v

B
v
C

B or C

A B or C

D
v
E

D or E
v
F

D E or F

A B C D E or F

F
v
BYE

G
v
H

G or H
v
I or J

G H I or J

I
v
J

K
v
L

K or L
v
M

K L or M

G H I J K L or M

M
v
BYE

LEGS

In competition the word 'leg' refers to one of two games which must be played to decide the winner. Each team or opponent plays one game at its own venue and one at its opponents. In the case of an equal aggregate score at the end of the two games, it is customary for the controlling official to spin a coin to decide the winner.

League Competition

A league is a number of teams or individuals. A specific number is laid down as being that which will constitute a league; this decision is made by the appropriate management committee. Usually it consists of sixteen or so units but can be as little as four.

COMPILING FIXTURE LISTS

Care must be taken not to plan a single league containing many teams. One authority in London made an attempt to run a competition which comprised a league of 32 teams – one for each London Borough. It was envisaged that each team would play one game per week throughout the season of 32 weeks, and that they would play against every other team in the league twice, one on their home ground and once on their opponent's ground. This would provide 16 games each Saturday. When compiling the code fixture list it was realized that 952 games would have to be arranged to complete the fixtures. As will be seen it would take 60 weeks to play off all the games, assuming that no games were postponed because of inclement weather. If the game was of national standing and affiliated to the appropriate body it would only be allowed to take place within the stipulated season. Official games are not played in the close season.

The table overleaf will give a rough idea of how many games will need to be arranged for leagues containing different numbers of units.

It has been mentioned before that a league fixture is prepared from a code list of which the symbols are either letters or figures. As application or entry forms are received so they should be given one of these symbols thus making it a fair system of 'first come first served'.

It is essential to reserve pitches or courts for replays on suitable dates.

No. of Units	Playing each other team once	Playing each other team twice
4	6 games	12 games
5	10 games	20 games
7	21 games	42 games
8	28 games	56 games
10	45 games	90 games
12	66 games	132 games
16	120 games	240 games
17	153 games	306 games
18	171 games	342 games
19	190 games	380 games
22	233 games	466 games
32	476 games	952 games

COMPILING A LEAGUE TABLE

In league competitions a points system operates whereby it is usual to award two points to a winning unit, one point to each unit who draws a game, and no points to a unit who loses a game.

A fully comprehensive table will give detailed information as to the following:

1. The number of games played at home by each unit.
2. The number of games played away by each unit.
3. The number of games won by each unit.
4. The number of games drawn by each unit.
5. The number of games lost by each unit.
6. The number of goals scored at home by each unit.
7. The number of goals conceded by each unit on its own ground.
8. The number of goals scored by each unit.
9. The number of goals conceded by each unit away from home.
10. The exact position in the table according to the points it has gained on a particular date.

A typical league table will read as shown in table on the next page.

To check whether your findings are correct or not count the total number of games played which in this case adds up to 32,

UNIT	P	W	D	L	F	A	Pts.
RED	4	3	1	0	10	6	7
PINK	4	3	0	1	12	4	6
GREEN	4	1	2	1	9	5	4
BLACK	4	1	2	1	8	8	4
ORANGE	4	1	2	1	8	12	4
WHITE	4	1	2	1	5	10	4
YELLOW	4	1	1	2	6	7	3
BLUE	4	0	0	4	6	12	0
	32	11	10	11	64	64	32

then add the next three columns together. Their total should also come to 32. Goals for and goals against should be exactly equal. The points column total should be the same as the games played total.

There is no need to explain in detail the procedure for organizing contests on the 'one versus the rest' system.

Prizes and incentives

It should not be expected that children will persevere in any activity – particularly one of a sporting nature – which requires a lot of training and self-discipline without the chance of winning some kind of material reward. Incentives are also desirable for children who take part in other activities – not necessarily competitive ones – designed to give help and services to others. Usually being able to be of service to others is sufficient reward for such children, others will work quite hard to achieve certain standards or acquire certain skills or abilities for very little reward, sometimes just for the sheer pleasure of it.

At the time of writing the cost of imitation gilt medals is approximately:

30 new pence each for gold
25 new pence each for silver
20 new pence each for bronze

Comparing the cost of a gold gilt medal with other commodities it roughly equals the price of about twenty cigarettes. An organizer should make sure that provision is made in the annual estimates for sufficient prizes of this kind to be purchased. It is important to work out how many prizes will be required during the whole year in order that sufficient publicity can be given to the fact that such prizes are offered. Publicizing the fact will certainly help to raise the number of participants.

Many acceptable prizes for young children can be obtained free of charge from various sources, in industry and from local government departments. For example the road safety officer usually has available miscellaneous small items of advertising media such as pencils and badges. Balloons and painting books, etc., can be had from the Public Relations Departments of large firms. The Blue Cross Society will provide judges and officials to organize a pet show and they will also provide the prizes for the winning children and their animals.

Sweets are always acceptable as prizes for small events such as races, scavenger hunts or artistic efforts. Sweets should always be of the wrapped variety for obvious reasons, but some authorities prohibit sweets because of dental implications. Therefore, as an alternative, good quality fruit is sometimes used as prizes.

Certificates may be used to great advantage and can be so designed that they can be presented for any activities. Naturally they must be signed by the Mayor of the authority.

Awarding points adds some little incentive but this naturally demands that a points awards system be established to implement the scheme. This could be designed as another activity to create playwork letting the children control the system.

Promoting children to prefect status can be reward for help and service to the scheme and this will act as a strong incentive to those children who are of an ambitious nature to gain this coveted award and the many privileges which go with it. This is also recognized as the first step on the ladder to becoming a trainee playleader. The experienced organizer will realize the importance of not making it too easy for children to become prefects, and will stimulate friendly competition amongst the children for the honour of being considered as a prefect candidate.

Reward for effort as against actual ability should be given to children who try very hard to become proficient enough to take part in shows and displays. Even if they do not reach the required standard they should be given the opportunity to take part in shows and displays in other items which do not require a great deal of talent. Such reward makes them strive even more to become proficient in the more difficult things for other occasions.

Photographs of stars of sport or the pop world are quite easily obtained in large numbers from secretaries of fan clubs at very little cost and sometimes free of charge; again, these are acceptable and sometimes coveted by children – more so if they eventually obtain a recognized complete set of pictures.

Older people taking part in 'organized games' should be persuaded to buy their own competition medals and trophies from subscriptions collected solely for this purpose.

It is also possible to persuade local firms, shops or newspapers and even individuals to donate trophies to the scheme for annual competition provided their name is given to the trophy.

Judging and adjudicating at competitions

Very seldom does an accolade come the way of a referee or an umpire. No matter how impartial he may be he nearly always falls victim to abuse and criticism.

The losers usually moan at his inefficiency and when a contest is drawn both sides slate him for having poor eyesight or for not knowing the rules of the game.

Organizers would be well advised to prevail upon neutral adjudicators for assistance if possible. They should never be found guilty of supporting any particular unit within their own organization. In the event of disputes arising it always is wise to have a league committee behind you to finalize any judgement.

In competitions where visual choice is made, for example a May Queen Festival, it is always wise to select a panel of volunteer lady spectators, put a piece of paper and pencils in their hands and let them do the choosing. Always have an odd number of judges to prevent a 'tie' occurring.

If the event is organized on a bona-fide basis make sure your adjudicators and judges are qualified or again you will find yourself subject to much criticism.

The best advice I can give in this respect is 'to be fair' to yourself make it fair for all those taking part.

8 · Marking out

One will notice that when a group of young boys arrive at an open piece of ground to play a scratch game of soccer, the first thing they do is to elect two boys who are to captain the teams or, to be more precise, the boy who owns the football and the boy who is the accepted best player elect themselves as captains. After performing a starting ritual – which could be something of a mystery to many an adult onlooker unless it simply involves the spinning of a coin – the two boys choose their players one at a time on an alternating system. This operation is usually carried out amidst much noise and disagreement and sometimes with threats being hurled at the team which is procuring all the star players. It culminates with the choice of a name for each team, and with much emphasis being placed on the fact that each boy wants to name his side according to the colours of his own soccer strip.

Next, the two teams, with all players talking at the same time, decide which way they will face. On deciding this the two physically weakest boys are detailed to play goalkeeper for their respective teams and after being given all the odd coats, shoes and bags, etc. are told to place these items in such a position that they will represent the two sets of goalposts.

It is at this point that a decision is arrived at concerning boundaries of the playing area and what best use can be made of existing facilities. For example they may decide to use a couple of trees for goalposts if suitably placed, or they may even use the gateway to a yard or the metal uprights of chain link fencing. Sometimes they chalk a set of goalposts on a wall, sometimes on the gable end of a house that belongs to 'that moaning old . . . '. Invariably it transpires that when such games take place in a public open space, at least one of the side lines is represented by a public pathway, the exact location of the second one is kept secret by both sides and appears to be an invisible line (like the equator) which moves about considerably and whose position is dictated when the cry 'Oy mate! where do you think you're going?' rings out.

This improvised marking out and use of existing features is applicable to a number of games other than soccer and it has been noticed that the duration of these games is more or less governed by how much they are parallel to the real thing. I feel that much enjoyment is obtained by youngsters who improvise for themselves in this way, but once they reach the age of about eleven years they take their games more seriously and it is then that they are likely to be attracted by more realistic facilities. Very rarely will they decide how long they are going to play, but this is governed by the following points.

A. The balance of playing ability of each team.
B. Whether any players wander off, thus making the teams uneven.
C. Whether any drastic disagreements take place between players.
D. The condition of the playing surface, and of course the weather.
E. Interference from older people.
F. Lost equipment, i.e. shuttles, play balls, etc.
G. Damage to property, i.e. broken windows, etc.
H. The calls of nature, hunger and certain television programmes.
I. Realistic playing facilities i.e. markings – nets – officials, etc.

This brings me to the question of how should we endeavour to cater for those young people who take their recreational sporting activities seriously? By this I refer not to play equipment but rather to space for play and the provision of courts and pitches for outdoor and indoor use.

Marking out these pitches can be something of a problem in itself in that the prerogative for carrying out the work is not always that of the playleader. More often than not it is the responsibility of ground staff. This right should always be respected by playleaders, otherwise trade unions may be brought in to enforce the ruling. Some playleaders on taking up their job find they are expected to do their own marking out and may know very little about it, and so it is always best to be prepared.

One of the first problems that one comes up against when

marking out is that of making a right angle. This is effected by first making a triangle using these measurements for the three sides:

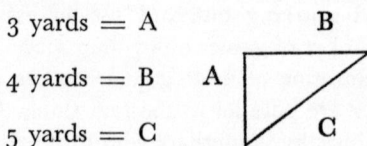

3 yards = A

4 yards = B

5 yards = C

It will be found that lines A and B constitute a right angle. (Sides of 3, 4 and 5 metres will give the same result.)

If it transpires that no marking machine or whitener is available, it is as well to remember that it is possible in an emergency to improvise by using white tape or string for very small courts, i.e. Batinton (not to be confused with Badminton) or sawdust for large pitches. Butchers usually keep a large supply of sawdust which could probably be acquired on the understanding that the same amount be returned at a later date. Spot markings for displays etc. can be done with small pieces of hardboard or plywood and nailed to the ground with a single large nail through each piece. They can be either numbered or painted different colours for place identification. Temporary improvised marking out has advantage in that it can be removed immediately after the game has finished and re-marked in a different place next time a game is played. This contributes in one way to help prevent the wear and tear of grass, which is often one of the reasons for disagreement between play-leaders and staff. I feel that wherever possible courts and pitches should be regularly moved about into different positions to save ugly patches appearing on the turf. Where soccer, rugby and hockey goalposts are sunk into the ground this of course is not possible, but for games like rounders, baseball, cricket and stoolball it is quite simple to move them about each time the game is played.

When marking out improvised playing areas for 'free play' type of small team games it is not essential to comply rigidly with full size measurements, but for competitive league games it is necessary. If improvising, one should endeavour to keep any reductions in size to roughly their correct proportions, and to take particular care not to have goal areas etc. backing on to rivers, lakes, railway lines, electricity cable compounds or glasshouse nurseries. It is an offence in some cases to put perimeter markings too near to public pathways or low fenced children's conventional playgrounds. Obviously the reason for this ruling is to prevent accidents to the general public and to safeguard against youngsters climbing over or going into danger areas to retrieve play balls etc. It is also advisable to keep ground markings well away from pet enclosures or aviaries and of course away from the resident park officer's back garden. If private property should back onto a public open space it would also be advisable to keep as far away from this area as possible with any kind of play provision or ground marking.

When making advance preparations to do any marking out on grass, it would be advisable to get the grass cut first because nothing causes more trouble for a referee or other games official than ground markings that are difficult to see. Cutting the grass after it has been marked out practically obliterates the lines.

Also it should be borne in mind that a weak mixture of whitener will very easily be erased by heavy rainfall, if the marking out has been done on a new grass site. Ideally the grass should be cut first, then the marking out done with a substance which retards any further growth of grass and finally with thickly mixed whitener. Try to get a flat piece of ground to mark out on for any ball games if you possibly can.

Marking out on Redgra area presents other problems to the uninitiated. Redgra is a fine sandy type of red gravel which is used for surfacing 'all weather' playing areas, usually effectively. A special type of marking machine of the no-contact type is used to apply whitener on Redgra. The standard type of grass marker – with a wheel applicator – is not very effective as the wheel is inclined to pick up the Redgra rather than deposit the whitener. To improvise marking out on Redgra in an emergency, the best bet is sawdust, white or yellow sand, industrial salt (usually used for sprinkling on icy pavements) during dry weather periods. I have known of flour being used, and on one occasion washing powder. It is of course possible to do marking out by scraping lines on Redgra with a sharp instrument but besides being unsatisfactory this is frowned upon by the groundstaff because it ruins the playing surface. Sandy gravel, although an asset in many ways, is not always popular with children if it is adjacent to a grass playing area, but where it is situated on its own it is used a great deal. It must be remembered that:

A. It can cause painful grazes to exposed parts of the body after a fall.

B. On dry windy days, dust may be blown into one's eyes and mouth.
C. Wet coloured gravel may stain clothing.
D. It wears out leather-case balls quicker than grass.
E. This also applies to footwear.
F. It is difficult to insert any kind of post or stake into the surface.

On playgrounds with concrete or tarmac surfaces it is comparatively simple to do improvised marking out with special playground chalk. This also applies to wooden floors in halls and gymnasiums, but permission should always be sought from the building caretaker before such action is taken. Ideally chalk could be used to mark out courts for such games as four court dodge ball, and for drawing wickets and goalposts on knockabout walls. Target circles and other kinds of aiming figures can be done in this way also. So can hopscotch markings and 'follow the leader' wiggly traverse lines. In this instance coloured chalks can be used for different markings. If such markings are to be made as a permanent feature of such a play area either in a hall or on a playground it is always advisable to engage the services of a reputable firm of experts to do the job properly.

Where no materials exist even to do improvised marking out, use can be made of existing markings of other games' pitches or courts. For example a netball court is ideal as an all purpose games court. It can be used for mini shinty, copstick or ringstick, three-a-side soccer, catch ball, quizling and many others.

The centre circle of an association football pitch can be utilized for numerous circle games, and the outer perimeter can be used as a running track for younger children, whereas half a full size soccer pitch would easily suffice for five-a-side soccer.

As far as conventional playgrounds are concerned, each one could be marked out for such games as hopscotch, and with giant markings for draughts, snakes and ladders and traverse lines.

In some games, for example Batinton, which is an Australian game, it is permissible to extend a line which is marked on the ground (assuming the area is not long enough) and carry it up the wall at the end of the playground or gymnasium. Another feature of ground markings, which I have mentioned before and which can be overdone, is that of marking different courts in various colours. Besides making it very difficult for players this can be extremely confusing for umpires and referees.

Before closing this chapter I would mention that several plastic playing surfaces for both indoor and outdoor use have been developed and a number of coloured adhesive plastic tapes are on the market which can be used for marking lines on these surfaces. Actually some of them can be used on ordinary wooden gymnasium floors. The advantage of using these tapes is that they are easier to remove than paint.

9 · Games for Fun

Gerald Haigh in his article 'Allow a Little Humour to Creep In', *Times Educational Supplement*, 21st May 1971, says:

'Humour, to me, is an art, a pleasure and a therapeutic; a maker of friends and a burster of bubbles. In a world of pollution, pestilence and Minutemen, the man without a sense of humour is half way to the psychiatric ward, if the ulcers do not get him first.

'Those of you who share my belief that laughter is important – and surely that means all of you – will also perhaps share my concern that we are failing in our job as teachers insofar as we make very little attempt to help our children in the development of their own sense of humour.'

A sense of humour is one of the many attributes of a good playleader, so if some teachers fail to help children develop a higher degree of appreciation of humour the playleader should regard it as a part of his everyday job to stimulate situations where this all-important aspect of a normal human being's make-up is prevalent because as Gerald Haigh says:

'... those who can neither laugh nor tolerate laughter are socially and emotionally handicapped ... '

Playleaders should be aware that because children are not involved or concerned in the everyday worries or responsibilities of adulthood, they see most things in a completely different light from grown-ups and in a lighthearted way which may be difficult to understand unless one possesses a sense of humour.

They are quick to sense any deficiencies in the characteristic makeup of adults with whom they come into contact. Such deficiencies are played upon in various ways, and playleaders not possessing the appropriate natural qualities – of which humour is one – may interpret them wrongly and subsequently take action which may aggravate the situation.

It may be argued that humour is a personal virtue and that

something which appears humorous to one person may appear ridiculously stupid to another. Be that as it may, the fact remains that between normal people humour is contagious, but to a person with the slightest form of neurosis or perhaps to a person with a suspicious mind, some kinds of humour can be misinterpreted as being of the 'mickey-taking' variety and treated by them with over-concern or even with bouts of bad temper or retaliation.

One of the many reasons why children play games – and there are many – is to have fun, so they naturally look to their playleader to help create a basis to fulfil this desire.

I am not intimating that the playleader should pre-arrange specific sessions with the express purpose of creating a 'silly half-an-hour' but that he should look to all aspects of playleadership technique – as much as possible – as through the eyes of carefree youngsters. If he can succeed in schooling himself to do this, he will enjoy his working hours as much as the youngsters enjoy his company.

The following games instructions have been prepared for a specific purpose, this being to create in the mind of the playleader student an insight into how some children, really the majority, interpret games in their own mind's eye, and to give an idea as to how they really see some games situations. The names of games' characters and the suggested prizes have been actually uttered by children and recorded in the mind of the author during his active participation as a playleader over the years. Some of the games for young children have been adapted from Sid Hedges' various books on games' rules. These books of his are a 'must' for all playleaders.

DOG AND BONE

(A waiting, circling teasing tag game)
A game which can be played indoors or outdoors.

Equipment

Any small object such as a stone, matchbox, handkerchief or a piece of wood.

PREPARATION

(a) Divide all those taking part into two equally numbered groups. On some occasions this is not as easy as it sounds.

(b) Arrange the groups so that they are formed into two straight lines standing nearly shoulder to shoulder, facing each other and about twenty-five feet apart. Pretend not to hear the threats of murder, bashing and spiflication which are sure to be hurled across no man's land.

(c) Every player is given a number starting with the youngster on the left who becomes number one to the competitor on the right of the line who is given the highest. This results in both number ones being on the opposite ends of each line. In other words they are not directly facing each other. If for example each group consisted of eight youngsters the line up would be so:

1	2	3	4	5	6	7	8
8	7	6	5	4	3	2	1

Having arranged both groups in their respective positions it is interesting to note their gentlemanly observation of one another or the 'weighing up' as it is sometimes termed. At this stage, on being told that they are to represent dogs trying to pinch a bone, one can expect to be serenaded with canine-sounding sweet rhapsodies. Finally the playleader places the small object – which represents the bone – in the exact centre of 'no man's land' and makes a hasty well-planned retreat.

Objective

To see who can first snatch the bone and make a return trip to his own line carrying the bone and without having been tagged by the opposing ferocious mangey unpedigreed hound. Or alternatively to play a waiting game, let the other unlicensed mongrel snap at the bone and then effect a well-aimed gentle clout behind his pointed ears, thus tagging him.

Scoring

One point for each Kennel Club member who successfully retrieves the bone and makes a return trip to his own pad unmolested.

One point for each wary hound, who because of his ungreedy and patient outlook manages to catch one of the other thieving pack of hounds with a bone in his possession before the said hound can reach his lair.

The pack with the highest number of thefts or arrests after ten minutes' rampaging is declared the winner.

Method

The playleader stands in a position where he can easily command – sorry, see – any dog fight which is more than likely imminent. Being in a safe place and having explained the intricacies and techniques of how to steal juicy marrow bones or how to stop a fleeing ravenous thieving miniature poodle he commences to talk to or at the youngsters. He speaks about anything but whatever he chooses to speak about he will need to mention a number. He must aim to approach the situation at the children's level and in this humour and noise are important. He can create excitement and fun by his very attitude to the situation. For example he can make remarks like:

'T – W – O spells – a different number than FOUR.'

After the word 'spells' has been uttered it will be found that both number twos are already standing over the bone ready for action. After the playleader has completed the sentence both number fours will have joined the number twos and the rest will probably be making choice remarks about the situation, but nevertheless these silly little things help to create fun and atmosphere. If he so desires he can repeat the same call to try to catch out those not 'with it'.

When the pattern has been established and the children know what to expect they will become cautious about their moves. On being called out they will become adept at feinting, probing and stabbing at the bone which actions are designed utterly to confound the other mongrel. It has been known for both contestants to become confounded at exactly the same moment. This occurs when both youngsters engage in the same play, which is to go straight to the bone, grab it whilst the other slow-thinking animal is making up his mind and beat a hasty retreat. Such action sometimes results in a clash of craniums, much to the delight of the remainder of the not so sympathetic participants, and the bewilderment of two confused youngsters who are both probably wondering what made the other one make such a ridiculously stupid move.

BLACKOUT BALL

Equipment

(a) Two different-coloured balls or – especially for indoors – two balloons.

(b) Two pieces of material or two masks which are used to cover the eyes of those taking part.

(c) A number of lusty-lunged boys and girls.

Objective

Two participants each representing opposing sides are selected to be blindfold and on the instructions of the rest of their side are directed to where they will find a ball or balloon of a particular colour. The first team to secure its ball three times is declared the winner.

Preparation

Having obtained the equipment the playleader divides the group into two sections. Boys versus girls nearly always produces the best results. By best results I mean noise, because noise is just about the most important ingredient of the activity.

Having divided the group he arranges that they sit in two straight lines facing each other about fifteen or twenty feet apart. All the well-behaved boys in one line and all the pretty girls in the other.

Having got them sat down with their legs crossed and their arms folded the playleader should seriously consider applying for another job in any firm which tackles impossible tasks. He should do well.

The playleader should then explain what is going to happen after which he will attempt to get the youngsters sat down again because by now they have all stood up and are wildly waving their arms about and clamouring to be first to have the privilege of being blindfold. It is at this stage that the playleader can create a temporary respite to all the noise and bring sanity back again simply by remarking that:

'I always choose those who sit with their legs crossed, their arms folded and their lips tightly shut.'

Then he simply selects the first boy and girl who make a reasonable attempt to comply.

Once effectively blindfold, both jabbering youngsters are rotated several times to their left and then several times to their right. This is supposed to make them lose their bearings, you hope.

Next they are asked to kneel down and place their hands on the floor in order to make it easy for them to traverse forward.

The playleader then places the two coloured balloons or play balls on the ground *away* from where the two youngsters are kneeling. Immediately he has done this he will find that the two lines of well-behaved boys and pretty girls are converging on our two contestants, screaming their heads off and gesticulating wildly in the direction of the balloons having no regard to the fact that the two competitors are unable to see these antics.

At times the excitement is so intense that some youngsters find it hard to contain themselves, particularly so when their representative has a near miss, or actually touches the balloon and pushes it away just out of reach.

The hilarious part of this activity happens when one of the competitors follows the instructions of one of the opposing group which usually has the effect of drawing him away from his own objective. 'Doing one's nut' is a mild description compared with some of the expressions – both facial and vocal – which are seen and heard at a game of Blackout Ball. One of the choicest I have heard came from a disquieted and over-exhausted young lad who screamed out:

'You must be ---- blind if you can't feel that fing under your bloody nose.'

BALLOON RACE

Equipment required

A balloon for each participant. It should be noted that balloons are graded into quality streams ranging from the 'easy to blow up' variety to the 'practically impossible to inflate' variety. An indication of quality is governed by price. The more expensive one is the easier it will be to inflate. Therefore playleaders with the right idea will attempt to procure balloons for this event free of charge.

Objective

A straightforward 'there and back' flat race in which those taking part are asked to blow a balloon up and then burst it.

Method

Each competing rosy-cheeked, leather-lunged and persistently jabbering youngster is politely asked by the playleader to take up his balloon and run from point A to point B and back again. The distance between points A and B is governed by the length of time which the person in charge wants to get rid of the happy throng.

On reaching point B the said balloon is to be inflated by giving it one or two lusty blows of nicotine-free puff, after which its neck is to be wrung and tied into a knot.

During this process it is to be hoped that one of the objectives will be achieved – at least for a short time – namely to stop the contestants from constantly jabbering. This cannot be guaranteed of course, because some youngsters can talk whilst doing anything, even swimming underwater I suppose. They are to be told to watch each other during the 'inflationary period' and to report to the playleader if they see anybody's ears flapping during this part of the event, because this is a disqualification.

Don't think for one second that such complaints will not materialize because they probably will. On one occasion a witty playleader remarked 'No blowing up balloons with your nose or you'll be disqualified'. At the usual end-of-race investigation one youngster is said to have remarked 'That's not fair, he blowed up his wiv his snitch the cheating b----'.

After the blowing, wringing and tying, the next stage is relatively simple. The competitors are asked to place the air-filled piece of rubber on the ground and – without the use of their hands – effect its total destruction with their posterior by sitting on it.

It is rather enlightening to witness a hurtling earthbound posterior – with the legs of its owner pointing heavenwards and its arms outstretched like the wings of an eagle of prey – aimed at a harmless piece of air-filled rubber – and miss. On making contact with the ground in this somewhat unorthodox manner the somewhat shaken owner may emit a sound resembling water gurgling down the plug hole of a bath. Of course the real strain comes when they are reminded by a vigilant playleader that they must regain their standing position without using their hands. After various experimental contortions and not a few uncomplimentary remarks about 'the brainy twit who fort abaht this stupid race' competitors regain their full posture and take off into mid-air again.

When the first balloon is burst, the sound of the bang seems to instil a mixture of despair and frenzy into the rest, particularly if prizes have been promised to first, second and third. Legs, arms and tongues continue their efforts with renewed vigour, spectators encourage bigger and better bounces, really hoping for bigger and better misses and in so doing they contribute much to the success of the occasion by creating a bigger and better unholy noise.

Armlock Wrestling (Two players)

Players sit back to back (emitting fearful threats), feet astride and elbows interlocked. Each attempts to force his opponent's right shoulder to the ground, and no more need be said.

Chinese Tug of War (Two players)

Opponents stand back to back (but not too close or they will knock each other over) bow politely to space and grasp right hands between their legs. In this most ridiculous position they try to pull each other to China.

Danish Wrestle (Two players)

'Bacon' and 'Cheese' stand sideways to one another, facing opposite ways, legs astride, the outside of their right feet together. Talking in Danish they grasp right hands and try by any means in their power to make the opponent move his hind leg.

Hand Wrestling (Two players)

Two players lie flat on their 'dinners' facing one another, feet astride, left arms behind their backs. They place their right elbows on the ground and grasp hands, their forearms vertical. The aim is to force the back of the opponent's hand to the floor without moving one's own body or elbow from the floor.

Ball Hit (Any even number up to 20)

As many small chalk circles as there are team members are drawn a yard or so apart and occupied by members of one team, who pass a football or tennis ball between them, occasionally throwing to

197

hit and put out of the game any snail-like members of the opposing team, who are allowed to dodge where they like. If the ball is thrown at a dodger and misses him, teams change places, after the usual arguments of course.

Circle Dodge Ball (Any even number)

One team is surrounded by the other on a small court, who throw a football to hit the besieged below waist level. Any hit 'collapses' and drops out. When one team is disposed of they change places.

Ground Ball (Twelve or more players)

This is similar to playing 'football' with the palm of the hands. There are two sets of goals, marked by bags of sweets or coats, one at each end of the room, two teams divided into forwards, backs and a goalkeeper. The game is started by a bounce from the centre; the ball must be struck or punched along the floor – never thrown, scooped, kicked or otherwise propelled; no body contact or obstruction, no holding the ball, no offside rule. A hit is taken from the goal-line by the goal keeper if the ball crosses the line from contact with an opponent's hand or body, a corner-hit if the goalkeeper's team touched it last.

Crab Football

This is played with players sitting down and kicking the ball.

Hot Rice (Any number above six)

'Flash Harry' dodges about in a circle of his enemies, trying to protect himself with his hands from being maimed below the waist with a tennis ball. When he is hit and the tantrums are finished he changes places with the thrower who is really in for it now.

Finnish Handball (From twelve players upwards)

Two teams are equally divided into defenders and attackers. Defenders link arms on their own goal-line, attackers move as they wish. A team scores by palm-hitting a football across the enemy goal-line; defenders stop the ball with their knees only, and must not break the 'arm lock' link with their neighbours or advance into the field of play. After each goal goodies and baddies change places with each other.

Lane Ball (Any even number from sixteen to twenty-four)

The area of play is divided into two equal-sized courts by 'no man's land' which is 6 feet wide. Each court is ruled by a team of from 8 to 12. Teams score by bouncing a play ball in no man's land so that it clean bounces again in enemy territory blowing them to smithereens.

Ball and Rope Relay (Any even number)

Teams line up in file behind the starting line; a one foot high rope is held ten yards away. Leaders jump the rope, pick up and throw a ball to number twos, who run, jump the rope and so on. The first team lined up beyond the rope wins.

Bombardment (Any even number up to thirty)

An equal number of skittles or moneyboxes are set up behind baseline at each end of the playroom. Teams appoint attackers and defenders in their own court. Both teams have an equal number of playballs and throw to up-end enemy skittles. Defenders intercept and feed their attackers. The team which first knocks down all the enemy skittles gets tickets for the F.A. Cup Final.

Moving Target (Any even number)

Two teams, both stand behind their end line of the main court, in possession of an equal number of tennis or playballs. In the centre of the main court is a large ball, doing no harm to anybody. The object is to move this ball over the enemy baseline by hitting it with tennis balls. Both teams gather loose playballs. The game becomes very exciting. No handling or footing of the large ball is allowed. No delivery may be made unless the bombardier is standing behind his end line.

Post Ball (Ten to twenty players)

A jumping stand in a circle at each end of the playhall with a guard of young Britons on the edge of the circle. Two teams play a handball short-passing game, holding only allowed for three paces or three seconds, score by throwing and hitting the stand. No tackling, obstruction, kicking, fisting, or tripping allowed.

Circular Pillar Ball (Any even number from twelve)

A circle of 40 feet in diameter is drawn and halved. A jumping stand is placed in the centre as a target. Teams divide their members, one half in one semi-circle, the other skulking outside their opponents' half-circle. The two sections of a team pass a playball between them until an opportunity occurs to score by throwing to hit the jumping stand.

Spokes (Any even number above twelve)

In a circle stands a thrower. Around it are spaced his own team and the enemy. He throws to members of his band in turn – who try to catch the ball while their opponents try to pinch it. A point or a pound of tripe is awarded for each successful catch and return. After each member of the first team has had a go the catchers become pinchers.

Chain Tag (Any number)

Each player tagged joins up with Looney Larry to form a chain and catch the scattered rabble. Only the end men of a chain can make a tag. A tag does not count if the chain is broken.

Japanese Tag (Any number)

Sili Suki is 'it', the rest are of course Yokohama Yobs. Those whom Suki touches become infected with the dreaded illness Suki Siki whether it is on the arm, ankle, nose, knee or haircut and so must put their hands to the afflicted spot and then change themselves by Japanese magic into another Sili Suki who helps to spread this contagious disease.

Prisoner Tug (Twelve players)

Six-a-side tug-of-war. As soon as the leading player in a team is pulled over the central line he falls out. The pull restarts with five children on one side and six on the other and continues until another team member is eliminated, and so on until the whole of one team is out. Over-confidence of the six often allows the five to draw level.

Relievo (Any even number from ten to thirty)

A prison with invisible walls is marked on the ground (6 feet square). The crooks hide and the coppers seek, leaving one warden to guard the clink. Anyone caught is led back to the nick and must stand with both feet inside. He may escape by a tag from one of his

200

gang. Only one prisoner may be freed at a time. After an agreed period sides change roles and cat calls.

Sprint Tug (From four to fifty players)

A large rope is stretched out on the ground between two teams who are lined up in file ten yards' distant from each end. On the command they rush for it and the tug begins. The team getting the rope back behind their starting line wins. Players may only touch their own half of the rope.

Three-Cornered Tug (Three players)

A knotted rope is laid on the ground in the form of a triangle, a boy's belt is placed equidistant from each corner. Three boys lift a corner each and holding the rope behind them with their right hands they face their belt and strain to reach it. The one who lifts his belt first wins. Unusual happenings occur.

Snake Tag (Any even number between twelve and thirty)

Two teams in file (Rattle and Viper), each player holding some part of the one ahead. Number one – or mouth – of each team tries to catch the last player – or tail – of the other.

Tail Tag (Any number above twelve)

Three tail-less lions pursue the crowd. Those tagged become the lion's tail, each clasping the shirt of the one in front. The lion with the longest tail after everyone's been bagged wins a park-keeper for dinner.

Batinton

Pat Hanna who hails from the Antipodes has contributed a great deal to the recreational pleasures of today's young people. His knack for inventing games which immediately become accepted is rather amazing. Wobldodge – Saladball – Under Polo and Hoop Golf are examples of his gift but I think his most successful game is Batinton.

Its main value lies in the fact that it takes very little time – only a matter of minutes – to acquire the basic skills required to play sufficiently well to enjoy it, which is of course an important point when deciding the kind of activities to provide for children in a Playleadership scheme.

It can be played indoors or outside and only a small area measuring 36 feet by 9 feet is needed to set up the court.

Having obtained the basic equipment comprising bats, shuttles, plastic play balls and the net and its supports, several different types of game can be played.

RULES AND OBJECTS

The rules of the game are similar to those of badminton.

The object of the game is to hit the shuttle across the net to a place in the opponent's court where he cannot reach it to strike back without hitting it out of court or into the net. A point is scored each time a player beats his opponent, and the first player, or side, to score 21 points wins.

Other games played with the same equipment and designed to suit all kinds of conditions are 'volley', 'tennis' and 'squash', all played with a small plastic ball, and 'batinton-quoits', when a rubber ring is used as in deck quoits.

KITE MAKING AND COMPETITION

Kite clubs for children and adults seem to be on the upward trend at the present time. As interest in the sport increases playleaders should look to this activity as a means of creating further interest in handicrafts and friendly competition.

As a hobby, kite flying held an important place in the recreational pursuits of people of the ancient Eastern world, particularly among the Chinese.

This is a clean activity demanding great skill and will prove to be an absorbing pastime both from the creative and operational aspects. Artistically it is also of interest and many very beautiful patterns and designs are to be seen in drawings and paintings of Chinese kites. Modern commercial creations, particularly in the United States of America depict effigies of Batman and Robin (heroes of the T.V. series). The private kite depicting a skull and cross bones is a favourite best-seller with American youngsters.

Andrée Brooks in the *Times Educational Supplement* of 10th December 1971 tells us of a game in India called 'Kite Fighting' and mentions how powdered glass is applied to the bridle of a kite and how the owners who are very adept at the art attempt to cut their opponents' kite free by severing the bridle.

Some kites can cost as much as £20 to make but they can cost as little as 25p or so. The following instructions show that really they are easy to make providing a little patience is exercised – particularly in waiting for glues and cements, etc. to harden properly.

How to construct a kite

1. Two large sheets of tissue paper, which should be heavy-duty quality and similar to that used for constructing model aircraft, or two thin sheets of plastic.
2. A quantity of balsa cement ⎫ Obtainable from any
3. A quantity of tissue cement ⎬ model making shops
4. Six pieces of ¼″ thick Obechi wood.
5. Reels of strong linen thread or fine string.

Mechanics of construction

THE FRAME

1. Construct a triangle of equilateral dimension using the Obechi. Allow the ends to overlap just a little – 26 inches will be sufficient – with an overlap of about half an inch (Fig. 9/1).
2. Securely bind the ends with strong thread and liberally glue them with balsa cement.
3. Construct a 'camp fire' type of tripod with the three other pieces of Obechi and glue and bind the overlapped apex (Fig. 9/2).
4. Place both sections together and securely bind and glue the

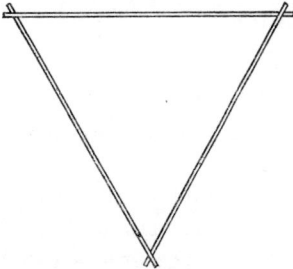

Fig. 9/1

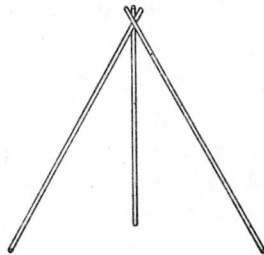

Fig. 9/2

three base points at A B and C as shown on Fig. 9/3 ensuring that dimensions and balance are correct.

5. Allow the cement to dry thoroughly and harden.

6. Cover *two sides only* with the heavy-duty tissue paper and firmly glue along the edges.

7. When the covering is completely dry attach the linen bridle. It should be attached to the kite at two points and therefore needs to be made in the shape of a two-pronged fork (Fig. 9/4) Ideally it should be wound around a fishing-line reel.

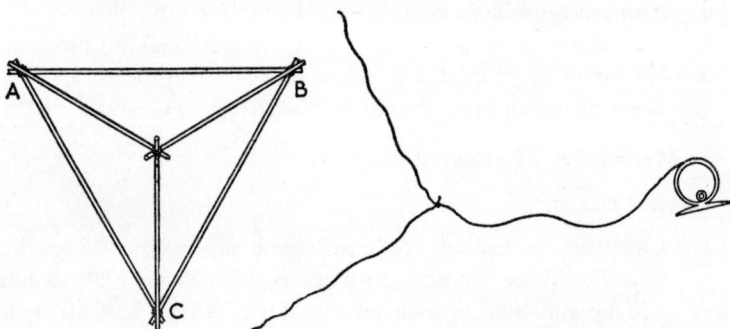

Fig. 9/3   Fig. 9/4

8 The tail of a kite should be about ten times as long as the body. It can contain paper or rag cloth bows or else used paper cups. They are spaced about twelve inches apart (Fig. 9/5).

Organization of a kite competition

Roughly about three weeks should be allowed between the announcement that a kite competition is going to take place and the date of the event.

A notice should be displayed in an appropriate position where it will attract most attention. It should impart information about the venue and the exact time when the different age groups will be judged.

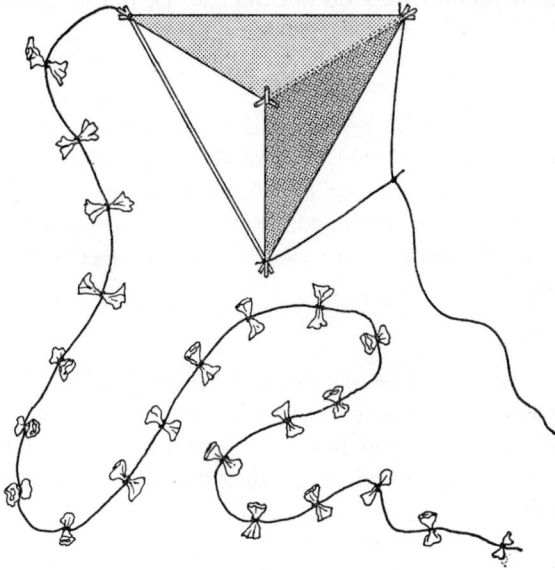

Fig. 9/5

In addition to this information a drawing should be displayed showing how a simple kite can be easily constructed. The playleader responsible for doing this should aim for simplicity and easy to understand instructions. It would serve a good purpose if an actual kite was available for the youngsters to see. Naturally it would not be advisable to leave a kite on show and unattended. They have a habit of 'taking off' on their own or in the hands of Mr. Nobody.

It should be made clear at the very beginning that the 'flying' or airborne part of the competition can take place only if climatic conditions are favourable, that is unless the playleader in question has the ability to whip up the winds at will. If he hasn't the ability to do this and conditions are unfavourable he had better have a good excuse up his sleeve because it is sure to be his fault for choosing a 'stupid day to have a kite fing on'. So for the sake of future success it is to be hoped that our playleader is blessed with information given him by an 'on form' long-range weather forecast expert.

VENUE

This should be on the highest ground available but on a site where telephone wires and trees do not impede the bridles or tails of the kites.

Competitors and unit representatives should assemble in their respective groups, preferably in straight lines and not too close to each other – if one has ever had the frustrating task of having to unwind two or more entangled kite tails he will understand why – in order that the judges can waste as little time as possible with the inspection.

JUDGES

At least three neutral people should be invited to adjudicate. They could include an art teacher from a local school, and likewise a handicrafts specialist and probably somebody from a Kite Flying Club. In the event of such people being unavailable, three parents would suffice.

PRIZES

Book tokens or model-making kits, wrapped sweets, fruit, certificates.

Classes of competitors

Group A Boys or Girls of Primary School age.

Group B Young people not yet 17 years of age.

Group C Open, any age, any design providing they are not commercially manufactured.

Group D Family section. Entries submitted by family units.

Group E GIANT KITES entered by play units and carrying a 'Play-leadership' slogan which can clearly be seen at a great height.

RULES

(These are rules which it is advisable to apply in addition to those drawn up by the local organizer).

1. Kites not actually competing should not be released when kites from other groups are airborne. Each group will be given 20 minutes 'flying time'.
2. Kites should be constructed by the person or persons entering them.
3. Any kite not airborne – i.e. 20 feet above ground – by the

stipulated time will be eliminated and will automatically lose any placing which it has received during the inspection for design, construction or decoration.

OBJECTS OF COMPETITION

To select:

1. The best constructed kite.
2. The best decorated or most colourful design.
3. The most magnificent tail.
4. The best flyer.
5. The highest climber.
6. The largest kite.

FINALE

Kites from all groups are invited to take part in the final 'all up' spectacular.

10 · Music and Playleadership

The main purpose of this chapter is to give the reader an insight into the tremendous importance and value of music in a play scheme and to help him to realize that its use can inspire many other interests, both good and bad. Its various values come under three headings:

1. Social
2. Cultural
3. Creative

These values become evident when youngsters come together to rehearse musical items for concerts or to organize their own dances or record sessions or, as they are sometimes called, 'musical appreciation' sessions.

The cultural aspects emerge when children are brought together to form any kind of musical group or dance troupe. This is particularly noticeable when older girls take it upon themselves to pass on their knowledge and teach their younger associates. Parents who are able to dance or play musical instruments are often quite willing to give up a little of their time to help the children.

Creative pursuits crystallize when young people busy themselves in making musical instruments, especially unconventional percussion items. Girls find creative occupation in making different types of attire which they wear during concerts. They also become very keen on creating new forms of music and movement, and choreography.

It would be very unwise of me to make any attempt to suggest a universal plan or policy for different types of playleaders on how to develop musical activities. I will say however that the aim of all playleaders should be to stimulate an interest in different forms of musical activity, and, to make the widest possible use of this very powerful attraction.

Making music

This will no doubt raise a question in the mind of the so-called unmusical playleader on whether some form of musical education is necessary before one can include musical activity in a programme. Personally I don't think so. It is not the responsibility of a playleader to teach musical theory, but it is his responsibility to create fun, and a great deal of musical creation can be tremendous fun.

Two different concepts exist about children and music making. One that it is imperative that they should not play any type of instrument unless they are reading music and the other advocates the aural side as being more important, and that – particularly in percussion band work – no sight-reading should take place at all. I feel that both concepts are wrong and that as far as percussion band work is concerned a happy medium should exist and children who are able to read music should be persuaded to help those who can't. Children should be encouraged to learn short simple repetitive and rhythmic melodies by heart.

It should be noted that few professional percussionists are able to sight read and play tuned percussion instruments at the same time. One needs to look at a xylophone or glockenspiel to play it properly, especially in quick tempo, when the music contains numerous semi-quavers. Most tubular bell (chimes) parts are memorized by professional players so it is fairly obvious that a youngster will be unable to do it, unless of course he is a prodigy. The aesthetic value of tuned percussion band work is very deep, but as I have intimated not many children are successful at it, unless they are taking piano lessons elsewhere.

If the playleader – in response to a request or otherwise – intends personally to create an authentic musical ensemble he naturally will need to have undergone some form of musical training. But, if his intention is to create an interest in various activities through the aid of music then theoretical training is not really necessary.

He will need only the very elementary fundamentals and natural musical instincts that most of us possess. These are:

A. To have a reasonable ear for music.
B. To be able to define the first beat of each bar.
C. To be able to deduce how many beats are contained in a bar of music, at least those of simple duple, simple triple and compound duple time.

D. To be able instinctively to feel the end of a musical phrase or sentence and to work out how many bars are contained in it.

E. To have a reasonably good sense of tempo.

Unless the playleader intends to form a band of any kind his ability to distinguish the difference in pitch between musical sounds and to name them correctly is relatively unimportant, but he should be capable of defining the difference between one melody and another.

As far as rhythm and note valuation are concerned, as long as the playleader has the ability to explain to the children that two beats are contained in a bar of two-four march tempo music, it is not really essential for him to know that it is two-four time or simple duple or two crotchets in a bar. Simply two beats to a bar. For example it could be a bar of six-eight instead, but it is still two beats to a bar as far as he is concerned (see Fig. 10/1).

Fig. 10/1

If a scheme has the necessary tuned percussion instruments – say two xylophones, two glockenspiels or tubaphones and a set of chromatic chimes (usually chimes are only manufactured to cover the diatonic scale of E flat) – it is amazing how immediate interest can be created by simple scale practice coupled with various uncomplicated rhythms played on various percussion instruments.

Glockenspiels are usually manufactured to give a two octave range, C natural to C natural, or a two and a half octave range G natural to C natural. Small percussion band xylophones are usually manufactured to give a two octave range, C natural to C natural, or G natural to A natural, which is not quite two and a half octaves. Some are manufactured giving only the major scale of C (no sharps or flats).

By utilizing the scale of C Major it is possible to have two children on each of the two glockenspiels and two on each of the xylophones and another youngster on the G – A xylophone. It is a good thing to give children a chance to perform on tuned percussion and untuned percussion in turn. When playing at scale practice in keys other than C Major it helps the children if a coloured mark (with sticky paper) is made on any sharp or flat notes involved. The paper can easily be removed afterwards without damage to the instrument. Children learn which notes are contained in different scales if they are given a chance of placing the coloured pieces of paper on the notes at the beginning of each session (see Fig. 10/2). They should be left to work out the musical intervals by themselves after being given the starting note, and care must be taken not to hurry the children during this process. The same thing applies with short easy melodies which they should be allowed to work out in their own time. For play purposes it is immaterial which key is used as long as the children derive pleasure from what they are doing.

It is important for organizers who have had no musical training to know that in the creation and fostering of musical activities in a play scheme it is not always the trained teacher or musician who will produce the best results. Likewise a qualified teacher of dancing may be unable to handle a large group of girls. Usually the reason for this is that experts are only concerned in devoting their time and energies to children who have potential.

At an age when children's emotions are sometimes balanced on a knife edge and when they are looking around themselves at their

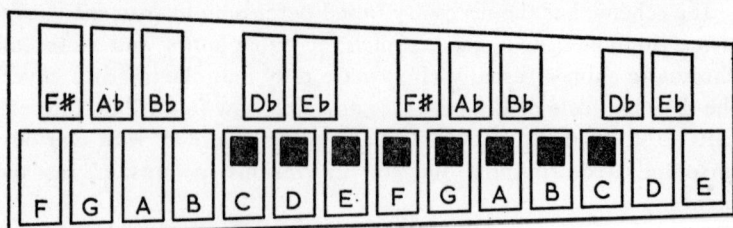

KEY OF C MAJOR ■

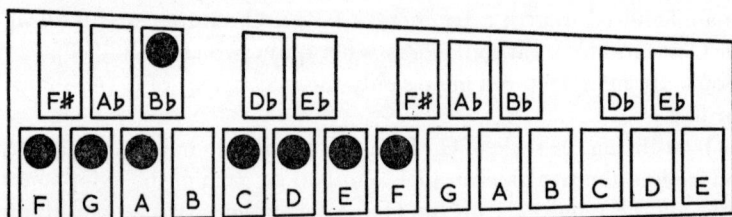

KEY OF F MAJOR ●

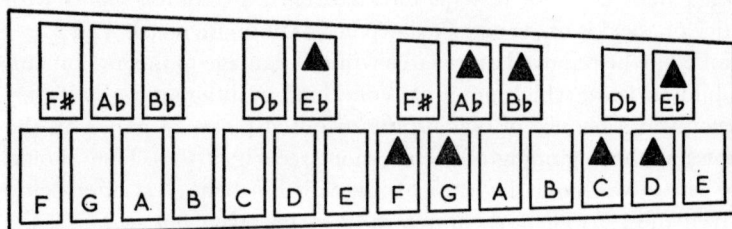

KEY OF Eb MAJOR ▲

Fig. 10/2

associates and acquaintances they will most certainly be inclined to react more readily to a person than to music.

In my last two paragraphs I do not mean that instrumental skill, musicianship and the ability to impart information correctly are handicaps, but I am suggesting that personality, warmth and the art of gaining ready acceptance are just as important as is a musical education.

Assuming that the reader has some form of musical education and intends eventually to form a musical ensemble, I would offer the following valuable advice, which comes from a Standing Committee on Musical Education.

'Touch them the wrong way at the start, let there be any aloofness, a lack of warmth at your first group meeting, and there will never be a second. But if they know you as a person and respect and admire you before they know anything about you as a musician, and if you can hold them, they will follow wherever you choose to lead; and their open-hearted response will be your greatest pleasure!!'

One problem which the conductor playleader may have to solve is that of procuring a place where the band or choir can practice without undue interference. He will also have to organize his musical rehearsals so that they are absolutely regular and held at least once each week or if possible twice. Security and storage of instruments is another problem and so is the selection of two or three keen and efficient band prefects who will be responsible for 'setting up' everything required for band practice and for replacing it in storage afterwards.

How music is going to be produced in the first place is of primary importance.

Consider first the absolute foundations of musical production which are of course, the voice, the hands and the lips. The voice and lips produce pitch and tone colour by singing or whistling and the hands produce elementary percussion by clapping. At this early stage it is not even necessary to use words to the songs. An alternative to singing is to use the voice and tongue and produce notes by uttering LA – LA – LA – LA – etc. or to close the lips and hum as in a lullaby.

PITCH

Other forms of tone colour can be produced by using simple and easily obtained materials such as a comb and piece of paper (tissue) or a set of thirteen bottles or tumblers each containing a different quantity of water which will determine the pitch of musical sounds when struck with a suitable beater. Thirteen notes will give a complete chromatic scale. Another simple form of pitch can be obtained by stretching pieces of elastic rubber band across a shallow box –

e.g. a cigar box – and dictating their pitch by using different lengths and tensions.

During the early skiffle era it became the 'done thing' to improvise a one-string bass. This was accomplished by using a tea chest as the belly and a broom handle as the neck. Instead of a proper gut or wire string a piece of strong cord was used and always used in a plucking or pizzicato manner.

The kazoo – a five inch long submarine-shaped plastic instrument containing a wire mesh and tissue paper covered opening in the centre – is about the cheapest form of non-mechanical wind instrument obtainable and costs only a few pence to buy as does the jew's harp. Both are useful for adding other forms of tone colour to a children's band. The next consideration should be the harmonica (mouth organ) as well as home-made pipes and whistles; also, many children possess their own recorders and great use can be made of these, as many children who own them can perform reasonably well and are usually able to read music a little.

A little more expensive but by no means unreasonable is the Melodica which is a small wind instrument with a two and a half or three octave piano-type keyboard.

Hygiene is important when using the above-mentioned wind instruments in the band. They should not be passed from one child to another without some form of disinfection. I would go so far as to say that each child should be encouraged to possess and use only his or her own wind instrument.

RHYTHM

Percussion rhythm instruments are fairly easy to improvise and can be utilized in almost any type of musical group.

To mention just a few:

Chocolo	Claves
Triangles	Bongos
Maracas	Tambourines
Castagnets	Timbales
Washboard	Whip
Conga Drum	Jingles
Cabaca	Scraper
Sandpaper blocks	Wobble board (Didgery Doo)

| Sizzle cymbal | Chinese wood block |
| Tin can cowbell | Jingle bells |

Novelty instruments include:

| Cycle bells | Motor horns |
| Knuckle bones | Musical saw |

CHOCOLO

A tubular-shaped metal or wooden (bamboo) container about one foot long. One end has a solid stop – so that it looks somewhat like an open cocoa tin – the other end is then covered with a piece of vellum or thin plastic and the whole contains a small number of beans or shot. It is played by being held at each end between the palms of the hands and held diagonally across the body about chest high, slightly tilted so that the shot falls to one end – the vellum-covered end – and then shaken forwards and backwards so that the shot strikes the inner walls of the tube, thus creating a high-pitched almost staccato sound. Sustained notes are created by an extremely rapid series of movements which can only be achieved by lots of practice. These instruments can be improvised by using cocoa tins and rice or other suitable hard pellets.

CLAVES

These are pieces of very hard wood about six inches in length and round in shape – like a tallow candle – usually made from lignum vitae, ebony or rosewood, and highly polished. When they are struck together in the correct manner they produce a highly pitched resonant sound which is extremely penetrating. One is held static in the cupped left hand between the index finger and the thumb, pointing forwards and down while its other end points towards the shoulder and rests on the lower wrist. The second one is held in the right hand between the forefinger and the thumb much the same as one would hold an ordinary side drum stick. The left-hand clave is struck by the right-hand clave with a clean blow. Without going into specific detail, claves are very easily obtained from many different sources.

TRIANGLE

A correctly suspended triangle will produce an absolutely clear ring if struck with a proper beater. These are made in several different

sizes and if used in the right way can be very effective. A holder
should be used in order to acquire the correct suspension and
freedom from any contact which will impair the triangle's ring.
Usually the holder is held in the left hand and the striker in the
right, but sometimes it is more convenient to suspend the triangle
from a music stand, thereby leaving the left hand free for other
movement. Care must be taken not to tie the gut or string too
tightly round the triangle as even this will deaden its ring. Single
notes are made by striking the base or horizontal bar of the instrument and trills or rolls are created by making a rapid side-to-side
movement against the apex of each of the slanting walls of the
triangle. Volume is increased by moving from the apex towards the
bottom of the triangle and diminuendos are created *vice versa*. Not
a great deal of imagination is needed to inspire the making of a
triangle and a beater.

BONGOES

Bongoes are made and used in pairs; actually they are fastened
together with the largest one (bass) on the left. They are tuned a
fifth apart – usually the tonic and dominant – and are snareless
with very tightly stretched heads. These Latin-American music
drums are played with the performer sitting down and clamping
them between his thighs. Alternatively they can be used clamped
to a special stand and raised to about hip height. They can be played
with the fingers – which is the correct way – or by using drum sticks
or timpani beaters. If played with the fingers a much greater
variety of sounds can be achieved. Bongo rhythms are difficult to
master, therefore simple extemporization must take place. Very
small bongoes are named bonguitos. Both types have no head on
the bottom of the drum. They can be improvised by using small
biscuit barrels and thin sheets of rubber or plastic.

MARACAS

These can be described as being similar to a baby's rattle from the
constructional point of view. They are played in pairs, one being held
in each hand. They are either round- or egg-shaped, roughly
about the size of a coconut with a handle attached. Like the chocolo
they contain a small amount of shot or beans. Maracas need a great
deal of control if they are to be played properly. The effect obtained
is very similar to that of the chocolo except that whereas the

chocolo has one sound only, maracas have two sounds, because no two maracas can be made to sound exactly the same. An effort should be made to obtain an almost staccato sound. Large movements produce a gushing sound as the pellets will not hit the inner walls of the maraca together. The best effect is acquired by gently tapping the top of the maraca with the forefinger of each hand. The high pitch of the sound is sufficient to carry it through without having to play *forte* (loud). Maracas can be improvised with plastic wool holders or with cocoa tins and dried peas.

CASTAGNETS

The authentic playing of castagnets or castanets is difficult to master. It is mostly attributed to Flamenco dancers, being part of the sound they produce in conjunction with their heel clicking rhythms. For percussion band work I feel that the handle-type castagnets – which can be played without much difficulty – are more appealing to children. They can be used rhythmically by beating out the rhythm with the heads of the castagnets against the palm of the hands. Sustained notes or rolls are accomplished by a rapid side-to-side movement of the wrist, with the head of the castagnets pointing downwards. A loose wrist action is necessary to obtain a really close roll. Any handyman can make a simple pattern pair of castagnets which will suffice for a children's band.

TIMBALES

Like bongos they are used in pairs, with the highest pitched or small one on the right; they are much larger in circumference and depth than bongos and have a copper shell. They have no bottom head and are joined together in pairs and clamped to a stand. Special sticks – without any taper of bead – are used to play them and much of the actual rhythms are played on the copper shell to produce a metallic sound contrasting to that of the head. Rim shots are played quite a lot on timbales and children love to accomplish the art of doing this. A rim shot is when one strikes a drum head and the metal rim with a drum stick simultaneously. Timbales can be improvised by using biscuit tins and thin plastic sheeting.

TAMBOURINE

This is normally held in the left hand with vellum or head facing towards the player's right. It is struck with the palm of the right hand (or the clenched knuckles) in the centre of the skin. As with most percussion instruments, a loose wrist action is the best. It will be found that a small hole is provided on the shell of the tambourine to facilitate a better grip. Sustained notes are achieved by a rapid half twist motion of the wrist. It is also possible to obtain a very close and quite sustained note by wetting a finger and pushing it across or round the edge of the tambourine so that it bounces very rapidly. This of course takes a little practice to accomplish correctly. Recently it has become the practice to use tambourines without skins on them, but this is mainly in pop music. It is possible to make a home-made tambourine, but this is not very easy.

TAMBOUR

This instrument is similar to a large tambourine but without any dingles. It may be used in lieu of a bass drum, and can be played with a hard drum stick or a soft tympani beater; or with the palm of the hand. By striking it in different places it will be found that different sounds can be obtained. Sometimes those tambours which are tunable are used on stands like a tympani. It should always be struck midway between the centre of the skin and the edge. A tambour can be made from the narrow lid of a large cheese container and a piece of vellum and some upholstery tacks.

SCRAPER (OR RESLO)

This very simple percussion instrument consists of a short piece of bamboo cane with a number of saw cuts or ridges evenly spaced in a single line on the outside. The sound is produced by scraping a piece of wire or produced by a thin sliver of bamboo cane over the ridges. The sound this action is intended to imitate is the croaking of a bull frog. Quite obviously this instrument, and many of the others, is only used in Latin-American numbers. No explanation is needed on how to make some of these instruments as it is so very simple.

CONGA DRUM

About the length of a walking cane, this tapered drum is slightly larger at the top than a dinner plate and a little larger at its base than a saucer. It is covered at both ends with thick vellum which is very tightly stretched. It is played with the hands and the fingers and a variety of different sounds can be produced by an experienced player. It can be either suspended from the neck by means of a strap which is secured to its shell or placed on a stand – sometimes in pairs – with the top head about lower chest level. I have seen an improvised one – without taper – made from a large tubular piece of aluminium. Although the sound was not correct, it served its purpose quite well in a children's percussion band.

SAND PAPER BLOCKS

Originally designed to imitate sand dancing they are oblong in shape and about the same size as an oil stone. They are made of wood with sandpaper stuck or nailed on them. Held one in each hand they are rubbed together to give a scraping sound. Lots of practice is required before the player becomes proficient in executing attractive suitable rhythms. No explanation is really necessary as how to make these simple instruments.

CHINESE WOOD BLOCK OR DRUM

Made of mahogany or other similar types of wood the wood block is a very simple piece of percussion equipment giving a high pitched hollow sound when played with side-drum sticks. It is oblong in shape and about a third of the size of a house brick; it contains a very narrow scooped-out aperture just beneath the surface of each face side. This is where it is struck with the stick. The best effect is obtained if the drum is not played with the bead of the stick but with the stem. Care must be taken when using one of these blocks as they are very easily damaged. They are fairly expensive to buy, but easy to make.

TOM TOMS

Basically these drums consist of a shell and either one or two heads. They can be improvised with large tins or wooden cheese cases and vellum or plastic sheeting. Normally they are played with felt beaters, but side-drum sticks or even the hands can be used.

Using the record player and tape recorder

This is the most popular way to produce music. When one considers activities based on listening to music, a number of obvious possibilities suggest themselves, and it is perhaps not necessary to elaborate them. The gramophone session of the 'Record Choice' type, with children bringing and playing their own records, is a useful start.

It is sometimes surprisingly difficult to get them to listen quietly to any records other than their own type of music, but with tact this can be done. From this one may proceed to programmes built round a particular broad subject such as music for films, traditional jazz or a programme presented by an individual member or outsider – 'Desert Island Choice' and so on. Programmes should be built where possible on a human interest. Variety in approach and variety within each programme are two more golden rules for the playleader. Every audience is made up of individuals with differing tastes and even to pop enthusiasts a programme centred entirely round one performer soon begins to pall. It is best to avoid such a theme as pop versus the classics, because it strengthens the false idea of an unbridgeable chasm between the two types of music.

Radios and tape recorders

I have noticed during the past year or so that teenagers tend to congregate near the park café if its radio is playing. Also I have noticed the almost magnetic attraction and the sudden popularity that the possessor of a transistor radio enjoys if the wave band is tuned to a pop programme. The louder the volume the greater the number of friends.

Personal appearances

If music is an attraction on the one hand, it can be a distraction on the other. It is noticed that when big-name pop entertainers come to Lewisham, many teenagers vanish from the play areas.

Tiny Tots

Teenagers are not the only group to be influenced by listening to music. A big attraction in our under-fives' centres during the summer happens to be Kenneth McKellar's record of Nursery Rhymes with top of the chart numbers like 'See Saw Margery Daw' and 'Little Bo Peep'.

Listening to music is always bound to have more practitioners than does music-making. Taking part in making music may have its drawbacks, like self-consciousness or lack of ability to play an instrument or sing, but most children can and *do* listen.

CHILDREN'S DRESS

Having acquired some means of producing music – for example a record player – and having created some form of movement it will then become desirous for the children to look the part. Ideas for costumes and dress will emerge – the children who up to now have been on-lookers will want to take part, for what young boy or girl does not like to dress up?

The wardrobe of my own scheme – which is vast – is available to any unit for use at shows, etc. It consists of literally hundreds of costumes, which have been collected over the years by my assistant. It comprises a large selection of Highland, Irish, Indian, Hawaiian and Chinese costumes, Sailors', Soldiers', Policemen's and Firemen's uniforms. Characters from nursery rhymes, coloured skirts, Astronauts' suits, Austrian clothes, Diddymen's outfits, Siamese dress, Bride and Groom's outfits, biblical characters, and many others.

PHOTOGRAPHS, ETC.

Another interesting aspect is that the games' hut is usually decorated with numerous coloured pictures or photographs of current pop favourites.

Making music

Instrumental music making has not been very highly organized in playleadership for several reasons:

A. Lack of instruments
B. Inadequate practice facilities
C. Inability of staff to take the subject
D. Irregular attendance of band members

This does not mean that nothing has really been accomplished in the past, in fact a lot has been done. I feel I am right in saying that several well known pop groups 'had the seed planted' as it were through Playleadership Schemes. There has been success also with the following:

A. Dance Band
B. Percussion Band
C. Percussion and Recorder Band

I feel that of all the various types of instrumental music to choose from, the Percussion Band is the most exciting as far as the play scheme is concerned.

11 · Music, Drugs and Rebellion

It is said that music can play havoc with our emotions. When I first heard this as a young soldier musician, I coupled it with the proviso that if one had a soul it probably could. Now, reflecting on this after a fairly varied musical career lasting over thirty-five years as a professional and semi-professional musician I am still of the same mind, but have realized that much depends on the mood and other circumstances of the listener at the time when the music is heard. For example, the place is important, as well as the presence of other people and the time. But most important of all is the type and style of music being played in relation to the likes or dislikes of the listener.

We all have our likes and dislikes of many things, but musically speaking we have either 'highbrow' or 'lowbrow' tastes. A high proportion of our younger generation are disciples of pop and some of the disastrous 'semi-cults' that unfortunately go with it. Thank goodness that only a small proportion of pop fans become seriously caught up in some of these unpleasant happenings. Perhaps this is because, as in other things, common sense prevails in the end.

Undeniably a distinct division exists between different musical worlds, and it is suprisingly difficult for a playleader to instil the idea that there is good music in all of them from pop to classics. Before much progress can be made he must successfully impress this upon his group. For the playleader this is quite often one of the hardest personal adjustments he has to make. For example, if he is a lover of classical music, he may be requested to organize a weekly pop record session by his organizer, in which he must try to take an attitude to pop music generally which will be informed, honest and sympathetic. It is no use his pretending to *understand* pop or jazz if he does not, for he will soon be found out. On the other hand he must not show a superior or destructive outlook or he will lose any sympathy he may have gained in other ways. This could be likened to a rugby-loving playleader trying to convert a group of boy-soccer-enthusiasts whose favourite team had reached the Cup Final. Assuming it was the week prior to Cup Final day I would not give our playleader friend a snowflake's chance in a furnace of succeeding. This is the kind of chasm which divides these different worlds of music and which a playleader may find himself trying to narrow.

Background music

For many youngsters it has become a favourite leisure-time occupation just to listen to recorded music. This is specially true of those who are knowledgeable about the groups and artists who are currently in the 'top ten' charts of the hit parade. In some teenage circles a person is not considered to be 'with it' if he is ignorant about such things as knowing who, or what, is at the top of the hit parade charts. As a result of this it will be found that large numbers of young people tend to be attracted to places where music is being played. They are happy if the music is played very loudly. Ideally for them it should be so loud that they literally need to shout at each other to be heard. I have heard several conflicting reasons as to why this is so: I know that there must be a reason for it, but I'm not really sure what it is. I do know, however, that it most certainly is not the best way to listen to music – any kind of music. The nearest acceptable reason to me is that the pitch of musical notes is not so important to the youngsters as the incessant throb of the beat. I find that many youngsters are in their element if vibrations from the amplification system can be felt through the floor. Personally when in such an atmosphere I find it very difficult to concentrate.

If this is indeed what some youngsters need to attract them to our recreation units, then we should make an effort to cater for them and at the same time introduce a modicum of reasonableness in order that their pleasure does not interfere with that of other users of the play unit. This is a very tall order, because some youngsters want their own way in everything and will strive to get it. A situation where several groups are seeking to participate in recreational activities of differing natures and where one activity jeopardizes another can strike up a chain of events which may lead to trouble. In such circumstances no set pattern of solution is laid down, and these problems must be solved on the spot by the leader. Usually the fault lies with the playleader in the first instance for lack of forethought and poor planning. For example, unless two different buildings or rooms are available, or one's intention is to operate the activities a good distance apart in the play area, very little purpose will be achieved in organizing a percussion band practice session and a pop record session simultaneously.

I would suggest that the following styles of recorded background music for various occasions will not give cause for much disapproval.

Under-fives play clubs etc: Nursery rhymes, children's songs, various sound-effects.

Games rallies and sports meetings: Marches and concert waltzes.

Festivals and displays where large crowds congregate: Light classical music and selections.

During normal play centre sessions: Big band swing arrangements and light orchestral music.

I feel that for indoor centres the music should be turned to a volume at which people are able to speak to each other without having to raise their normal speaking voice.

THE INFLUENCE OF MUSIC

In an endeavour to find an answer as to why young people like to have their music played at a deafening volume, a number of young people were asked to give their reasons voluntarily.

One 16-year-old girl who has been part of the play scheme at Lewisham for four years and who thinks of this as being 'a place where you can enjoy yourself at your own leisure', says that noise – to her way of thinking – is a shield against embarrassment. She gives as an illustration the picture of a young person making an entrance into a place frequented by young people and where constant noise is part of the scene; she maintains that the noise tends to allay any feeling of embarrassment which may be experienced if the place was otherwise quiet.

Another 16-year-old girl states:

'Noise makes fun.'

She expanded on this by declaring that:

'It goes a long way towards creating a lively exciting atmosphere.'

The same girl said that although it was not her personal outlook, she felt that some young people did it as 'an outward protest, endeavouring to annoy older people who do not like it.'

A 14-year-old who is in the seventh stream at school said 'It makes you really want to go.'

On being asked 'Where to?' she replied 'Dance'.

Only one 15-year-old boy out of a group of ten could give an answer:

'So you can hear what's going on in the record.'

Four girls aged either eleven or twelve years of age, out of a group of fifteen, gave the following answers:

'So that everyone can hear.'

'So as we can dance to it and jump about.'

'It's all in the fashion.'

'So they can hear it all over the place and upstairs.'

The other eleven girls all replied 'Don't know' with no further comment.

As a result of further discussions which took place between a group of playleaders and a number of children and young people the following rather startling points emerged. All are in one way or another relevant to music.

The majority of young people belong to a 'we-group' which is a kind of social recreational band of either all girls, all boys, or one of mixed sexes. They meet whenever and as often as they can. The assemblage takes place at school, the youth club, the street corner, or the discothèque. Sometimes they meet at the home of one of its members.

An interesting point brought up by a teenage girl was her statement that:

'When I am with the group, the real me never comes out.'

A very intelligent thirteen-year-old whose home background is very correct and proper and who has twin 26-year-old brothers who are both married, says:

'I'm fighting my own war between two me's. I am a member of a group of girls who are all fanatical on pop music, reggae and motown, but I like orchestral music. I play 'cello in an orchestra. I feel that if the group find out they will reject me.'

A young girl approaching the age of seventeen said that the we-group:

'... provides security of environment outside the home, and

gives us opportunity to live and act to a completely different code of behaviour which suits our outlook on life.'

She also indicated that young people have fears of being a 'loner' when she said:

'Fear of rejection compels one to conform to the wishes of the majority of the group. Even to one's choice of listening to music.'

If a youngster deliberately makes the effort to be an individualist in this day and age, he or she will be the secret envy of many a 'groupy' of whom one, a thirteen-year-old, says:

'It takes guts to be an individualist these days', she follows this remark with a reference to 'groupies' in which she says:

'I suppose we are all defeatists at heart really.'

The clothes one wears or the type of music one listens to can be indicative of the type of group a young person belongs to.

Each group favours its own type of music according to its classification which at the time of writing is one of the following: Skin Heads, Greasers, Dropouts, Hippies, Suede Heads.

Music is also classified according to its style, which at the present time has the following names:

Reggae (Jamaica Ska), Rock and Roll, Tamla Motown, Blue Beat, Soul, Underground (or progressive), Trad, Modern Jazz, Folk Music (protest), Swing.

These types reach a zenith of popularity each time one of their records gets to the top of the musical poll charts.

The name of some types of music are apt to change, for example Reggae is two-beat music which was once named Jamaican Ska.

A fourteen-year-old said of pop lyrics:

'Words to pop music is reality, it tells about what is going on in the world, older people don't realize it.'

But an eighteen-year-old man who volunteered the information that he had been a 'dropout' for a year or so: (a dropout is one who drops out of society and no longer conforms, one who is contumacious) said:

'In me, heavy music tends to eliminate any feelings of aggression. I have experienced feeling of being 'sent' by just listening to music, but I think this happened because I wanted it to. It must be a form of self-hypnosis I suppose, but of course one must have other heads around, doing the same thing, it's sort of infectious.'

The term 'head' means a person, for example a 'Suede Head' is one who wears his hair long, wears such things as stay-press trousers and items of suede clothing and shoes.

A seventeen-year-old boy brought back the subject of volume when he said:

'Lots of music is already recorded loud, because this is an ingredient of selling power, especially with second-rate groups. I don't buy a record just because it is recorded loud but I know lots of people who do. But good melody still commands respect.'

'Loud music' commented a sixteen-year-old, 'is played like that because it stops you thinking about things.'

This concept of an escape from reality led to an outburst from a seventeen-year-old girl who declared:

'Discussions like this spark off feelings I didn't realize I was capable of having.'

She said this after another sixteen-year-old had remarked:

'You need to have the feeling of being against somebody or something, that's why I don't like some kinds of music'.

Further discussion led back again to the we-group when one of the girls said:

'These bleeding shoes are killing me.'

It would appear that youngsters will readily suffer physical pain to wear fashions dictated by the group's majority. But one of the most startling facts came to light when one of the youngsters said that her eyes were smarting and that she should really be wearing her spectacles.

'I can't wear them because of fear of rejection by the group. It is a sign of being intellectual to wear glasses so none of us do.'

It was discovered that four of the girls who were present should have been wearing spectacles.

'I'm going to wait until I get the new kind of contact lens first', said one of the girls.

'When will that be?' asked one of the playleaders.

'Oh I don't know. Years maybe.'

Another young girl remarked:

'You know, we're always trying to get the admiration of the rest of the group by doing something that they think is good. It could be anything from playing a record on a jukebox to clobbering someone we don't like.'

Another element showed itself in that some youngsters are anti-parent and that a favourite topic of discussion is about the inhibiting influence which parents impose on them and how they in turn make retaliation. I should imagine that many of the claims made by children as to how they 'stood up' to their 'old man' are rather exaggerated, and invented to create pseudo-admiration for themselves from the group. The main avenues of disagreement between young people and their parents appear to be:

(a) Their choice of music, and the volume at which it is played.
(b) Mode of dress.
(c) The company they mix with.
(d) Smoking.
(e) Provision of spending money.
(f) General untidiness in the home.

One or two interesting points about smoking emerged during the discussion and one young girl remarked that some youngsters smoke deliberately because their parents tell them not to, before they even contemplate it.

'I don't smoke' remarked an eighteen-year-old, 'because my parents are non-smokers, so they never left any fags around the house for me to try. I don't see any point in starting now, because I'm the envy of all the blokes in my group. They keep trying to make me start but I don't want to anyway.'

'I stopped smoking to prove to my leader at the centre that I had the willpower to stop. I don't think my own group would have been able to sway me.'

Generally speaking indications were that it was the thing with young people to reject ideas from older people, unless of course such people were held in high esteem.

Prejudices against coloured youngsters were discussed as a side-issue which came out of a suggestion that the majority of coloured people liked one particular kind of pop music. On the suggestion that this was a free country and that one was entitled to his own choice it was remarked that some coloured youngsters resented any approach to friendliness and that the younger a child the more spiteful it was. This outlook was not really accepted by the play-leaders who were all of the opinion that no colour bar existed among small children but unfortunately several of those present had experienced open aggression at a local discothèque, and they could not be convinced that these were probably only isolated incidents.

'Hysteria is infectious within a group and can easily give birth to violence.' This statement was made by a sixteen-year-old girl. She maintains that trouble between groups of youngsters, and sometimes between an individual and a group is often prompted by differences in musical tastes.

Musical taste for young people has become on the one hand a status symbol and on the other a stigma to the individual which could instigate violence. I think that a playleader on being aware of this should consider very carefully what type of music he should allow to be played at certain times and for various events. He should also ensure that no private transistor radios are played inside a playleadership building when other events are taking place. What young people do in this respect – outside – is of course their own business, but I think it will be found that unless permission has been granted many parks have bye-laws which prohibit the playing of music in any form if it disturbs the public. The responsibility for enforcing this rests with the parks' staff.

DRUGS

The most disturbing issue which came to light during the discussion was that which pinpointed the serious state of affairs which prevails amongst children and young people, namely their familiarity with another subject closely associated with the 'music scene', *drugs*.

Undoubtedly none of those young people present at the discussion were personally involved in drug-taking, but they were very well aware of what was going on around them, in their schools and in different groups with which they were familiar.

'Yes a lot of them try different things, mostly purple hearts' said one young person. 'Some of the older ones get blocked at parties and the disco', she said.

The expression 'blocked' was new to me and to the other play-leaders present; it soon became apparent that unless we did something about the situation we would be unable to communicate properly with these people on the subject of drugs and other allied subjects. Within a few minutes, after my suggestion that we were interested in these 'expressions' we had learnt much about different types of drug used by young people. Some of them really had a lot to say, probably to impress the other young people that they were well up on the subject.

As a result of this discussion I became convinced that all play-leaders should know something about the drug scene. After contacting the Home Office to seek their advice I offer the following edited information from *Drugs in your Town* with kind permission of the author, Councillor Simon Randall of Bromley Borough Council. I strongly advise all potential playleaders to read this book throughout.

DRUG-TAKING

The reasons for taking drugs

There are many reasons behind a young person's need to take drugs, and one writer suggested that three basic factors must be present to lead to drug dependence – personality weakness, personal crisis and availability of drugs. Drugs have been called detectors of psychic weaknesses, and it is the personality of the drug-taker which so often determines his eventual dependence or addiction to the drug and not the qualities of the drug itself.

During adolescence personality is forming, and the youngster is turning from his home environment and parental love, to that of society at large and friendships with his own age group outside the family. This stage of growing up is punctuated by stresses at school from examinations, and for many there is the change from school to work when they have money in their pockets and plenty of time to spend it. During this turbulent period young people are at risk and whilst the vast majority will come through unscathed, some will be caught up along deviant paths.

Many authors have outlined some of the reasons behind drug-taking, and the writer owes much to the Rev. Kenneth Leech and others for the thoughts which follow.

Rebellion

Some take drugs as an opportunity to rebel against society, knowing that drug-taking is disapproved of by the older generation. Kenneth Leech wrote that in doing this the drug-taker is hurting himself for the pleasure of seeing how it hurts his parents. Young people often feel that their parents should not bring them up for the parental world, but for the one they themselves are going to have to live in.

Boredom

There is a need for a meeting place where young people will be accepted as they are and 'not get thrown out if they can't afford to keep stuffing themselves'. If young people are unable to find some excitement in existing facilities, they may turn to those drugs which bring them 'out of themselves', such as amphetamines.

Experimentation – 'Youth is wholly experimental'

When young people hear about the exciting side of drug-taking as publicized in the press, which recounts the stories about pop stars' experiences with drugs, they are inquisitive and wish to experiment themselves. Through ignorance few of them realize how they may be affected by the drug, and even if they do realize there may be some danger that they are not prepared to resist the temptation. Many drugs stimulate the senses in a way which no other substance can.

'One of the best ways of using marihuana is when listening to music. You can hear music as you've never heard it before', one famous film star was recently quoted as saying:

'Drug-takers say they feel happy and elated, wishing to speak to everyone. Cannabis makes them more aware of their existing feelings, and amphetamines give them a false sense of courage, when they are easily led into committing petty crimes.'

Where are drugs taken?

As the vast majority of soft drug-taking by young people is illegal it will obviously rarely take place in public, and then always so as not to attract attention. Some may smoke cannabis by rolling their own 'joint' in a public house or dimly-lit coffee bar when the characteristic sweet smell is disguised by the smell of tobacco smoke, and others may take their drugs in public parks away from the crowds.

Most drug-taking however, takes place in a group context at 'pot parties' or pill parties which, contrary to the belief of most members of the public, do not end in mass sexual orgies. The availability of drugs at parties is clear from both the evidence of the school-children's questionnaire and the indications appearing from time to time in the local press. The indoor parties often take place at the home of one of the group's members or in derelict premises.

The 'joints' are passed round the room, or the bottle of pills divided up between those present – one hears cases of young people who take up to 30 pills on a Saturday night. At all-night parties amphetamines, the drug used during the Second World War to keep troops alert, are taken by the young people to keep them awake to enjoy themselves.

Short notes on the pharmacological effects, symptoms, description and nicknames for some of the drugs abused by young people

It is very difficult to recognize accurately whether or not a young person is under the influence of drugs, as some of the symptoms and general behaviour of the individual may simply be signs of adolescent behaviour or depression, etc.

Whilst each drug has its own peculiar effects, there are some general points which may be indicative of drug-taking.

A relatively sudden change in the individual's behaviour, standard of appearance and contrasting moods are perhaps suspicious factors. The drug-taker will be rather secretive, less willing to associate with his family and may appear rather irritable.

School teachers may notice extra tiredness or sleepiness after the week-end, accompanied by a lessening of interest in class activities. Patchy attendance at school, particularly on Mondays, often indicates that drug-taking may have taken place. Some studies have shown that a major cause of truancy, particularly in the last few terms at school, arises from the after-effects of drug-taking.

SEDATIVES OR SLEEPERS

These include methaqualone and diphenhydramine hydrochloride (Mandrax), amylobarbitone sodium (Sodium Amytal), quinalbarbitone sodium and amylobarbitone sodium (Tuinal), pentobarbitone sodium (Nembutal). Mandrax is a small white tablet with a slightly bitter taste. The others, all barbiturates, are generally in the form of white powder contained in coloured gelatin capsules.

This type of drug is often misused by young people and the main effect is that of sleepiness. By depressing the central nervous system it removes fears. Effects, which are increased with alcohol, include slurred speech, slow thinking, giddiness, clumsy movements and unsteadiness on the feet.

Barbiturate addiction is almost as serious as heroin addiction, causing severe withdrawal symptoms with convulsions. Although young barbiturate takers are found among the heroin users, throughout society the drugs are used as sleeping tablets, mainly by the middle-aged.

STIMULANTS OR PEP PILLS

These include Dexedrine, Benzedrine, Methedrine, Durophet, Preludin, Drinamyl – known as dexies, bennies, meth, black bombers, french blues, purple hearts, doobs, etc.

Dexedrine – small yellow tablet – dexamphetamine sulphate.

Benzedrine – white tablet about 1 cm. in diameter – amphetamine sulphate. (Benzedrine is not now marketed.)

Methedrine – small white tablet – also ampoule containing liquid with the same appearance as water – methylamphetamine hydrochloride. (Methedrine is not now marketed.)

Durophet – three kinds of capsules with different quantities and coloured all white, black and white, and all black – dexamphetamine three parts and laevoamphetamine one part.

Preludin – white tablet about 1 cm. in diameter – used as a slimming tablet – phenmetrazine hydrochloride.

Drinamyl – light blue tablet nearly 1 cm. in diameter containing amphetamine and barbiturate, used to be heart-shaped – hence 'purple heart' – dexamphetamine sulphate and amylobarbitone.

The effects of these drugs are almost the opposite to those of barbiturates. There is a marked stimulant effect on the central nervous system, with increased blood pressure, pulse rate and breathing. They cause a lessening of fatigue, an increase in mental activity, and a general feeling of well-being. There is a tendency to increase muscular movement so that takers appear restless, unable to relax, with loud laughter, talkativeness and dilatation of the pupils. They may also be very flushed, have a dry mouth and no appetite. Also associated with these drugs are headaches, aggression perhaps leading to violence, delinquency and susceptibility to 'dares' and risks. The morning after brings with it tiredness, a lack of interest in work and school, resulting in absence from both. Large doses bring about a paranoid psychosis, fever, cardiovascular reactions, respiratory failure, disorientation, hallucinations (known as 'the horrors'), convulsions and coma.

In small doses the effects are almost imperceptible to an observer and only familiarity with the personality of the individual could detect any change which is attributable to the drug. Dexedrine does not give the twitchy feeling of Benzedrine, and is occasionally used as a 'pep' pill in sport, for example by car rally drivers to prolong alertness – at the cost of reduced judgement.

Drinamyl is probably one of the most popular pills among young people as it combines both dexamphetamine sulphate and amylobarbitone producing disinhibition and heightened energy.

Methylamphetamine hydrochloride can be injected intravenously, and was widely used by addicts as a substitute for heroin when this latter drug was withdrawn from general circulation and restricted to registered doctors at treatment centres. As it created tremendous problems during the course of 1968 it was then restricted to hospital pharmacies only. Its effects are immediate and similar to those described above.

Cocaine: this is also a stimulant. It is available as a white crystalline powder with a bitter numbing taste. It may be taken by sniffing and can cause ulcers of the septum between the nostrils. It leads to states of wild excitement, euphoria and hallucinations. Cocaine addiction can also lead to digestive disorders, rashes and skin infections. The drug is most often taken with heroin and is then known as 'speedball'.

PAIN KILLERS OR ANALGESICS

These include morphine, heroin and methadone hydrochloride (available as Physeptone). Heroin is known as horse, H., shit, gear, etc.

An almost white, odourless powder in crystalline form with a bitter taste – heroin or diamorphine – is the last step in drug addiction. It is sniffed, taken by injection beneath the skin ('skin-popping') or intravenously ('main-lining'). The addict carries his injection kit or 'works' with hypodermic syringe and needles in a tin box. The fix is so important it becomes an almost ritualistic exercise. Multiple pinpricks on the addict's arms and tattooing of veins caused by injections are strong indications that a person is addicted to heroin.

The long and short-term effects of heroin on health and otherwise are well known, and they can be disastrous. Addicts tend to be convincing liars, deceitful and always trying to 'score' or obtain drugs from others. When waiting for their supplier they stare intensely, often oblivious of anything or anyone else.

The withdrawal symptoms, which become severer as addiction progresses, include sweating, yawning, sneezing, muscle twitching, anxiety, insomnia, nausea, vomiting, diarrhoea, dehydration, dilated pupils and general physical deterioration.

MOOD CHANGERS AND HALLUCINOGENS

These include cannabis and L.S.D.

Cannabis has many names, including bhang, charge, grass, hash, hashish, hemp, herb, marihuana, mary-hane, pot, rope, tea, weed, etc.

It comes in three main forms – firstly, as the flowers and leaves of the female cannabis plant (marihuana); secondly as a cube of hard brown resin which has been cut from a large block (hash) and thirdly, as hash crumbled into a powder, when it is sold in brown or silver paper packets.

In addition ready-made cigarettes, reefers, can be obtained, but otherwise they have to be rolled. It is a good indication of familiarity with cannabis-smoking if a young person through no apparent need to save money, starts rolling his own cigarettes. The reefer is rolled with a filter usually made with a small roll of paper, and then double-wrapped with an ordinary cigarette paper. The 'stick' or 'joint' may be passed round a group of young people. When smoking the smell resembles burning grass or cabbage, and is different from that of Eastern cigarettes.

The effects of the drug depend to a large extent on the individual taking it and the experiences which are expected by him, since there is a great deal of self-priming involved in the reactions. The Wootton Report considered them in great detail, and they include a tendency to make one more aware of one's surroundings, euphoria, distortion of time, giggling, laziness – often characterized by takers sitting round just dozing. Takers often have drooping eyelids, bloodshot eyes, dry mouth and throat, accompanied by increased thirst and appetite. There is a sense of well-being, with a benevolent attitude to the world. As the Wootton Report put it, cannabis users often tend to concentrate their attention on their aches, pains and anxieties without helping to resolve them, and to induce passivity without removing suffering. The drug makes one feel the necessity to do things, tell everyone how happy one is etc., but at the same time removes the need for action. It could be called the great procrastinator. However unlike alcohol it produces no hang-overs.

*

L.S.D. is known as sugar, sugar lumps, acid, etc., and S.T.P. or Serenity, Tranquillity and Peace.

A colourless liquid, L.S.D. 25 or lysergic acid diethylamide is taken on a sugar lump or soaked into blotting paper. It is a most dangerous drug, as the reactions from person to person vary so enormously and only a minute dose produces an uncontrollable reaction. In a much more marked way than cannabis it produces distortions of time, colour and sound in the setting of a mystical experience.

In appropriate doses it produces changes in the perceptual functions, especially the visual system, with changes of colour, illusions and hallucinations. There are also alterations of insight and awareness of one's own personality and alterations of the sense of time and space. Auditory hallucinations occur so that a small noise may be magnified many times, and one's sense of smell and taste can be similarly altered.

PRODUCERS OF STUPOR

These include model glue, ether, chloroform, petrol, paraffin, nutmeg, etc.

These substances, or their volatile fumes, are sniffed and often produce dizziness, accompanied by a sense of well-being. Prolonged sniffing is very dangerous and many organs of the body can be seriously damaged, particularly the liver.

12 · Diary for a Week

To give a rough idea about the various kinds of personal involvement which befall an organizing playleader this extended extract from my own diary refers to a week during the Summer recess of 1970.

My assistant organizer was not on duty during this period and a certain amount of the work load would have been taken over by her. Nevertheless many organizers – including the reader – may find themselves faced with similar situations and will be expected to cope with numerous problems during long, tedious or interesting hours depending, of course, on how they look at it. During these rather hectic periods, one takes refreshment or relaxes if and when the opportunity presents itself. It is nearly impossible to work to a fixed time table. One plays the rules of this game as they fit in with the circumstances and it does not pay to be optimistic about full co-operation from one's part-time staff. Careful study of the following events of a week's history will tell several stories.

Monday (3rd week of school recess)

9.35 *Visit my office* at the Town Hall. Deal with correspondence and a number of telephoned queries.

As my assistant will not be available for the remainder of the week I make arrangements to have all telephone calls to me diverted to a clerk in the parks' section. He will make notes of them and deal with any queries he is able to answer.

11.05 *Arrive Southend Park.* Discover leader-in-charge has gone to my office to see me on an urgent matter. Chat for a few minutes with a park keeper on the subject of his entering one or two five-a-side football teams from his club into one of the scheme's leagues. Only 15 children present.

11.12 *Arrive Home Park* (Situated 400 yards away from Southend Park). Children's entertainment (clown, Punch and Judy, etc.) in progress. Have discussion with Entertainments'

Officer. About 145 children were seated on the grass watching the entertainment, half a dozen older boys were kicking a ball around. Playleader requests a further quantity of white crepe paper from me. This is to make paper flowers which will eventually be used to decorate a float which is going to be entered in a parade later that month. I make my way to the adjacent adventure playground (about thirty yards distant) which is completely devoid of children because they are all either watching or 'taking the mickey' out of the entertainer. I am informed by the leader that one of the playground's rabbits has had another litter of young. I am thinking that this is becoming a meticulously regular occurrence when George, the trainee, informs me that he is starting a regular job and will be leaving at the end of the week. I make a note to the effect that a replacement will be needed. The playleader-in-charge of the adventure playground comes over, so I ask him to keep on the lookout for a likely replacement for George.

11.27 *Arrive back at Southend Park.* Deliver time sheets. Have the unpleasant task of giving one week's notice to one of the playleaders for breach of regulations.

11.50 *Arrive Forster Memorial Park.* Deliver time sheets. Instruct playleader-in-charge also to take charge of Southend Park (half a mile distant) for the time being. Meet ten European students who are working on a voluntary project and who have brought 120 children from Deptford to this semi-urban district of Lewisham to organize playleadership sessions during the day. There is a slight language problem and my prisoner-of-war camp German or my Linguaphone French is of little help. The students don't seem to be doing so well with their English either. They have absorbed a few expressions from their charges and this became evident when a swarthy smiling young male playleader loudly remarked that their charges, although noisy, were 'very good basteds from taligraeff ill' (Telegraph Hill). I try my best to issue what instructions I feel should be given and ask my staff to assist as best they can with a very difficult situation. It would appear that a feeling of resentment is creeping in from the park's locals. The situation could need very careful handling.

12.12 *Arrive Sports Centre.* Urgent message awaiting me. A number of the previous week's time sheets have been mislaid, can I clarify the situation? Although my assistant is not on duty I telephone her to ascertain the situation. The problem is resolved and I telephone the pay office. The centre is not open for playleadership on Monday.

1.15 *Lunch.* I have a sandwich and a glass of beer.

2.00 *Equipment Store Room at Sports Centre.* Sort out a few small miscellaneous items of equipment: crepe paper, chalk, paint etc. which have been requested by various leaders.

2.37 *Arrive Blythe Hill Play Area.* Find Senior Playleader has not arrived: she has custody of the play building keys: assistant leader playing with about half a dozen children. Senior leader arrives 2.45 (13 minutes late), number of children had grown to about twenty. Reprimand leader for being late (car trouble, fourth time), leave instructions about handicrafts work that evening.

2.57 *Arrive Luxmore Gardens (Under-fives only).* Complement of twelve children with parents. Deliver time sheets. Find myself drawn into discussion with a park keeper about union affairs. Playleaders very happy. No complaints. Meet lady ex-playleader. No luck when I made attempt to persuade her to come back to work: I was thinking of the vacancy which had arisen that morning.

3.05 *Arrive Brookmill Park.* Everything normal. Several methylated spirit drinkers are lying around on the grass, but the children just ignore them and keep to other parts of the park to play. It is a little windy and dust is flying around from the adjacent Redgra play area. Receive request for some glue. Did I know that – – – (one of my playleaders) was pregnant and did I think she would be leaving? If she was could – – – take her place? These remarks of course come from the girls. I promised to give it some thought. Interesting point – four white children and 27 coloured children in the play area.

3.25 *Arrive Northbrook Park.* Deliver time sheets. Playleader in charge suggests that indications point to the possibility that in that particular area it may prove to be a good thing if the morning session was moved back half an hour to run from 10.00 a.m. until 12.00 because the play area became virtually deserted by 12.15 as many children went to lunch. Had a report that letters have been received by some parents from the Parks' Department (this park is under the control of another authority) to the effect that certain children are barred from the park. Promise to investigate.

3.50 *Arrive Chinbrook.* Normal play session in progress, about 65 children occupied with various activities in the play area, another 15 just lying around. A larger number are playing in the paddling pool. Under-fives' area contains about 5 children with their parents. Playleader wants to know if he can be issued with a track suit. Council workmen are digging trenches in the grass area, foreman appears to be apprehensive about dangers of children interfering with tools and wheelbarrows and hurting themselves. I try to enlighten him that no harm is likely to result and that some children would much prefer to dig than do anything else. But he informs me that this is not the point. It would appear that after digging a section of trench in another area, his gang went for refreshments and when they came back part of the trench had been filled in by children before the necessary work had been carried out. Could I leave somebody to guard the holes whilst the workmen were away? I cautiously hint that it may be better if they put their tools out of reach of the youngsters before they went for the tea break. They'll give it a try and let me know how things go.

4.15 *Arrive Warren Avenue.* Deliver time sheets. Attendance four. Leader informs me that about 35 children had been the maximum during the afternoon. A large window had been broken in the equipment hut. The damage had been done from the inside, by 'Mr. Nobody'. I must arrange to have this repaired quickly. Can I also arrange to have the pitches marked out as the older boys and young men had made a complaint the previous Friday that the lines were barely discernible. Can I telephone my office as somebody wants to speak to me urgently? The park staff room telephone is not working. I telephone from the public 'phone box outside the park gates. A message has been left that a complaint has been lodged by the parents' committee of our under-fives' club with the Public Health department that the floor of the play hall was dirty on the previous Friday. Can I throw any light on the situation? I comply with this request and agree to send a written report, thinking to myself that during school holidays attendance at the play clubs drops drastically and that the children play outside anyway.

5.00 *Arrive Forster Park.* I have a cup of tea and a hot dog at the park café. Telephone my wife at the surgery. Park keeper tells me that the foreman is pretty annoyed at the visitors from Deptford. It would appear that the overseas' students had little if any control over the children, who had run riot in the park. They had been picking flowers from the flower beds and 'look at their picnic area on the grass, like a damn refuse dump'. When I explained about the difficulty of language he reiterated 'They've got no difficulty understanding each other mate. It's been one long snogging session by them playleaders. No wonder the kids went wild. If the parks' superintendent had paid a visit, we'd all of got the push.' I waited until my own staff came on duty. My senior playleader confirmed the park keeper's remarks, and so left me with a problem. The problem was that the project had been organized by a church. A little later at 5.50 another problem arose. A young boy about six or seven years old was discovered lost in the woods adjacent to the playing area. He had been left behind by the foreign students who had brought the party of children on a number of small education authority school coaches. The child was not very coherent and all we could get out of him was that he lived in Deptford. He was concerned more about 'getting fumped' for being late home. Together with a playleader I took him to Deptford to the pick-up point in the hope that he would know his way from there. He did. I explained the situation to his mother who quite obviously was dubious as to my identity until I convinced her who I was. Nevertheless I did not give the youngster much chance of getting away without a 'fumpin'.

7.00 *Arrive Sports Centre.* Discuss the situation about the floor with Supervisor and two attendants. Agree to ask playleaders to co-operate by mixing the water colour paint to a thicker consistency, and to withdraw the blue paint completely because for some unknown reason it emits a very unpleasant odour. I ask the Supervisor if the first-aid treatment book has been found as it has been missing for several weeks from the office. Receive telephone call from playleader at

Northbrook Park. Please can they have some batteries for the portable record player? By this time the dog training session had commenced so I decide to call it a day. On arrival home a message requested me to ring Forster Park. I do, no reply.

Tuesday

9.30 *Sports Centre.* Discuss and have re-arranged into a different pattern all the major items of play equipment such as climbing-frame, slide, benches etc. Make arrangements to have a billiard table slate recovered.

10.00 Receive delegation from the Under-Fives' Play Club parents' committee. They request me to obtain the services of a professional entertainer, preferably a Punch and Judy man for their children's Xmas party on 19th December. Also they would like me to book a well-known celebrity to open their Xmas fair on 21st November. Telephone call from office. Would I go over and see the Principal Engineer (my Chief).

11.05 *Office.* I go immediately and we discuss minor items about the forthcoming annual display. Answer four letters. Telephone several professional acts for the parents' Xmas party etc. Have great difficulty. All of them seem to be booked up. Contact Civic Recreation Officer. Please can he help? Leave it with him, he will try. What about a celebrity? Would Pearl Carr and Teddy Johnson do because they will be around at that time doing rehearsals for the Council's pantomime Robin Hood? Yes please. Leave it to him. As the roneo duplicator is not being used, I take the opportunity to run off a few stencils of the minutes of the last parents' committee meeting. Telephone call from a playleader, please can she have an immediate interview? Yes! Make it snappy. I have a cup of tea and wait for her to arrive. Telephone call from a park keeper at Warren Avenue. What are the dimensions of a mini shinty pitch? I tell him, 'Same as a netball court exactly, including internal markings.' He asks 'What is shinty?' So I tell him and he says he should have a plan anyway. Playleader arrives, domestic problems, rather serious, can I help? I think so. I ring the appropriate department and pass her on to more capable hands. As she leaves I receive another visitor, a young boy. Can he see the application form of a certain team in his league because he 'finks they been

fiddlin'. I ask him if his team have played them yet. 'Yes.'
When did the game take place? 'Last night.' What was the
score. '18–nil'. He looks at the form. I ask 'Who won?' He
squints at me and replies 'They did but they had two
unregistered players, so we did didn't we, and according to
rule five they're out of the league and the cup, aren't they?'
How does he know that they had two unregistered players
playing? Because they go to his school, and their names are
not on this form. He gives me their names, addresses, telephone number and launches into their life histories, so I tell
him to give me his particulars and he will be notified in due
course. He wants to know now because he's going on holiday
tomorrow etc. Finally he departs saying 'I'll come in after
I get back.' I feel sure he will. I leave a note for my assistant
to check his complaint when she returns to duty.

12.00 *Town Hall.* Take letter of authority to draw small amount of
cash from the paymaster with which to buy refreshments for
visitors from another London scheme later in the week.

1.15 *Lunch.* In staff canteen.

1.50 *Office.* Telephone message. Will I please telephone Padding-
ton Recreation Ground? Information re our set-up at Lewisham, and does the playleadership scheme own its own
mini-bus? If so how did we raise the cash to buy it, and are
there any legal snags about insurance etc? After several
attempts I make contact and give all the necessary information.
Another telephone call from the organizer at Ealing. Who
do we purchase our track suits from, how much do they cost
and do we buy in bulk? I answer these queries and invite
Tom Sullivan, the Ealing scheme organizer, to our annual
display, and he accepts.

2.30 *Workshops at Council Depot.* Have a look at a new hut which is
being constructed for the scheme, chat to the foreman and
one of his carpenters who is doing the work. Have a cup of
tea with them during their tea break and thank them for
their help and co-operation, which incidentally is always
first class. I then go over to the Sports Centre which is 50
yards away.

3.10 *Sports Centre.* Leader reports broken basketball backboard. It
looks dangerous, so I immediately telephone the carpenters'

foreman and ask him if he can help. Yes, he can if it is an emergency. Will I send a 'works' order' to the workshops' superintendent first thing tomorrow morning please? Yes, I will. I watch a rehearsal for an old folks' concert and find some amusement in the performance of a cod ballet dance performed by a number of boys dressed in ballet skirts, football boots and stockings. The dirty knees stand out in sharp contrast to the spotless white of the borrowed skirts and I try not to deceive myself by thinking that this is part of the act. Those three pairs of knees have been the same colour for weeks. One of the Sports Centre attendants asks if I can clarify which qualifications it is necessary to hold in order to become accepted as a coach in various sports. I refer him to the Central Council for Physical Recreation.

3.15 *Visit Police Station.* One of the under-fives' club mothers notifies me that a five pound note had been taken out of her purse while she was washing tea cups. The lady is well known to me, and has been for some considerable time. I make a few tentative enquiries and then accompany her, at her own request, to the local police station which is adjacent to the Sports Centre. After registering the loss we return to the Centre. The lady is somewhat distressed at having lost all her housekeeping money so I replace the money for her myself until she is able to repay it. It is too late for her to go to the bank and she has to purchase food for the evening meal.

3.35 *Ladywell Centre.* Arrive back at the Centre to be informed that another purse had been stolen from a perambulator basket. Luckily this purse contained no cash at all, but it did contain the key to the owner's house. As I leave the Centre to go back to the police station with victim number two I am handed my five pounds back by victim number one who has found her five pound note tucked inside another piece of paper in an unused compartment of her purse.

3.45 *Visit Police Station.* Report loss of second purse.

3.55 *Ladywell Centre.* Hold discussion with parents about the possibility of introducing a scheme to safeguard valuables. Make out a written report. Have a cup of tea during this time.

4.15 Discuss the situation with the Centre Supervisor.

4.25 Terminate play session and disperse children from the Centre.

4.45 Take reports over to my office and discuss the situation with my Senior Officer.

5.35 *Visit Police Station.* Arrange with Station Officer for local patrol to pay regular visits to the Centre in the hope that it will create a better relationship between the police and local children.

6.00 *Sports Centre.* Supervise trampoline session of girls club. Four trampolines and forty-two girls. This club is normally under the supervision of my assistant. Render first-aid to trainee playleader who landed awkwardly, hurting her ribs.

7.05 *Visit Forster Park.* Receive report about vandalism and inspect broken windows in play building. Advise on temporary repair. Have a look at the work which is being done on their handicrafts' contribution to our annual event. Have discussion with a voluntary playleader who would like to come on to the official staff. As he is an asset to the scheme, and well experienced, I decide to employ him.

Playleader-in-charge advises me that she is of the opinion that a petition is going around for signature. Its aim is to reverse the decision of the parks' foreman who has had small teams' pitches marked out on a sloping piece of ground, away from the main playing area. I advise her not to become personally involved and to let the public get on with it in their own way. Attendance about 95.

8.10 *Visit Southend Park.* About 35 children present. Leader tells me that a sudden craze for tennis has arisen. Can I let them have an extra volley ball net with which to improvise a tennis court? What about tennis rackets? 'Oh! lots of them have their own rackets.' I don't venture to ask where the rackets came from, but I hazard a guess. My attention is drawn to a coloured youth who has been constantly hanging around the play area all day. It appears that he never speaks to anybody, but he periodically takes a stroll round the small park and then back to sit on the same park bench again. Has she reported the situation to the park staff? Yes, and they have kept him under surveillance, but he has committed no breach of regulations. Speculation is running high amongst the youngsters, particularly the girls, one of whom says he

245

possesses a large knife. It appears that this lad, about sixteen years of age, has not been seen to eat anything all day. One or two of the children are beginning to venture over to him and make probing remarks. I instruct their leader to persuade them to keep away. I decide to make an effort to make conversation with him. The boy appears to be quite respectable and well mannered, not particularly bright but perhaps this is only because of the language difficulty. No, he does not live near here, he is from 'a long way'. He can't find his uncle's shop because he has only been there once before. It is near this place because he can remember the pond with the ducks. He is waiting here for his cousin who comes through the park on his way home from work. The park is a much used short cut, so this is quite feasible. What kind of shop does his uncle own, what does he sell? He replies 'All kinds'. When I ask him his uncle's name I can't really understand what he is saying. Is he hungry? No, plenty of chocolate. He indicates a nearby litter cage which contains several wrappers of chocolate biscuits. If his cousin does not come shortly – because the park will be closing in ten minutes' time – will he go back home? No he does not want to and he has only a 'little lot' of money left. I suggest that he should go along to the police station where he will receive help and that if he waits until I get my brief case from the hut I will go to the police with him. I go to the hut and when I return he has gone. I leave the park at 8.55 and telephone the police giving a description of the boy and of my conversation with him. Quite obviously something is out of order.

9.15 *Arrive Sports Centre.* Table tennis club in session with about 30 boys and girls whose ages range from about 12 years to 17 years. Receive rather serious complaint from a playleader from Home Park about a new lady playground attendant who is employed by the Park's Superintendent in the conventional playground. It would appear that she shows signs, by her activities, that she dislikes children intensely and spends much of her time evicting them from the playground. It was even suspected that she had struck some children and that parents have had occasion to visit the playground to speak to her about it.

One of the Centre attendants gives me a message. Will I

please ring the Parks' Superintendent. I do, and it concerns the woman at Home Park. He has also had complaints and can I get him any proof from some of my youngsters? Yes, I will try. I discuss plans for the following day – we have a party of children coming from Heston and Isleworth – with another member of my staff. I instruct him to notify the Centre supervisor that the visitors will be having a look round the Centre. Activities terminate at 9.55. Meet my wife and go for a meal and a drink.

Wednesday

9.30 *Sports Centre (Play Hall)* Discuss another suggestion relating to a new layout for play furniture.

10.15 Telephone office to take any messages which have been left for me. Ask for works' order to be made out to have the basketball backboard repaired. Receive a telephone call from Playleader at the Municipal Playing Fields. 'Please can the youngsters paint and decorate the inside of the play building?' 'Yes, they can.' 'What colour can they do it?' 'Any colour, blue with dotted stripes if they like.' 'Please can I get them some paint?' 'Yes I think so, but I'm not going to promise.' 'And some paint brushes?' 'Yes, if I can scrounge some.' I ask what this is all in aid of. 'You'll see', I'm told. They ring off. I telephone the painters' section at the maintenance depot of the Housing and Estates Department. 'Please have they any unwanted or unserviceable paint, distemper, wallpaper, brushes, dynamite anything?' I'm told by an efficient sounding familiar voice 'You're a bloody nuisance. This is the third time this year.' I tell the voice, 'I know, and it won't be the last time either.' 'You'll have to pick it up yourself after twelve o'clock', the voice says. I make thanks and ring off. I make another 'phone call and arrange for the stuff to be picked up and delivered to the playleader at the Municipal Playing Fields. (The Municipal Playing Fields or Brookmill Road as the children prefer to call it, is plagued with a number of those unfortunate beings who drink anything alcoholic and who have a habit of sleeping on the grass near the play area). A fleeting picture passes through my mind of blue and dotted striped drunks wandering around Deptford Broadway that evening.

I collect the refreshments which have been prepared for our visitors by the playleaders and some of the older children. The refreshments are in the form of a luncheon bag containing a sandwich roll, a piece of cake, an apple and a few wrapped sweets. The visitors were also served lemon or orange drinks. A small sum of money is allocated for this purpose in the annual estimates each year.

11.20 *Arrive Forster Park.* Deliver refreshments to the playleader. The parks' foreman would like to see me as soon as I have time. I have time now so I go over to his office. He complains about the state of the toilets after the Deptford party had left. The lady employed to clean them was more than concerned, I promise to get in touch with the organizers of the visiting play scheme to see if they can organize some form of supervision. They will be visiting the park twice a week from now on, so if something is not done now I can foresee staff problems arising. The park café had been burgled during the night. Would I wait for the C.I.D. officers in case any of the play scheme regulars were involved. As I have to wait for an unspecified length of time I decide to get the trampoline out to give the youngsters a session. Eventually 68 children become involved, but this is far too many to cater for with only one trampoline, so I decide to let them have 30 bounces each.

12.30 No C.I.D. detective had arrived. Have the trampoline put away and discover that I have acquired a new nickname from several small coloured children, I hope it does not stick because I would hate to be called 'Mister jumpin man'. Attendance 120.

I have a cup of tea with the park keepers and have a general discussion as to how we can improve certain facilities and overcome some difficulties. Two C.I.D. men arrive. They make a routine check and inform us that a wave of this kind of thing is happening all over the district. They don't think that it is any person who regularly frequents the park as the break-in operation has all the characteristics of similar happenings throughout the area.

12.30 *Sports Centre.* Lady waiting to see me. She would like to be a playleader. Her first question was 'How much do you pay' then 'I'm not really interested in Saturday work or weekday afternoons, but I could manage Thursday and Friday evenings and perhaps Tuesday if you can place me at Northbrook Park. Of course I would have to stop work at 7.00 o'clock.' Unfortunately for her I have no vacancies at the present time which would suit her requirements.

12.45 Go home for a meal. My wife is not working on this particular day, and she gives me a message that the party from Heston will not be staying with us for as long as they originally intended. Change of plans, something to do with their coach. They will only be staying for a couple of hours. The press have been on the 'phone: can I give them further information about Play Day? I have been given the job of organizing the publicity and public relations for the National Association of Recreation Leaders first National Play Day. I ring them, but the person concerned is not there. Will I please ring them back. Sorry I'm busy, will they please ring me later in the day.

1.25 *Sports Centre.* Coach arrives with visitors from Heston, bringing 38 children and 6 playleaders. Conduct a tour of the Sports Centre which is mainly used for gymnastics and playleadership activities. The playleaders and children are interested in the spacious play hall with its facilities for many activities. Their interest stems from the fact that the Sports Centre is a converted swimming baths building containing two very large halls.

1.55 *Arrive with Visitors at Forster Park.* After a quick look around the park, which consists of 11 acres of grassed playing area surrounded by 14 acres of natural woodland (which to my way of thinking is a wonderful adventure play area for children) the children themselves decide the programme of activities which they would like. It involves trampoline, soccer, cricket, netball. As they have their refreshments a little while later the visitors are entertained by the local children who give a display of dancing and music and movement. Afterwards some of the children from Heston join the locals in some music and movement. Attendance about 250.

3.15 See visitors away after their short stay.

3.25 *Arrive Adventure Playground.* I am advised by one of the children that Hoppity the rabbit has had his operation and that the children are very proud of the fact that they possess the only rabbit in Sydenham with a silver pin in its leg. I make my way down to the conventional playground in Home Park to observe the lady whom we had received complaints about. She is not on duty and the several children who I succeeded in getting to speak about her have not noticed anything unusual, in fact one or two of them rather like her. One thinks she is a 'silly old bitch' and another one 'wouldn't go in the bleeding place' so he 'wouldn't know, would he guv?' The adventure playground leader comes over and draws me away from a park keeper who is seeking sympathy after indignantly telling me that '"they" took over ten bob too much income tax off me pay'. As I work at the Town Hall can I do anything about it?

3.45 *Southend Park*. About 40 children present. Somebody tried to get into the hut last night. He was unsuccessful – I think of the young coloured boy. Have I got time to go over the music and movement routine for display day, as the girls who are going to be in it are all present? Yes, I think I can remember it. Get them ready. Two girls argue as to who sits next to who, so we get them both to agree as to who will sit where as dictated by the spin of a coin. One place is heads and the other one tails. They take their choice, the coin is spun, and the argument is finished – at least for the time being. A park keeper comes across to speak to me about a number of boys who are constantly attempting to catch goldfish in the pond. Can I do anything about it? I say that staff will be given instructions to co-operate but the responsibility rests with the parks staff. My staff are told to keep their eyes open for such offenders, but they tell me that 'fishing sessions' go on in between playleadership sessions when they are not usually in the park.

4.05 *Blythe Hill*. Deliver time sheets. Attendance about 45. Not a great deal of activity taking place. Majority of the young people are listening to the battery-operated record player. A gentleman approaches me with a complaint about the number of occasions when young people climb his garden fence to regain balls which are kicked over into his garden. He does not wish to be a spoilsport and he applauds the efforts of the scheme, but would it not be sensible to mark the games pitches in the centre of the playing field instead of close to the private gardens at the edge of the park? I promise him that I will endeavour to do my best, adding that this particular aspect does not come under the jurisdiction of me or my staff. It is purely the park keeper's prerogative to do marking out when and where they see fit. He also makes mention of the deplorable language which goes on, particularly during the later evening period. I sympathize with him and ask him if he can think of or suggest any solution which one could put into operation to stop groups of 16 or 17-year-olds from swearing. He can't think of one but still insists that it should not be allowed. I feel that the problem hinges round the fact that when the play scheme activities terminate in the evening, the older lads still tend to congregate around the playleaders' temporary building which is near the gentleman's garden fence. If the building was moved to the centre of the field it would draw the young men away. Of course this may create another problem in that their voices would then be heard by tenants of properties on more than one side.

4.30 *Sports Centre.* Message for me to ring Captain Forbes of the National Playing Fields Association. Can he come along with two of his associates to view the Lewisham Scheme? He is particularly interested in adventure playgrounds. Yes, he can come along. If he can give me sufficient warning I will arrange for a meal to be prepared by the senior girls – on the understanding of course that they partake at their own risk. I will be able to arrange transport for them during their tour of the play units. I am just in time to receive a delegation from the parents' committee. They would like to organize a dance for our senior boys and girls. Can they use the Town Hall? I say I will find out as this depends on several factors. No, I am unable to give an immediate answer. If they give me a date and an alternative I will start from there. What are the proceeds for? The play club. Have they got any particular band or group in mind? No, its going to be a discothèque. Have they got sufficient stewards? They think so. Can we get tickets printed for them? I don't think so, but I will see what can be done.

4.45 Have a cup of tea with attendants in the kitchen. Urgent message. A gang of youths are attempting to overturn the small shed which contains play materials and equipment at Blythe Hill. The young lady playleader has gone home. By now it is pouring with rain and my staff have gone off duty. One of the centre's attendants offers to run me up in his mini bus because I have decided to take my alsatian dog for a run. It is the attendant's tea break.

4.55 *Blythe Hill.* Arrive during a rainstorm. The shed is still in its position but slightly turned to face another direction. I hear the sound of distorted flat-sounding music coming from the direction of the hut. I make a quiet approach. The shed door is jammed tight as the door frame has been pushed slightly out of alignment because of the attempt to push the shed over. The sound of giggling and laughter comes from behind the hut which is where the music is coming from. I have the dog on a tight lead. He is very large, black, and vicious-looking but he is really very gentle. His wet long-haired coat gives him a rather wolfish appearance. The attendant and I go round the hut each approaching from a different side. I look round the gable end to see a girl and two young lads all about 17 years of age. They are sitting on the grass with their backs against the gable wall of the shed. I ask how long they have been there. One of the lads looks around towards me, the other one without even a glance tells me where to get off – and in no uncertain terms. I gently ease Bruce the dog forward so that his head is level with that of our young man who has just spoken. 'Do you mean both of us?' I ask. He turns his head around and finds himself within licking distance of a large tongue. He freezes. All three have seen the alsatian by now. Absolute silence. I say 'Well, don't sit there on the wet grass, get up, but slowly.' They comply. The dog wants to go home, but he looks the part. 'Whatever you do don't run', I tell them. 'This fellow is like greased lightning and he needs some exercise.' They ease a few inches away and then stop. I don't know any of them and it is quite obvious they do not know who I am. This is a good point. In answer to my queries, they speak but tell me very little. They have just arrived. They have not seen anybody else. The record player was already there, and the records. No, the park keeper has not been near them. Have they seen any keys belonging to the hut? 'Which hut?' 'The one you're propping up.' 'Oh no, the girl took them.' This remark came from the young girl. 'Shurrup you silly twit', says one of the lads. I ask them if they realize that technically they can be charged with damaging and stealing public property. After further discussion in which I learn nothing except that they are not locals, but one of them 'use to live near here years ago', I get them to put the record player back in the shed, and secure the door with a wedge until I can procure a hammer and nails or a few screws from the park keeper to effect a better form of temporary security. Their respect for the dog is obvious but for me it is rather dubious because they still do not know who I am except that I am from the Town Hall. After telling them that I am responsible for the hut and its contents I get them to move it back into position – they do this by rocking the small hut backwards and forwards, obviously quite experienced. After casually advising them that the hut is constantly under surveillance from a nearby house whose owner has been asked to telephone the police at the slightest sign of trouble I tell them to make themselves scarce, which they quickly do.

5.15 *Sports Centre*. Have a general discussion with playleaders and several of the older girls before they commence their national dancing session. Have a cup of tea and a ham roll. My assistant arrives to take charge of the dance session although she is officially on leave.

6.35 Receive a visit from the Blythe Hill playleader who would like to discuss the present situation at her play park. This discussion covers many aspects of the play unit and its users, concluding with an agreement that many of the upsets within the play park are caused not by the regulars but rather by young people who come from some distance expressly to make trouble. It is felt that certain elements are anti park staff and that only occasionally do they turn their attentions towards the play scheme. They do not intentionally interfere with activities or younger children but they do direct their vandalistic efforts towards unattended public property. This is of course in keeping with the problem created by vandalism in many other ways. Short of keeping somebody on duty 24 hours each day – possibly with a guard dog – we agreed that very little could be done and to be thankful that interference with young children's activities was negligible. The answer seemed to be that it was best not to take too much apparent notice of their antics.

7.55 *Sports Centre Basketball Club.* Session commences, I catch up with a certain amount of paper work. Club activities terminate at 9.40. I go home. Telephone message from my assistant. She thinks she has left her cardigan in the play hall, please can I check? I do this and find the cardigan on the balcony. My wife tells me that my dinner has been on the stove for hours. I'm sorry, I do understand. No I don't blame her, yes I would like soup. Bed? Most certainly.

Thursday

Normally my day off. As my assistant is not on duty I decide to work during the morning.

10.00 *Sports Centre.* Visit the play hall. Discuss work on the preparations for our annual display. Receive telephone message, will I telephone one of my staff. She would like an interview today if possible. I ask her to come down immediately.

10.30 *Office.* Interview the playleader and find it necessary to rearrange another meeting later in the day.

11.00 *Home Park.* Routine visit. Everything normal. Attendance had dwindled to six. Had a discussion in the shed about cycling and road safety in very wet weather. Had a cup of adventure playground brew. No ill effects.

12.30 *Lunch.* One of the youngsters volunteered to go to the local fish shop for fish and chips. Playleaders and children all had lunch together 'out of the paper'. Much amusement was caused by having each person read a pre-selected line or heading from the paper his food was wrapped in.

2.15 *Office.* Playleader came back for interview. Domestic problem which was affecting her job as a playleader. This interview lasted two and a half hours.

5.20 *Home.*

Friday

10.00 *Town Hall.* Interview with Social Worker about one of the youngsters who frequents one of our play areas. Unable to help with the problem. Had a visit from the Old People's

Employment Officer who is attached to the Council of Social Service. He would like to know if the scheme can use people over 60 years old for any type of work relating to playleadership. Discuss the possibilities quite fully without making any promises or commitments in any way. Spend the rest of the day working on reports and draft programme for our annual event. Such an event needs much attention to detail which requires that a number of memoranda have to be sent out to various departments. A cue sheet for staff must be prepared and checked and letters sent out to the Performing Right Society to obtain a licence. I also make out a list of points which must be raised at Saturday's weekly meeting of playleaders.

5.35 *Visit Brookmill Park.* Find that only the trainee is present. She tells me that the lady playleader did not feel well during the afternoon and that as far as she knew the man playleader was not coming in that evening. On my way to the park's office I meet the man playleader who tells me that he had received an urgent request by telephone from the lady playleader to get down to the park as soon as possible because she was ill. Apparently she had made an unsuccessful attempt to contact me, and had taken matters into her own hands and asked him. I stay in the play area and work as a playleader until 6.45 when I am relieved by two adults who are voluntary helpers. I then go home for a meal.

Saturday

10.00 *Sports Centre.* Preside at playleaders weekly meeting. The main item of the agenda was about the annual playleadership display, and concerned the cue sheet which is prepared for all playleaders to guide them in their duties on the day. As is to be expected some of them adhere strictly to it and others are only interested in the various displays which involve children from their own play units. This naturally adds extra chores to those leaders who are willing to do a little extra, and who are now making their protest. Collect several time sheets.

11.15 *Sports Centre Stores.* Issue and exchange a few items of equipment for playleaders in charge of units.

11.35 *Playleadership Depot.* Visit this new depot to see some work which has just been completed.

11.45 *Visit Forster Park.* Attendance about 65. Everything normal. Chat with foreman about the erection of a temporary chestnut fence around the main activities arena on the forthcoming display day.

2.30 *Sports Centre.* Lunch. Take dogs out for a run.

2.00 Distribute application forms for winter activities at the sports' centre.

2.20 *Visit Blythe Hall.* Attendance 15. Routine visit. Everything normal.

2.40 *Visit Adventure Playground.* Starts to rain heavily. Attendance about 10 children.

3.15 *Visit Warren Avenue Playing Fields.* Raining very heavily. Attendance five children.

4.45 *Visit Forster Park.* Torrential rain. Deliver some Polycell. Go home.

Appendix I

SOME USEFUL ADDRESSES

This list was compiled in 1972. It will be realized that the names and addresses of secretaries frequently change.

Adventure Playground Workers' Association, F. McLennon,
    57a Burton Road, London S.W.9.
All England Netball Association, Miss A. D. Cairncross,
    26 Park Crescent, London W1N 4EE. (01-580 3459)
All England Women's Hockey Association, Miss A. G. Browne,
    45 Doughty Street, London W.C.1. (01-405 7514)
All England Women's Lacrosse Association, Miss G. Mott,
    26 Park Crescent, London W.1. (01-636 1123)
All Wales Ladies' Lacrosse Association, Miss J. Donovan,
    51 St. Nicholas Road, Barry, Glam.
Amateur Athletic Association, B. E. Willis, 26 Park Crescent,
    London W1N 4BQ. (01-580 3498/9)
Amateur Basketball Association, K. K. Mitchell,
    P.O. Box 1W3, Leeds LS16 6RE. (Leeds 677469)
Amateur Boxing Association, W. T. Lovett,
    Clutha House, 10 Storey's Gate, S.W.1. (01-930 9207/8)
Amateur Fencing Association, Commander S. A. Booth,
    83 Perham Road, London W.14. (01-385 7442)
Amateur Rowing Association, M. C. Stamford,
    Portland Court, 160 Great Portland Street, London W1N 5TB.
Amateur Swimming Association, N. Sarsfield, M.C.,
    314 Grays Inn Road, London W.C.1. (01-278 6751)
Amateur Wrestling Association, A. Wishart,
    60 Calabria Road, London N.5. (01-226 3931)
Badminton Association of England, J. B. H. Bisseker,
    81a High Street, Bromley, Kent. (01-460 5722)

Bicycle Polo Association of Great Britain, Mrs. D. Corby,
  31 Shipman Road, Forest Hill, London, S.E.23. (01-699 3932)
British Amateur Gymnastic Association, R. G. Taylor,
  23a High Street, Slough, Bucks. (Slough 34383)
British Amateur Weight-Lifters' Association, W. Holland,
  3 Iffley Turn, Oxford. (Oxford 44630)
British Canoe Union, 26 Park Crescent, W.1. (01-580 4710)
British Cycling Federation, L. A. Unwin,
  26 Park Crescent, London W.1. (01-636 4602/3)
British Judo Association, A. J. Reay,
  26 Park Crescent, London W.1. (01-580 7585)
British Olympic Association, K. S. Duncan, M.B.E.,
  12 Buckingham Street, London W.C.2. (01-930 1761)
British Sub-Aqua Club, R. L. Vallintine,
  160 Great Portland Street, London W1N 5TB. (01-636 5667)
British Trampoline Federation Ltd.,
  174 Wood End Lane, Northolt, Middlesex. (01-422 1079)
British Water Ski Federation, T. G. Richardson,
  Virginia Water, Surrey. (Wentworth 3988)
Camping Club of Great Britain and Ireland, G. A. Cubitt,
  11 Lower Grosvenor Place, London S.W.1 (01-828 9232)
Canoe Camping Club, G. Halfacre,
  9 Glebe Road, Sandy, Bedfordshire.
The Cricket Council, S. C. Griffith, D.F.C., T.D.,
  Lord's Cricket Ground, London N.W.8. (01-289 1611)
Croquet Association, V. Robinson,
  Hurlingham Club, London S.W.6. (01-736 3148)
Dalcroze Society, Mrs. A. Heron,
  16 Heathcroft, Hampstead Way, London N.W.11. (01-455 1268)
English Bowling Association, J. Elms,
  Merville Hotel, Exeter Road, Bournemouth, Hants. BH2 5AW.
  (Bournemouth 22233)
English Folk Dance and Song Society, K. F. Goode,
  Cecil Sharp House, 2 Regent's Park Road, London N.W.1.
  (01-485 2206)
English Lacrosse Union, C. D. Coppock,
  3 Chessington Avenue, Bexleyheath, Kent. (Erith 36067)
English Schools Swimming Association, E. H. Burden,
  190 Nether Street, West Finchley, London N.3. (01-346 6338)

English Table Tennis Association, D. R. Tremayne,
26 Park Crescent, London W.1. (01-580 6312)
English Volleyball Association, T. A. Jones,
45 Fairford Avenue, Barnehurst, Kent. (01-383 1605)
Football Association, D. Follows, C.B.E.,
16 Lancaster Gate, London W.2.
Football Association of Wales, T. Morris,
3 Fairy Road, Wrexham, Denbighshire. (Wrexham 2425)
Grand National Archery Society, J. J. Bray,
117 Keene Way, Galleywood, Nr. Chelmsford, Essex.
(*Home* Chelmsford 52453 *Office* Chelmsford 57982)
Hockey Association, R. J. W. Struthers,
26 Park Crescent, London W.1. (01-580 4840)
International Playground Association, W. D. Abernethy,
57b Catherine Place, London S.W.1.
Institute of Park and Recreation Administration, K. L. Morgan,
F.C.C.S., Lower Basildon, Reading, Berks. (Goring-on-Thames
2314)
Institute of Playleadership,
57b Catherine Place, London S.W.1.
Irish Football Association, W. H. Drennan,
20 Windsor Avenue, Belfast 9, Northern Ireland.
Keep Fit Association, Mrs. J. Worrall,
26 Park Crescent, London W.1. (01-637 3152)
Keep Fit Association of Northern Ireland, Miss G. Casement,
23 Agnes Street, Belfast BT13 1GF.
Laban Art of Movement Guild, Miss E. A. Osgathorp,
Art of Movement Studio, Woburn Hill, Addlestone, Surrey.
(Weybridge 42464)
Ladies' Amateur Fencing Union, Mrs. A. K. Payne,
99 Hazon Way, Epsom, Surrey.
The Lawn Tennis Association, S. B. Reay, O.B.E.,
Barons Court, London W.14. (01-385 2366)
National Anglers' Council, P. H. Tombleson,
17 Queen Street, Peterborough, Northants. PE1 1PJ.
(Peterborough 4084)
National Association of Boys Clubs, Sir Reginald Goodwin, C.B.E.,
D.L., 17 Bedford Square, London W.C.1. (01-636 5357)
National Association of Recreation Leaders,
The Secretary, The Town Hall, Woolwich S.E.18.

National Council of Social Service, J. K. Owens,
26 Bedford Square, London W.C.1. (01-636 4066)
National Federation of Community Associations, K. M. Reinold,
26 Bedford Square, London W.C.1. (01-636 8944)
National Playing Fields Association, Major-General Sir John
Nelson, K.C.V.O., C.B., D.S.O., M.C., O.B.E.,
57b Catherine Place, London S.W.1. (01-834 9272)
National Rifle Association, Air Commodore A. B. Riall, C.B.E.,
R.A.F.(Ret'd), Bisley Camp, Brookwood, Woking, Surrey.
(Brookwood 2213)
National Roller Hockey Association, E. E. Newbury,
c/o Radio Conversions Ltd., Clarendon Road, London N.8.
(01-888 3043)
National Rounders Association, Miss B. E. Harrison, Secretary,
1 Chantry Close, Beeston, Nottingham.
National Ski Federation of Great Britain, Major-General I. R.
Graeme, C.B., O.B.E., 118 Eaton Square, London S.W.1.
(01-235 8228)
Northern Branch Badminton Union of Ireland, Mrs. A. Kinkead,
64 Ballymacash Road, Lisburn, Co. Antrim, Northern Ireland.
Northern Cricket Union of Ireland, Major G. C. Ormsby,
M.B.E., E.R.D., 49 Malone Road, Belfast, Northern Ireland.
BT9 6RY.
Northern Ireland Amateur Athletic Association, G. E. Wilson,
72 Woodview Crescent, Lisburn, Co. Antrim, Northern Ireland.
Northern Ireland Cycling Federation, S. Finlay,
10 Newry Street, Banbridge, Co. Down, Northern Ireland.
Northern Ireland Netball Association, Miss M. McNeilly,
3 Pound Street, Newtownards, Co. Down, Northern Ireland.
Northern Ireland Women's Amateur Athletic Association,
Mrs. M. Kyle, 'Tir-Na-Nog', Old Galgorm Road, Ballymena,
Co. Antrim, Northern Ireland.
Outward Bound Trust, Commander H. E. B. Jenkinson,
Iddlesleigh House, Caxton Street, London S.W.1. (01-222 2926/7)
Pre-School Playgroups Association,
Alford House, Aveline Street, London S.E.11.
Ramblers' Association, C. Hall,
1-4 Crawford Mews, London W1H 1PT. (01-262 1477)
Royal Academy of Dancing, B. G. Dumont,
251 Knightsbridge, London S.W.7. (01-584 9335)

Royal Scottish Country Dance Society, Miss E. R. Grubb,
12 Coates Crescent, Edinburgh 3. (Edinburgh 225 3854)
Royal Life Saving Society, Brigadier P. de C. Jones, O.B.E.,
Desborough House, 14 Devonshire Street, London W.1.
(01-580 5678)
Rugby Fives Association, A. Maltby,
28 Devonshire Road, Bexhill-on-Sea, Sussex. (Bexhill 347)
Rugby Football League, W. Fallowfield, O.B.E.,
180 Chapeltown Road, Leeds 7. (Leeds 624637/8)
Rugby Football Union, R. E. Prescott,
Whitton Road, Twickenham, Middlesex. (01-892 8161)
St. John Ambulance Brigade Cadets, Miss P. Morison or
Lieut.-Colonel A. Goring, 8 Grosvenor Crescent, London S.W.1.
(01-235 5231)
Save the Children Fund,
29 Queen Anne's Gate, London S.W.1. (01-930 2461)
The Sports Council,
26 Park Crescent, London W.1. (01-580 6822)
Squash Rackets Association, J. H. Horry,
26 Park Crescent, London W.1. (01-636 6901)
Swimming Teachers' Association, R. Clements, D.S.T.A.,
1 Birmingham Road, West Bromwich, Staffs. (West Bromwich
5828)
Table Tennis Association of Wales, Mrs. H. Roy Evans,
198 Cyncoed Road, Cardiff, Glam.
Ulster Amateur Gymnastic Association,
c/o CCPR Offices, 49 Malone Road, Belfast BT9 6RZ.
Ulster Archery Association, E. Dougan,
35 Norglen Drive, Belfast 11, Northern Ireland.
Ulster Branch of the Irish Amateur Swimming Association,
R. Fergusson, 13 Knockbreda Park, Belfast 6, Northern Ireland.
Ulster Branch of the Irish Rugby Football Union, F. C. Humphreys,
85 Ravenhill Park, Belfast 6, Northern Ireland.
Ulster Council of the Irish Lawn Tennis Association, P. S. F. Bayliss,
88 Marmount Park, Belfast 4, Northern Ireland.
Ulster Women's Hockey Union, Mrs. H. W. Templeton, M.B.E.,
36 Ardenlee Avenue, Belfast 6, Northern Ireland.
Welsh Amateur Basketball Association, J. Garretty,
28 Brundall Crescent, Culverhouse Cross, Cardiff, Glam. CF5
4RU.

Welsh Amateur Boxing Association, V. J. Thomas,
3 Davies Avenue, Westpark, Nottage, Porthcawl, Glam.

Welsh Amateur Swimming Association, W. Hopper,
45 Devon Place, Newport, Mon.

Welsh Badminton Union, N. T. Ramsden,
30 Lon Isa, Rhiwbina, Cardiff, Glam.

Welsh Baseball Union, E. J. Fowles,
70 Lon-y-Celyn, Whitchurch, Cardiff, Glam. CF4 7BU.

Welsh Folk Dance Society, Mrs F. Mon Jones,
Bryn Mair, Llanfair Caereinion, Montgomeryshire.

Welsh Hockey Association, K. H. Ingledew,
9 Cathedral Road, Cardiff, Glam.

Welsh Netball Association, Miss M. Williams,
Brentwood, Gwerthonor Road, Bargoed, Glam.

Welsh Rugby Union, W. H. Clement, M.C., T.D.,
Royal London House, 28/31 St. Mary Street, Cardiff, Glam.
CF1 2PP.

Welsh Women's Hockey Association, Miss N. Roblin,
107 Monthermer Road, Cardiff, Glam.

Women's Amateur Athletic Association,
41 Hayward Court, Levehurst Way, London S.W.4.
(01-622 8079)

Women's Amateur Rowing Council, Miss J. Filkins, W.A.R.C.,
20 Wensleydale Road, Hampton, Middx. (01-979 3808)

Women's Cricket Association, Miss A. Sanders,
34a Millway, Mill Hill, London N.W.7. (01-959 0385)

Women's Football Association, A. H. Hobbs,
95 College Road, Deal, Kent. (Deal 4387)

Women's Squash Rackets Association, Miss J. M. Wilson,
4 Denbigh Gardens, Richmond, Surrey. (948 2811)

World Billiards and Snooker Council, Mrs. B. P. Holliday,
1-5 Salisbury Promenade, London N.8. (01-802 6222)

Youth Camping Association of Great Britain and Ireland,
Mrs. W. Graham, 25 Longmoor, Cheshunt, Herts.
(Waltham Cross 20884)

Youth Hostels Association of England and Wales,
H. B. Livingstone, Ll.B., Y.H.A., Trevelyan House,
8 St. Stephens Hill, St. Albans, Herts. (St. Albans 55215)

Appendix 2

ACTS OF PARLIAMENT UNDER WHICH
ASSISTANCE CAN BE GIVEN FOR PLAYGROUND
AND PLAYLEADERSHIP SCHEMES

Public Health Act 1875
Recreation Grounds Act 1859
Town Gardens Protection Act 1863
Public Improvements Act 1860
Public Health Amendment Act 1890
Public Health Act 1961
Local Government Act 1894
Open Spaces Act 1906
Public Health Act Amendment Act 1907
Public Health Act 1925
Physical Training and Recreation Act 1937
Local Government Act 1948
Local Government Act 1958
Local Government Act 1966
Social and Physical Training Grant Regulations 1939
Education Act 1944
Nurseries and Child Minders Act 1948
National Health Service Act 1964
Children Act 1948
Children and Young Persons Act 1963
Local Government (Financial Provisions) Act 1963
Recreational Charities Act 1958
Charities Act 1960
Housing Act 1957
Street Playgrounds Act 1938
Commons Registration Act 1965

Index

265